4800 WISECRACKS, WITTY REMARKS, AND EPIGRAMS FOR ALL OCCASIONS

4800 WISECRACKS, WITTY REMARKS, AND EPIGRAMS FOR ALL OCCASIONS

Edited by
EDMUND FULLER

He misses what is meant by epigram
Who thinks it only frivolous flim-flam.
                                    MARTIAL

AVENEL BOOKS · NEW YORK

This book was originally published as *Thesaurus of Epigrams*.
Copyright © MCMXLIII, MCMLXXI, by Crown Publishers, Inc.
All rights reserved.

This 1980 edition is published by Avenel Books, distributed by
Crown Publishers, Inc., 225 Park Avenue South, New York, New
York 10003.

Printed and Bound in the United States of America

Library of Congress Cataloging in Publication Data

Fuller, Edmund, 1914–
    4800 wisecracks, witty remarks, and epigrams for all
occasions.

    Reprint of the ed. published by Crown Publishers,
New York under title: Thesaurus of epigrams.
    Includes index.
    1. Epigrams. I. Title.
PN6281.F8 1980   808.88'2   80-16661
ISBN 0-517-320908

s r q p o

INTRODUCTION

What is an epigram? What sets it apart from the quip, the quiddity, the *bon mot,* the *jeu d'esprit,* the retort, the reply courteous, the anecdote, or the gag? Wits or sages, if indeed they be not the same, of all ages have ventured to identify and isolate the epigram. It is Oscar Levant who has definitively scored it for our time with a fine sensitivity to the fact that stuffing is out of place in a humorist's shirt. By Oscar, "An epigram is a gag that's played Carnegie Hall." It is Bob Hope at Harvard; it is Sinatra singing with the Philharmonic. It is the irreverent leaven of earthy humor, however polished, that keeps the arteries of intellect from hardening.

Let the epigrammatists speak for themselves. An anonymous Latin distich requires that:

> Three things must epigrams, like bees, have all,
> A sting, and honey, and a body small.

Samuel Taylor Coleridge bears witness:

> What is an epigram? a dwarfish whole,
> Its body brevity, and wit its soul.

The Oxford Dictionary defines it as (1) an "Epigraph" (or "An inscription; *esp.* one placed upon a building, tomb, statue, etc., to indicate its name or purpose; a legend on a coin"); (2) "A short poem leading up to and ending in a witty or ingenious turn of thought." (3) "A pointed or antithetical saying."

To attempt to assemble a broad collection of epigrams, one must first make up his mind that epigrams are where you find them and what you want them to be. They overlap with many other classifications of the gnomic, or aphoristic, wisdom of the race and no bones about it. They should be brief, but how short is brief? They should be witty, but where does wit begin and end? They should be paradoxical, but one man's paradox is another man's faith. They should be true, but as Pontius Pilate asked . . .

vii

So, if epigrams are so vague and disputatious a form of thought, what good are they? At once everyone with a definition will drop his particular view and rush forward to unite in proving the values that make the epigram one of the most ancient and one of the most modern capsules for ideas.

> He misses what is meant by epigram
> Who thinks it only frivolous flim-flam.

So says Martial, perhaps the greatest epigrammatist of them all. "An epigram often flashes light into regions where reason shines but dimly." So says the American essayist, E. P. Whipple. Hendrik Willem Van Loon assures us that "Somewhere in the world there is an epigram for every dilemma." But when you are searching for it, cautions C. W. Thompson, remember that, "No epigram contains the whole truth." In fact, many of the best epigrams aren't true.

This book attempts to present a sampling of the epigram from Martial to Mizner, from Heraclitus to Hope. It contains the greater part of the rich body of Greek and Roman epigrams, excluding only such as were of too narrowly local interest and a substantial number that are unprintable. Here it might as well be noted that the *risqué* or the downright bawdy are elements which have been and remain of the essence of the best in epigrammatic tradition. The form is inevitably inclined toward irreverence, deflation, and cynicism.

Those unfamiliar with them are urged to pay special attention to the Greek and Roman epigrams. Some are so short and sharp as to hit home at once. Many, however, require one to get the hang of them. In general, the classicists are an acquired taste but they are easier to take than olives and better when you get to like them. Try it. You will find them, among other things, past masters of the gentle arts of insult and abuse.

HOW ARE YOU GOING TO USE THIS BOOK? You will use it, with its wide breakdown under subject headings and its extensive cross-reference, to supercharge your conversation, your speeches, or your writings at the right time. It can serve you as a spear or a shield, as a clincher or as an opener. The conversational adversary whom you fell with a good epigram will never rise again.

Whatever your own capacities as a wit, this book has a usefulness for you. If you are yourself "witty and the cause of wit in others" it will sharpen, refresh, remind and divert you. If you are not yourself witty, or if you are a mere fledgling at the art, remember, with Bovée, that "The next best thing to being witty one's self, is to be able to quote another's wit." This, in itself, requires some ability and is a recognized credit to a man's discrimination. "Next to the originator of a good sentence," says Emerson, broadening out the idea, "is the first quoter of it."

Another challenge is offered to the ingenious user of this material, one which is indeed a kind of school or whetstone for wit. This is the task of *adaptation* of the material. The potentialities of this process render this collection virtually the ultimate of possible wit in the sense that a dictionary is the ultimate in possible literature, *if you use the words.*

Change these epigrams around forty ways from Sunday. Make them your own. That is the whole of originality, anyhow. Lowell notes that:

> Though old the thought and oft exprest,
> 'Tis his at last who says it best.

Take these epigrams, change the subjects or objects which you find in them and let them fit your purpose of the moment. The fact that many of them are paradoxical contains a clue to this process. A paradox is a kind of reverse twist rendering the outcome of a thought otherwise than that which was expected at the outset. True or false, when you find it you can twist it once more, forwards or backwards, and lo, it will be either a new epigram or a mess. If it's a mess, don't use it.

This may be illustrated by a flash of genius with which the famed agnostic, Robert Ingersoll, took the old saw, "An honest man is the noblest work of God" and brought it forth as "An honest God is the noblest work of man."

The switch can be done on your feet if you're sure-footed. Paul Bourget ventured an epigram to the effect that "When an American has nothing else to do he can always spend a few years trying to discover who his grandfather was." Mark Twain made the heroic retort, "And when all other interests fail for a Frenchman, he can always try to find out who his father was."

Discretion should be applied, however, in the use of epigrams. They are edge tools and are not to be used by fools and children. You can commit a kind of conversational suicide with them as well as do a murder.

Always use your own brains first. To rely indiscriminately upon epigrams will take the life out of the spoken or written word. Think out what you are saying. Use the epigram *thoughtfully,* not as a shortcut to avoid thought. We might attempt a "switcheroo" with Shakespeare and caution, "O God! that men should put an epigram in their mouths to steal away their brains!" It is wisely said, "Enough wit places one above his equal; too much of it lowers him to the rank of mere entertainer."

Here they are, then, some five thousand of them, more or less. In any case, enough, for as Martial says, "No amount of misfortune will satisfy the man who is not satisfied with reading a hundred epigrams." If your own favorite is left out, we must ask forgiveness. It is impossible to include all and there are many that would have appeared had we thought of them or succeeded in finding them. A scrupulous effort has been made to be correct and complete in making attributions. If errors have occurred, or if some one or two epigrams, which are well known to be the words of this or that individual, have been listed as anonymous, it is by accident and with the editor's apologies.

Acknowledgment is necessary of the indispensable and patient spadework done by Bertha Krantz and Nathan Ausubel. It is their book, too.

Edmund Fuller

New York

4800 WISECRACKS, WITTY REMARKS, AND EPIGRAMS FOR ALL OCCASIONS

TABLE OF CONTENTS

HOW TO USE THIS BOOK

The epigrams in this book are classified according to subject and numbered for cross-reference. The subjects are in alphabetical order. An index of subjects will be found at the back of the book. The key numbers are not for the purpose of counting but of locating. In order to keep the book from being frozen by reference numbers it was necessary to break their numerical sequence, leaving "expansion joints." The practice has been followed, at the end of each category, of advancing the numbers to begin the next category with the next decade—thus a 7 to 11, a 16 to 21, a 45 to 51. This has made it editorially practical to readjust and perfect this book up to the last minute. It will permit the expansion of further editions without disrupting the entire editorial organization. It is suggested that the constant user may also avail himself of the opportunity to make his own up-to-date supplementary collection of epigrams, using the blank numbers to correlate it with the material in this book—a uniquely useful device.

If you want to find an epigram on any subject turn to that subject. You will find there a number of epigrams from which to choose. In addition to this you will find, at the end of the group, a list of Related Subjects. One or more of these may guide you to what you are seeking. Also, at the end of almost every group, you will find a list headed See Also. These represent specific epigrams pertaining to the subject at hand but listed under other headings for more direct meanings. Thus, No. 254: "Choler hates a counsellor," is listed under Anger but is referred to as a See Also under Advice.

Finally, read the Introduction: it will help you to get the greatest service and enjoyment from this book.

EPIGRAMS

A

ACTION

1 Better to sink beneath the shock
Than moulder piecemeal on the rock.
    —*Byron*

2 The best way to keep good acts in memory is to refresh them with new.
    —*Cato*

3 We should pray with as much earnestness as those who expect everything from God; we should act with as much energy as those who expect everything from themselves.
    —*Colton*

4 We are taught by great actions that the universe is the property of every individual in it.
    —*Emerson*

5 A man's action is only a picture book of his creed.
    —*Emerson*

6 Every noble activity makes room for itself.
    —*Emerson*

7 The materials of action are variable, but the use we make of them should be constant.
    —*Epictetus*

8 Adventure is not outside a man; it is within.
    —*David Grayson*

9 Our acts our angels are, or good or ill,
Our fatal shadows that walk by us still.
    —*John Fletcher*

10 Action is the proper fruit of knowledge.
    —*Thomas Fuller*

11 A man of action, forced into a state of thought, is unhappy until he can get out of it.
    —*Galsworthy*

12 An ounce of performance is worth more than a pound of preachment.
    —*Elbert Hubbard*

13 Positive anything is better than negative nothing. —*Elbert Hubbard*

14 The great end of life is not knowledge, but action. —*T. H. Huxley*

15 We would often be ashamed of our finest actions if the world understood all the motives which produced them. —*La Rochefoucauld*

16 Although men flatter themselves with their great actions, they are usually the result of chance and not of design.
    —*La Rochefoucauld*

17 The actions of men are the best interpreters of their thoughts.

—*Locke*

18 Every man feels instinctively that all the beautiful sentiments in the world weigh less than a single lovely action. —*Lowell*

19 Execute every act of thy life as though it were thy last.

—*Marcus Aurelius*

20 Ah! Valere, all men say the same thing to women; all are alike in their words; their actions only show the difference that exists between them.

—*Molière*

21 Stability itself is nothing else than a more sluggish motion.

—*Montaigne*

22 Life is act, and not to do is death. —*Lewis Morris*

23 Inactivity is death.

—*Mussolini*

24 Dreams grow holy put in action. —*Adelaide Procter*

25 Only actions give to life its strength, as only moderation gives it its charm.

—*J. P. Richter*

26 Action is eloquence.

—*Shakespeare*

27 Count that day lost whose low descending sun
Views from thy hand no worthy action done.

28 Actions speak louder than words.

29 Actions speak louder than words—but not so often.

30 Actions are the insipid reflections of our motives.

31 The draft that blows out a match makes a furnace burn better, and what prostrates a coward excites a brave man to action.

32 The acts of this life are the destiny of the next.

33 Amongst other advantages: a rolling stone gathers no moss.

SEE ALSO
Desire 1532
Experience 2002
Sin 5066

RELATED SUBJECTS
Decision
Deeds
Work

ACTORS

41 An actor is a sculptor who carves in snow. —*Lawrence Barrett*

42 To see Kean act was like reading Shakespeare by flashes of lightning.

—*Coleridge*

43 Let him who plays the monarch be a king;
Who plays the rogue, be perfect in his part.

—*Erskine*

44   The actor who took the role of King Lear played the king as though
he expected someone to play the ace.   *—Eugene Field*

45   Our Garrick's a salad; for in him we see
Oil, vinegar, sugar and saltiness agree.   *—Goldsmith*

46   On the stage he was natural, simple, affecting,
'Twas only when he was off, he was acting.   *—Goldsmith*

47   Actors are the only honest hypocrites.   *—Hazlitt*

48   At the Academy Award Dinners all the actors and actresses in
Hollywood gather around to see what someone else thinks about
their acting besides their press agents.   *—Bob Hope*

49   It sure has been a pleasure for us to broadcast for the sailors and
soldiers; besides, it's part of the National Defense Program to
prepare our boys for anything.   *—Bob Hope*

50   Some of the greatest love affairs I've known have involved one actor
—unassisted.   *—Wilson Mizner*

51   Bores to themselves, to others *caviare.*   *—Phaedrus*

52   The stock actor is a stage calamity.   *—Bernard Shaw*

53   Foote from this earthly stage, alas! is hurled;
Death took him off, who took off all the world.

SEE ALSO
Character 692
Courtesy 1119
Dictators 1590
Preachers 4611

RELATED SUBJECTS
Art
Theater

ADMIRATION

61   All things are admired either because they are new or because they
are great.   *—Bacon*

62   A fool always finds a greater fool to admire him.   *—Boileau*

63   Distance is a great promoter of admiration!   *—Diderot*

64   Admiration begins where acquaintance ceases.   *—Johnson*

65   There is an admiration which is the daughter of knowledge.   *—Joubert*

66   We always love those who admire us, and we do not always love
those whom we admire.   *—La Rochefoucauld*

67   Yet let not each gay turn thy rapture move;
For fools admire, but men of sense approve.   *—Pope*

68   Admiration and familiarity are strangers.   *—George Sand*

69   Admiration is the daughter of ignorance.

SEE ALSO   RELATED SUBJECTS
Character 693   Fame
Vanity 5633   Flattery
Wickedness 5823   Greatness
                                 Praise

ADVERTISING

71   Advertising is the mouthpiece of business.   —*James R. Adams*

72   You can tell the ideals of a nation by its advertisements.
                                                      —*Norman Douglas*

73   If you don't advertise yourself you will be advertised by your loving
     enemies.   —*Elbert Hubbard*

74   Publicity eliminates pretense. The faker cannot work in a club.
                                                      —*Elbert Hubbard*

75   The sign brings customers.   —*La Fontaine*

76   One-third of the people in the United States promote, while the
     other two-thirds provide.   —*Will Rogers*

77   We are advertis'd by our loving friends.   —*Shakespeare*

78   Emerson's remark that the landscape belongs to the man who looks
     at it was made a long time before billboards became rampant.

79   Samson had the right idea about advertising. He took two columns
     and brought down the house.

80   Sales resistance is the triumph of mind over patter.

81   Hark! the herald angels sing,
     Beecham's Pills are just the thing;
     Peace on earth and mercy mild,
     Two for man and one for child.

SEE ALSO   RELATED SUBJECT
News 4174   Business

ADVICE

91   We give advice by the bucket, but take it by the grain.
                                                      —*W. R. Alger*

92   The worst men often give the best advice.   —*Philip J. Bailey*

93   *Advice:* the smallest current coin.   —*Ambrose Bierce*

94   He loves who advises.   —*Burton*

95   Good but rarely came from good advice.   —*Byron*

96 Advice is seldom welcome; and those who want it the most always like it the least. —*Chesterfield*

97 Nobody can give you wiser advice than yourself. —*Cicero*

98 Advice is like snow; the softer it falls, the longer it dwells upon, and the deeper it sinks into the mind. —*Coleridge*

99 To profit from good advice requires more wisdom than to give it. —*Churton Collins*

100 To ask advice is in nine cases out of ten to tout for flattery. —*Churton Collins*

101 When we feel a strong desire to thrust our advice on others, it is usually because we suspect their weakness; but we ought rather to suspect our own. —*C. C. Colton*

102 We ask advice, but we mean approbation. —*C. C. Colton*

103 When Thales was asked what was difficult, he said, "To know one's self." And what was easy, "to advise another." —*Diogenes Laertius*

104 No vice is so bad as advice. —*Marie Dressler*

105 They first condemn that first advis'd the ill. —*Dryden*

106 He that won't be counselled can't be helped. —*Franklin*

107 Good counsel failing men can give, for why?
He that's aground knows where the shoal doth lie. —*Franklin*

108 He who will not answer to the rudder, must answer to the rocks. —*Hervé*

109 Advice is offensive—it shows us that we are known to others as well as to ourselves. —*Johnson*

110 Nothing is given so profusely as advice. —*La Rochefoucauld*

111 Ask a woman's advice, and whate'er she advise,
Do the very reverse and you're sure to be wise. —*Thomas Moore*

112 It is the part of a fool to give advice to others and not himself to be on his guard. —*Phaedrus*

113 Be niggards of advice on no pretence,
For the worst avarice is that of sense. —*Pope*

114 It is bad advice that cannot be altered. —*Publilius Syrus*

115 Many receive advice, few profit by it. —*Publilius Syrus*

116 To one who knows, it is superfluous to give advice; to one who does not know, it is insufficient. —*Seneca*

117   The belly will not listen to advice.
             —Seneca

118   When a wise man gives thee better counsel, give me mine again.
            —Shakespeare

119   Direct not him whose way himself will choose:
 'Tis breath thou lack'st, and that breath wilt thou lose.
            —Shakespeare

120   Good advice is one of those injuries which a good man ought, if
 possible, to forgive, but at all events to forget at once.
           —Horace Smith

121   How is it possible to expect mankind to take advice when they will
 not so much as take warning?   *—Swift*

122   How we do admire the wisdom of those who come to us for advice!

123   Who needs advice most, usually likes it least.

124   He who takes advice is wiser than the one who gives it.

125   Write down the advice of him who loves you, though you like it
 not at present.

126   When in doubt give advice.

127   It is safer to hear and take counsel than to give it.

128   A woman's counsel is not worth much, but he that despises it is no
 wiser than he should be.

129   Take your wife's first advice, not her second.

SEE ALSO	RELATED SUBJECTS
Anger 254	Caution
Bee 411	Help
Difficulty 1591	Judgment
Discretion 1634	Listening
Money 4039	Wisdom
Success 5250	

AGE

132   In wine and man this difference appears:
 The old man bores you, but the wine cheers.
 Men do not, like your wine, improve by age;
 The more their years, the less their ways engage.
          —Alexis of Thurii

133   You are not permitted to kill a woman who has injured you, but
 nothing forbids you to reflect that she is growing older every
 minute. You are avenged 1440 times a day. *—Ambrose Bierce*

134   'Tis said that persons living on annuities
 Are longer lived than others.
             —Byron

135 A man is as old as he's feeling,
     A woman as old as she looks.   —*Mortimer Collins*

136 Antiquity is the aristocracy of history.   —*Dumas*

137 We do not count a man's years until he has nothing else to count.
                                                         —*Emerson*

138 One of the many things nobody ever tells you about middle age is
     that it's such a nice change from being young.
                                              —*Dorothy Canfield Fisher*

139 They say women and music should never be dated.   —*Goldsmith*

140 To be seventy years young is sometimes far more cheerful and hope-
     ful than to be forty years old.   —*O. W. Holmes*

141 The Grecian ladies counted their age from their marriage, not
     their birth.   —*Homer*

142 The best of friends fall out, and so
     His teeth had done some years ago.   —*Thomas Hood*

143 Old men are only walking hospitals.   —*Horace*

144 Forty is the old age of youth; fifty is the youth of old age.
                                                     —*Victor Hugo*

145 Whenever a man's friends begin to compliment him about looking
     young, he may be sure that they think he is growing old.
                                              —*Washington Irving*

146 Age is the most terrible misfortune that can happen to any man;
     other evils will mend, this is every day getting worse.
                                                 —*George James*

147 No man is so old but thinks he may yet live another year.
                                                     —*St. Jerome*

148 Women's hell is old age.   —*La Rochefoucauld*

149 You give your cheeks a rosy stain,
     With washes dye your hair,
     But paint and washes both are vain
     To give a youthful air.   —*Lucianus*

150 Why, Thais, do you constantly call me old? No one, Thais, is too
     old for some things.   —*Martial*

151 You ask, Matrinia, whether I can love an old woman. I can, even
     an old woman. But you are not an old woman; you are a corpse.
                                                       —*Martial*

152 If a man of many years prays Zeus still for more,
     Answer, Zeus, his vow by granting another score.   —*Nenecrates*

153   Beauty and ugliness disappear equally under the wrinkles of age;
      one is lost in them, the other hidden.   —*Petit-Senn*

154   From forty to fifty a man is at heart either a stoic or a satyr.
                                                           —*Pinero*

155   One is always of his age and especially he who least appears so.
                                                      —*Sainte-Beuve*

156   The young man who has not wept is a savage, and the old man who
      will not laugh is a fool.   —*Santayana*

157   Crabbed age and youth cannot live together,
      Youth is full of pleasure, age is full of care.   —*Shakespeare*

158   Old men are dangerous: it doesn't matter to them what is going to
      happen to the world.   —*Bernard Shaw*

159   That sign of old age, extolling the past at the expense of the
      present.   —*Sydney Smith*

160   No man loves life like him that's growing old.   —*Sophocles*

161   Deaf, giddy, helpless, left alone,
      To all my friends a burden grown;
      No more I hear my church's bell
      Than if it rang out for my knell;
      At thunder now no more I start
      Than at the rumbling of a cart;
      And, what's incredible, alack!
      No more I hear a woman's clack.   —*Swift, about himself*

162   Old men must die, or the world would grow mouldy, would only
      breed the past again.   —*Tennyson*

163   He that is not handsome at twenty, nor strong at thirty, nor rich
      at forty, nor wise at fifty, will never be handsome, strong, rich,
      or wise.

164   Man knows his age; woman computes hers.

165   Man has reached middle age if he can't repeat his follies with
      impunity; woman, with grace.

166   Women never refer to their age until it would be wiser to ignore it.

167   With a little practice any woman can remain thirty years old.

168   Man is old when he begins to hide his age; woman, when she be-
      gins to tell hers.

169   Religion often gets credit for curing rascals when old age is the
      real medicine.

170   Old men become frolicksome, that is their second childhood;

middle-aged women become naive—one might suspect them of second virginity.

171   Antiquity cannot privilege an error, nor novelty prejudice a truth.

172   An old goat is never the more reverend for his beard.

173   Wrinkles are the deathbed wherein women bury their illusions.

174   When an old man frolics, he flirts with ridicule.

175   A woman is no older than she looks.

SEE ALSO
Beauty 366
Bed 407
Coquetry 1075
Death 1325
Love 3711
Wine 5881

RELATED SUBJECTS
Children
Time
Youth

AIM

181   If I shoot at the sun I may hit a star.   *—P. T. Barnum*

182   What I aspired to be,
And was not, comforts me.   *—Browning*

183   'Tis not what man Does which exalts him, but what man Would do!   *—Browning*

184   Perhaps the reward of the spirit who tries
Is not the goal but the exercise.   *—E. V. Cooke*

185   Ambition aspires to descend.   *—Corneille*

186   Ambition is like love, impatient both of delays and rivals.   *—Denham*

187   Look not too high,
Lest a chip fall in your eye.   *—Dykes*

188   When a man is no longer anxious to do better than well, he is done for.   *—Haydon*

189   What we earnestly aspire to be, that in some sense we are.   *—Anna Jameson*

190   Ambition is but avarice on stilts and masked.   *—Landor*

191   They make glorious shipwreck who are lost in seeking worlds.   *—Lessing*

192   When a man imagines, even after years of striving, that he has attained perfection, his decline begins.   *—Theodore Martin*

193   Lord, grant that I may always desire more than I can accomplish.
                                                              —*Michelangelo*

194   The mere aspiration is partial realization.   —*Anna Cora Mowatt*

195   It is more important to know where you are going than to get
      there quickly. Do not mistake activity for achievement.
                                                              —*Mabel Newcomber*

196   To be what we are, and to become what we are capable of becom-
      ing, is the only end of life.   —*Stevenson*

197   The world will never disarm until disambitioned.

198   Devotion to duty is a fire that warms us but worldly ambition is a
      fire that consumes us.

SEE ALSO   RELATED SUBJECTS
Conviction 1041   Character
Failure 2070   Competition
Youth 6210   Deeds
                            Purpose

AMERICA

201   I am willing to love all mankind, except an American.   —*Johnson*

202   The United States never lost a war or won a conference.
                                                              —*Will Rogers*

203   America is one long expectoration.   —*Oscar Wilde*

204   Americanism consists in utterly believing in the principles of
      America.   —*Woodrow Wilson*

205   The early North American Indian made a great mistake by not
      having an immigration bureau.

206   Immigration is the sincerest form of flattery.

207   The fault in aliens is that those easiest to exploit are hardest to
      assimilate.

SEE ALSO   RELATED SUBJECTS
Advertising 76   Democracy
Diplomacy 1612   Patriotism
Patriotism 4336
Politics 4510
Youth 6211

ANCESTORS

211   The pride of ancestry increases in the ratio of distance.
                                                              —*G. W. Curtis*

212   Prodigious actions may as well be done,
      By weaver's issue, as by prince's son.
                                                              —*Dryden*

213   Every man is an omnibus in which his ancestors ride.
—O. W. Holmes

214   My nobility begins in me, but yours ends in you.
—Iphicrates to Harmodius

215   Ah, sir, I know nothing about it; I am my own ancestor.   *—Junot*

216   I don't know who my grandfather was; I am much more concerned to know what his grandson will be.   *—Lincoln*

217   The man who has not anything to boast of but his illustrious ancestors is like a potato—the only good belonging to him is underground.   *—Thomas Overbury*

218   It is indeed a desirable thing to be well descended, but the glory belongs to our ancestors.   *—Plutarch*

219   I didn't come on the wrong side of the blanket.   *—Smollett*

220   Each has his own tree of ancestors, but at the top of all sits Probably Arboreal.   *—Stevenson*

221   Nothing like blood, sir, in hosses, dawgs, and men.   *—Thackeray*

222   Whoever serves his country well has no need of ancestors.
—Voltaire

223   You should study the Peerage . . . It is the best thing in fiction the English have ever done.   *—Oscar Wilde*

224   They that on glorious ancestors enlarge
Produce their debt instead of their discharge.   *—Young*

225   You've got to do your own growing, no matter how tall your grandfather was.

226   Send your noble blood to market and see what it will buy.

227   Generations are needed to make a gentleman; mere circumstances make a lady.

228   Great birth is a very poor dish at table.

229   He that boasteth of his ancestors, confesseth he hath no virtue of his own.

230   So yourself be good, a fig for your grandfather.

231   The younger brother is the ancienter gentleman.

232   From our ancestors come our names; but from our virtues our honors.

233   Gentility without ability is worse than plain beggary.

234 A man can't very well make for himself a place in the sun if he keeps continually taking refuge under the family tree.

235 A man who boasts only of his ancestors confesses that he belongs to a family that is better dead than alive.

SEE ALSO   RELATED SUBJECTS
Farming 2143   Courtier
                                  Family

ANGER

241 'Tis said that wrath is the last thing in a man to grow old.
—*Alcaeus*

242 Anger makes dull men witty, but it keeps them poor.   —*Bacon*

243 Never forget what a man says to you when he is angry.
—*H. W. Beecher*

244 An angry man opens his mouth and shuts his eyes.   —*Cato*

245 Whenever you are angry, be assured that it is not only a present evil, but that you have increased a habit.   —*Epictetus*

246 The worst tempered people I've ever met were people who knew they were wrong.   —*Wilson Mizner*

247 An angry man is again angry with himself, when he returns to reason.   —*Publilius Syrus*

248 The anger of lovers renews the strength of love. —*Publilius Syrus*

249 Anger wishes all mankind had only one neck; love, that it had only one heart.   —*J. P. Richter*

250 Epileptics know by signs when attacks are imminent and take precautions accordingly; we must do the same in regard to anger.
—*Seneca*

251 When angry, count four; when very angry, swear. —*Mark Twain*

252 He is a fool who cannot be angry; but he is a wise man who will not.

253 Two things a man should never be angry at; what he can help, and what he cannot help.

254 Choler hates a counsellor.

255 Anger punishes itself.

256 Anger makes a rich man hated, and a poor man scorned.

RELATED SUBJECTS   Insults
Contempt   Quarrel
Fight   Soldiers

ARCHITECTURE

261 Old houses mended,
Cost little less than new before they're ended. —*Colley Cibber*

262 Too many stairs and backdoors make thieves and whores.
—*Balthazar Gerbier*

263 Architecture is frozen music. —*Goethe*

264 To build is to be robbed. —*Johnson*

265 Architecture is the work of nations. —*Ruskin*

266 To build many houses is the readiest road to poverty.

267 Building is a sweet impoverishing.

RELATED SUBJECT
Art

ART

271 The little dissatisfaction which every artist feels at the completion
of a work forms the germ of a new work. —*Auerbach*

272 Art is man's nature; nature is God's art. —*Philip J. Bailey*

273 Art is choice. —*Bezard*

274 I must confess, mine eye and heart
Dote less on Nature than on Art. —*Catullus*

275 Art is limitation; the essence of every picture is the frame.
—*Chesterton*

276 Emotion resulting from a work of art is only of value when it is
not obtained by sentimental blackmail. —*Jean Cocteau*

277 When a work of art appears to be in advance of its period, it is
really the period that has lagged behind the work of art.
—*Jean Cocteau*

278 Too nicely, Jonson knew the critic's part;
Nature in him was almost lost in Art. —*Churton Collins*

279 There are only two styles of portrait painting, the serious and the
smirk. —*Dickens*

280 A photograph is a portrait painted by the sun. —*Dupins*

281 In the vaunted works of Art,
The master-stroke is Nature's part. —*Emerson*

282 Art is the surest and safest civilizer. —*Charles B. Fairbanks*

283 Nothing so resembles a daub as a masterpiece. —*Paul Gauguin*

284   A highbrow is the kind of person who looks at a sausage and thinks
      of Picasso.   —*A. P. Herbert*

285   Art is the only thing on earth, except holiness.   —*J. K. Huysmans*

286   Only God Almighty makes painters.   —*Sir Godfrey Kneller*

287   Menodotis's portrait here is kept;
      Most odd it is
      How very like to all the world,
      Except Menodotis.   —*Leonidas of Alexandria*

288   You see these fish carved finely in relief by Phidian art? Add
      water; they will swim.   —*Martial*

289   The true work of art is but a shadow of the divine perfection.
                                                            —*Michelangelo*

290   There are three arts which are concerned with all things; one
      which uses, another which makes, a third which imitates them.
                                                                   —*Plato*

291   A room hung with pictures is a room hung with thoughts.
                                                        —*Joshua Reynolds*

292   When love and skill work together expect a masterpiece.   —*Ruskin*

293   What garlic is to salad, insanity is to art.   —*Homer Saint-Gaudens*

294   An artist may visit a museum, but only a pedant can live there.
                                                               —*Santayana*

295   Every time I paint a portrait I lose a friend.   —*John Sargent*

296   More matter with less art.   —*Shakespeare*

297   Painting is silent poetry, and poetry is painting with the gift of
      speech.   —*Simonides*

298   To sit for one's portrait is like being present at one's own creation.
                                                          —*Alexander Smith*

299   Good painting is like good cooking: it can be tasted, but not ex-
      plained.   —*Vlaminck*

300   An artist's sphere of influence is the world.   —*Carl von Weber*

301   An artist's career always begins tomorrow.   —*Whistler*

302   Every portrait that is painted with feeling is a portrait of the
      artist, not of the sitter.   —*Oscar Wilde*

303   In art I pull no high-brow stuff,
      I know what I like, and that's enough.   —*William W. Woollcott*

304   Art is life seen through a temperament.   —*Emile Zola*

305   To stone the gods have changed her—but in vain;
      The sculptor's art gave her to breath again. —*On a statue of Niobe*

306   Take a quart of nature, boil it down to a pint, and the residue is
      art.

307   All works of art are the autobiographies of liars.

308   He that lives with the muses shall die in the straw.

309   An artist lives everywhere.

310   The perfection of art is to conceal art.

311   Art helps nature, and experience art.

312   A gilded frame makes a good picture in the eyes of nearly all the
      world.

313   No man is his craft's master the first day.

ATHEISM

321   The fool hath said in his heart,
      There is no God.   —*Bible*

322   Nobody talks so constantly about God as those who insist that
      there is no God.   —*Heywood Broun*

323   An atheist's laugh's a poor exchange
      For Deity offended!   —*Burns*

324   Atheism is the last word of theism.   —*Heine*

325   Regius maintains that there are no gods and that heaven is unoccu-
      pied. His evidence in favor of atheism is that he is a prosperous
      man.   —*Martial*

326   A man cannot become an atheist merely by wishing it.   —*Napoleon*

327   By night an atheist half believes a God.   —*Young*

328   Some are atheists only in fair weather.

329   An atheist is one point beyond the devil.

SEE ALSO   RELATED SUBJECTS
Hypocrisy 3031   Belief
                                  Christianity
                                  Church
                                  Doubt
                                  Faith
                                  God
                                  Religion

AUTOMOBILES

331   The Ford car is Henry Ford done in steel, and other things.
                                            —Samuel S. Marquis

332   Reckless automobile driving arouses the suspicion that much of the horse sense of the good old days was possessed by the horse.

333   Too often a grade crossing is the meeting place of headlights and light heads.

334   The fool that used to blow out the gas now steps on it.

335   All the pedestrians ask is a little more cooperation between horse-power and horse sense.

336   The reason there were fewer wrecks in the old horse-and-buggy days was because the driver didn't depend wholly on his own intelligence.

SEE ALSO   RELATED SUBJECT
Business 572   Travel
Courtship 1180

B

BEAUTY

341   Personal beauty is a greater recommendation than any letter of introduction.   *—Aristotle*

342   There are no ugly women; there are only women who do not know how to look pretty.   *—Antoine P. Berryer*

343   'Tis distance lends enchantment to the view,
And robes the mountain in its azure hue.   *—Campbell*

344   Beauty without grace pleases, but does not captivate, being like bait without a hook.   *—Capiton*

345   The expression a woman wears on her face is far more important than the clothes she wears on her back.   *—Dale Carnegie*

346 It matters more what's in a woman's face than what's on it.
—*Claudette Colbert*

347 Cheerfulness and content are great beautifiers, and are famous preservers of youthful looks. —*Dickens*

348 Lovely female shapes are terrible complicators of the difficulties and dangers of this earthly life, especially for their owner.
—*George Du Maurier*

349 Truth, and goodness, and beauty are but different faces of the same all. —*Emerson*

350 It is the soundness of the bones that ultimates itself in the peach-bloom complexion. —*Emerson*

351 He thought it happier to be dead,
To die for beauty, than live for bread. —*Emerson*

352 If eyes were made for seeing,
Then Beauty is its own excuse for being. —*Emerson*

353 In beauty, faults conspicuous grow;
The smallest speck is seen on snow. —*John Gay*

354 Beauty is eternity gazing at itself in a mirror. —*Kahlil Gibran*

355 The rose's prime lasts one brief hour of morn,
That past, I find no rose—only a thorn. —*Greek Epigram*

356 I cannot spare the luxury of believing that all things beautiful are what they seem. —*Fitz-Greene Halleck*

357 There are beautiful flowers that are scentless, and beautiful women that are unlovable. —*Houillé*

358 Not only does beauty fade, but it leaves a record upon the face as to what became of it. —*Elbert Hubbard*

359 That which is striking and beautiful is not always good; but that which is good is always beautiful. —*Ninon de l'Enclos*

360 Nycilla dyes her locks, 'tis said,
But 'tis a foul aspersion;
She buys them black, they therefore need
No subsequent immersion. —*Lucillius*

361 Thais's teeth are black, Laecania's white. Why? Laecania bought hers, Thais's are her own. —*Martial*

362 You are pleasing when felt. You are pleasing when heard. If not seen, you are altogether pleasing. If seen, you please in no way whatever. —*Martial*

363 When you try to conceal your wrinkles, Polla, with paste made from beans, you deceive yourself, not me. Let a defect, which is

possibly but small, appear undisguised. A fault concealed is pre-
sumed to be great.   —*Martial*

364 Philaenis always weeps with one eye. "How is this?" you ask.
     She has only one.   —*Martial*

365 Do you wish me, Fabullus, to tell you in few words how ugly
     Philaenis is with her one eye? Philaenis would be better looking
     with no eye at all.   —*Martial*

366 Your friends, Fabulla, either are
     Old cronies or beldames uglier far:
     These frumps you trot around with you
     To parties, plays, and galleries too:
     And so, my dear, such hags among
     You look quite pretty and quite young.   —*Martial*

367 In Tibur's sun, the nut-brown maid was told,
     Ivory grows white though yellow turned and old.
     Thither she hies her, but ere long comes back
     (So strong the upland air) not blonde, but black.   —*Martial*

368 On Dora's brow the flower may fade
     The garland may decay:
     But she herself, the sweetest flower,
     Blooms fresher day by day.   —*Meleager*

369 How does he know I have a hump?
     He has never seen my back.
              —*Duke Francois Henri de Montmorency-Bouteville*

370 My only books
     Were woman's looks,
     And folly's all they've taught me.   —*Moore*

371 Cleopatra's nose: had it been shorter, the whole aspect of the
     world would have been altered.   —*Pascal*

372 If to her share some female errors fall,
     Look on her face, and you'll forget 'em all.   —*Pope*

373 If she undervalue me,
     What care I how fair she be?   —*Walter Raleigh*

374 One may live without bread, not without roses.   —*Jean Richepin*

375 Beauty provoketh thieves sooner than gold.   —*Shakespeare*

376 Mollis abuti
     Has an acuti;
     No lasso finis,
     Molli divinis.
                                                                —*Swift*

377 'Tis hard with respect to Beauty, that its possessor should not have a life-enjoyment of it, but be compelled to resign it after, at the most, some forty years' lease. —*Thackeray*

378 The perception of beauty is a moral test. —*Thoreau*

379 What a strange illusion it is to suppose that beauty is goodness! A beautiful woman utters absurdities: we listen, and we hear not the absurdities but wise thoughts. —*Tolstoi*

380 Those who find beautiful meanings in beautiful things are the cultivated. For these there is hope. —*Oscar Wilde*

381 Beauty is worse than wine; it intoxicates both the holder and the beholder. —*Zimmerman*

382 A woman's beauty is not a gift to man—only a bribe.

383 Perfect beauty is always cold; only touches of the commonplace add warmth to it.

384 Beauty skins deep.

385 Blind men's wives need no paint.

386 If all the world were ugly, deformity would be no monster.

387 When the candles are out all women are fair.

388 Beauties without fortunes have sweethearts plenty, but husbands none at all.

389 Beauty may have fair leaves, yet bitter fruit.

390 She who is born a beauty is half married.

391 Beauty without virtue is a curse.

SEE ALSO	RELATED SUBJECTS
Mirror 3973	Art
Poverty 4579	Flattery
Quarrel 4740	Vanity
Wit 5936	Women

BED

401 No civilized person ever goes to bed the same day he gets up.
—*Richard Harding Davis*

402 In bed we laugh, in bed we cry,
And born in bed, in bed we die;
The near approach a bed may show
Of human bliss to human woe. —*Johnson*

403 Whoever thinks of going to bed before twelve o'clock is a scoundrel.
—Johnson

404 The bed comprehends our whole life, for we were born in it, we
live in it, and we shall die in it.   *—Maupassant*

405 To go to bed after midnight is to go to bed betimes.—*Shakespeare*

406 All that are in a bed must not have quiet rest.

407 Age and wedlock bring a man to his nightcap.

408 If a bed would tell all it knows, it would put many to the blush.

409 Bed is a medicine.

RELATED SUBJECTS
Sickness
Sleep

BEE

411 No good sensible working bee listens to the advice of a bedbug on
the subject of business.   *—Elbert Hubbard*

412 That which is not good for the swarm, neither is it good for the
bee.   *—Marcus Aurelius*

413 A swarm of bees in May is worth a load of hay but a swarm in
July is not worth a fly.

414 The bee, from her industry in the summer, eats honey all the
winter.

415 Bees that have honey in their mouths have stings in their tails.

416 Honey is sweet, but the bee stings.

RELATED SUBJECTS
Nature
Work

BEGGING

421 The petition of an empty hand is dangerous.   *—John of Salisbury*

422 Better a living beggar than a buried emperor.   *—La Fontaine*

423 Beggar that I am, I am even poor in thanks.   *—Shakespeare*

424 Beggars mounted run their horse to death.   *—Shakespeare*

425 Neither beg of him who has been a beggar, nor serve him who has
been a servant.

426 Give a beggar a bed and he'll repay you with a louse.

427 Better to die a beggar than live a beggar.

428   Beggars can never be bankrupts.

429   Beggars fear no rebellion.

430   Begging a courtesy is selling liberty.

431   Beggars breed and rich men feed.

432   I am unable, yonder beggar cries,
      To stand, or go;—if he says true, he lies.

SEE ALSO	RELATED SUBJECTS
Ancestors 233	Borrowing
Courtier 1150	Charity
Love 3699	Debt
Work 6083	Hunger
	Poverty

BELIEF

441   A belief is not true because it is useful.   *—Amiel*

442   Lord, I believe; help thou mine unbelief.   *—Bible*

443   There is no unbelief;
      Whoever plants a seed beneath the sod,
      And waits to see it push away the clod,
      Trusts in God.
                                                    —Bulwer-Lytton

444   He who does not believe that God is above all is either a fool or
      has no experience of life.   *—Caecilius Statius*

445   Men freely believe that which they desire.   *—Julius Caesar*

446   Alas, the fearful Unbelief is unbelief in yourself.   *—Carlyle*

447   In politics, as in religion, we have less charity for those who believe
      the half of our creed, than for those who deny the whole of it.
                                                    —C. C. Colton

448   A man must not swallow more beliefs than he can digest.
                                                    —Havelock Ellis

449   We are born believing. A man bears beliefs, as a trees bears apples.
                                                    —Emerson

450   A little credulity helps one on through life very smoothly.
                                                    —Mrs. Gaskell

451   Credulity is the man's weakness, but the child's strength.*—Lamb*

452   Credulity is the common failing of inexperienced virtue; and he
      who is spontaneously suspicious may justly be charged with radi-
      cal corruption.   *—Johnson*

453   Nothing is so firmly believed as what we least know.*—Montaigne*

454   Infidelity does not consist in believing or in disbelieving: it consists
      in professing to believe what one does not believe.

—*Thomas Paine*

455   I know of a charm by way of a prayer that will preserve a man
      from the violence of guns and all manner of fire-weapons and
      engines, but it will do me no good because I do not believe it.

—*Rabelais*

456   Creeds grow so thick along the way,
      Their boughs hide God.   —*Lizette W. Reese*

457   Tell that to the marines—the sailors won't believe it.   —*Scott*

458   You believe that easily which you hope for earnestly.—*Terence*

459   While men believe in the infinite, some ponds will be thought to
      be bottomless.   —*Thoreau*

460   The temerity to believe in nothing.   —*Turgeniev*

461   Orthodoxy is my doxy—heterodoxy is another man's doxy.

—*William Warburton*

462   Better believe it than go where it was done to prove it.

463   He does not believe that does not live according to his belief.

464   He that believes all, misseth; he that believes nothing, hits not.

SEE ALSO   RELATED SUBJECTS
Lies 3531   Atheism
Reason 4781   Conviction
Speeches 5201   Faith
Understanding 5597   God
                         Trust

BLUSHING

471   Once he (Diogenes) saw a youth blushing, and addressed him,
      "Courage, my boy! that is the complexion of virtue."

—*Diogenes Laertius*

472   A blush is no language; only a dubious flag-signal which may mean
      either of two contradictories.   —*George Eliot*

473   The blush is beautiful, but it is sometimes inconvenient.—*Goldoni*

474   Men blush less for their crimes than for their weaknesses and
      vanity.   *La Bruyère*

475   Innocence is not accustomed to blush.   —*Molière*

476   He blushes: all is safe.   —*Terence*

477   Man is the only animal that blushes. Or needs to.—*Mark Twain*

478   The man that blushes is not quite a brute.   *—Young*

479   To blush at vice shows the world you are ashamed of it.

480   Better a blush in the face than a spot in the heart.

SEE ALSO   RELATED SUBJECTS
Bed 408   Chastity
Vanity 5628   Coquetry
                            Decency
                            Modesty
                            Virtue

BODY

481   The body is but a pair of pincers set over a bellows and a stewpan
      and the whole fixed upon stilts.   *—Samuel Butler*

482   Most of the people who came for dancing lessons had Rhumba am-
      bitions and minuet bodies.   *-Bobe Hope*

483   This body is my house—it is not I:
      Triumphant in this faith I live and die.
                            —Frederic Lawrence Knowles

484   Body and spirit are twins: God only knows which is which.
                                                  —Swinburne

485   Every man is the builder of a temple, called his body.—*Thoreau*

486   The body is the socket of the soul.

SEE ALSO   RELATED SUBJECTS
Gravity 2623   Health
Man 3813   Sickness
Modesty 4001
Theatre 5365

BOOKS

491   If bread be what you seek, O little mice,
      Go to some other shelf, is my advice;
      But if upon my books you whet a tooth,
      Your revel you shall rue in bitter truth.   *—Ariston*

492   The printing-press is either the greatest blessing or the greatest
      curse of modern times, one sometimes forgets which.
                                                  —J. M. Barrie

493   Where is human nature so weak as in the book-store?
                                                  —H. W. Beecher

494   Books are embalmed minds.   *—C. N. Bovée*

495   If the whole be greater than a part, a whole man must be greater
      than that part of him which is found in a book.—*Bulwer-Lytton*

496 Through and through the inspired leaves,
Ye maggots make your windings;
But, oh, respect his lordship's taste,
And spare the golden bindings!   —*Burns*

497 'Tis pleasant, sure, to see one's name in print;
A book's a book, although there's nothin' in 't.   —*Byron*

498 There are books of which the backs and covers are by far the best
parts.   —*Dickens*

499 Many thanks; I shall lose no time in reading your book.
—*Disraeli, to an Author who had sent him a book*

500 If we encounter a man of rare intellect, we should ask him what
books he reads.   —*Emerson*

501 Every book is a quotation.   —*Emerson*

502 I would define a book as a work of magic whence escape all kinds
of images to trouble the souls and change the hearts of men.
—*Anatole France*

503 I wrote a book when impotent to fight a battle.
—*Francesco D. Guerrazzi*

504 He might be a very clever man by nature for aught I know, but he
laid so many books upon his head that his brains could not move.
—*Robert Hall*

505 Half of your book is to an index grown;
You give your book *contents,* your reader none.   —*Hannay*

506 The readers and the hearers like my books,
But yet some writers cannot them digest;
But what care I? for when I make a feast
I would my guests should praise it, not the cooks.
—*Sir John Harrington, after Martial*

507 No gentleman can be without three copies of a book: one for show,
one for use, and one for borrowers.   —*Richard Heber*

508 You can cover a great deal of country in books.   —*Andrew Lang*

509 For people who like that kind of a book—that is the kind of book
they will like.   —*Lincoln, on being asked for an opinion*

510 There are excellent bits here, you'll find,
And bits of a so-and-so kind.
Still more than the latter
Are bad bits—no matter!
A book is of all sorts combined.   —*Martial*

511 'Tis easy to write epigrams nicely but to write a book is hard.
—*Martial*

512   A good book is the precious life-blood of a master-spirit, embalmed
      and treasured up on purpose to a life beyond life.   —*Milton*

513   Retirement without the love of letters is a living burial.   —*Seneca*

514   A best-seller is the gilded tomb of a mediocre talent.
                                                  —*Logan Pearsall Smith*

515   Read the best books first, or you may not have a chance to read
      them at all.   —*Thoreau*

516   Man builds no structure which outlives a book.   —*E. F. Ware*

517   Camerado, this is no book,
      Who touches this touches a man.   —*Whitman*

518   We go to a book as Narcissus went to the fountain, see ourselves
      therein, and are enamored.

      SEE ALSO   RELATED SUBJECTS
      Beauty 370   Art
      Censorship 625   Censorship
      Genius 2485   Criticism
      Marriage 3877   Literature
      Science 4941   Pen
      Soul 5173   Philosophy
      Tolerance 5453   Poetry
      War 5734   Writers

BORES

521   *Bore, n.* A person who talks when you wish him to listen.
                                                  —*Ambrose Bierce*

522   Society is now one polish'd horde,
      Formed of two mighty tribes, the *Bores* and *Bored.*   —*Byron*

523   His room is better than his company.   —*Robert Greene*

524   Out of sight, out of mind: this may run right;
      For all be not in mind that be in sight.   —*Heywood*

525   He is not only dull himself, but the cause of dullness in others.
                                                         —*Johnson*

526   Perhaps no man ever thought a line superfluous when he wrote it.
      We are seldom tiresome to ourselves.   —*Johnson*

527   We often forgive those who bore us but we cannot forgive those
      whom we bore.   —*La Rochefoucauld*

528   Got the ill name of augurs, because they were bores.   —*Lowell*

529   The basic fact about human existence is not that it is a tragedy, but
      that it is a bore.   —*Mencken*

530   A prating barber asked Archelaus how he would be trimmed. He
      answered, "In silence."   —*Plutarch*

531   I assure you it requires no small talents to be a decided bore.
                                                                —*Scott*

532   Nature makes a fool; a bore belongs to civilization.

533   If the good people have not made the world better, they have surely
        made it duller.

534   Bore: one who is interesting to a point—the point of departure.

535   Dullness has depth.

536   There is nothing so pathetic as a bore who claims attention—and
        gets it.

See Also   Related Subjects
Actors 51   Conceit
Hero 2882   Conversation
                             Fools
                             Speeches

BORROWING

541   Be not made a beggar by banqueting upon borrowing.—*Apocrypha*

542   The borrower is servant to the lender.   —*Bible*

543   If you would know the value of money, go try to borrow some;
        for he that goes a-borrowing goes a-sorrowing.   —*Franklin*

544   Th' feller that calls you "brother" generally wants something that
        don't belong to him.   —*Kin Hubbard*

545   He who prefers to give to Linus the half of what he wishes to bor-
        row, rather than to lend him the whole, prefers to lose only the
        half.   —*Martial*

546   I have bought a property in the country for a good round sum,
        Caecilianus, and ask you to lend me a thousand. Won't you give
        me an answer? I fancy from your silence you are saying, "You
        won't pay it back." That is just why I am asking for it,
        Caecilianus.   —*Martial*

547   Let us all be happy and live within our means, even if we have to
        borrow the money to do it with.   —*Artemus Ward*

548   The man who never lends money never has many friends. Also, he
        doesn't need them.

Related Subjects
Begging
Credit
Debt
Money

BREVITY

551 For brevity is very good,
Where we are, or are not understood. —*Samuel Butler*

552 Let thy speech be short, comprehending much in few words.
—*Ecclesiasticus*

553 There is need of brevity that the thought may run on.—*Horace*

554 But what is the use of brevity, tell me, when there is a whole book
of it? —*Martial*

555 As man is now constituted, to be brief is almost a condition of being
inspired. —*Santayana*

556 Since brevity is the soul of wit,
And tediousness the limbs and outward flourishes,
I will be brief. —*Shakespeare*

557 Be brief; for it is with words as with sunbeams, the more they are
condensed the deeper they burn. —*Southey*

558 Not that the story need be long, but it will take a long while to
make it short. —*Thoreau*

SEE ALSO
Drinking 1746
Life 3567

RELATED SUBJECTS
Epigrams
Wit

BUSINESS

561 Christmas is over and Business is Business. —*F.P.A.*

562 The market is the place set apart where men may deceive each
other. —*Anacharsis*

563 The playthings of our elders are called business. —*St. Augustine*

564 Our grand business is not to see what lies dimly in the distance,
but to do what lies clearly at hand. —*Carlyle*

565 Without some dissimulation no business can be carried on at all.
—*Chesterfield*

566 Promptness is the soul of business. —*Chesterfield*

567 Business will be either better or worse. —*Calvin Coolidge*

568 A business with an income at its heels
Furnishes always oil for its own wheels. —*Cowper*

569 Here's the rule for bargains:
"Do other men, for they would do you." —*Dickens*

570 Never shrink from anything which your business calls you to do.
The man who is above his business may one day find his business
above him. —*Daniel Drew*

571   Business? It's quite simple. It's other people's money.
                                                    —*Dumas the Younger*

572   A business, like an automobile, has to be driven, in order to get
       results.   —*B. C. Forbes*

573   No nation was ever ruined by trade.   —*Franklin*

574   Where wealth and freedom reign contentment fails,
       And honor sinks where commerce long prevails. —*Goldsmith*

575   The firm is really ahead of the times. It has a stock market ticker
       that prints its reports on thin aspirins.   —*Bob Hope*

576   Big business makes its money out of by-products.—*Elbert Hubbard*

577   The merchant has no country.   —*Jefferson*

578   Talk of nothing but business, and despatch that business quickly.
                                                       —*Aldus Manutius*

579   Business is a combination of war and sport.   —*André Maurois*

580   It is easy to escape from business, if you will only despise the re-
       wards of business.   —*Seneca*

581   Of all the damnable waste of human life that ever was invented,
       clerking is the very worst.   —*Bernard Shaw*

582   He had talents equal to business, and aspired no higher.
                                                             —*Tacitus*

583   When two men in a business always agree, one of them is unneces-
       sary.   —*William Wrigley, Jr.*

584   Go to your business, pleasure, whilst I go to my pleasure, business.
                                                     —*William Wycherley*

585   It is not the crook in modern business that we fear, but the honest
       man who doesn't know what he is doing.   —*Owen D. Young*

586   A handful of trade is a handful of gold.

587   Trade is the mother of money.

588   A merchant's happiness hangs upon chance, winds, and waves.

589   Trade knows neither friends nor kindred.

590   Men that have much business must have much pardon.

591   He that thinks his business below him will always be above his
       business.

592   Boldness in business is the first, second, and third thing.

593   He who findeth fault meaneth to buy.

594 It is a bad bargain, where both are losers.

595 Make every bargain clear and plain
That none may afterwards complain.

596 It is naught, it is naught, saith the buyer; but when he is gone his way, then he boasteth.

597 In business the man who engages in the most adventures is surest to come out unhurt.

SEE ALSO
Bee 411
Crime 1234
Eating 1785
Fools 2291, 2294
Honesty 2914, 2927
Idealism 3060
Preachers 4620
Sacrifice 4902
War 5742

RELATED SUBJECTS
Advertising
Competition
Money
Work

C

CAT

601 Those who'll play with cats must expect to be scratched.
—Cervantes

602 The Cat in Gloves catches no Mice. *—Franklin*

603 There are more ways of killing a cat than choking her with cream.
—Kingsley

604 When I play with my cat, who knows whether I do not make her more sport than she makes me? *—Montaigne*

605 When the cat's away the mice will play.

606 When all candles be out all cats be grey.

607 Keep no more cats than will catch mice.

SEE ALSO
Fidelity 2195
Lawyers 3415
Love 3734

RELATED SUBJECTS
Dogs
Nature

CAUTION

611 Confident because of our caution. *—Epictetus*

612   When the cup is full, carry it even.   —*Scotch Proverb*

613   'Tis better to bear the ills we have
      Than fly to others that we know not of.   —*Shakespeare*

614   The early worm should read the proverbs.

615   He that a watch would carry, this must do,
      Pocket his watch, and watch his pocket too.

616   Consideration gets as many victories as rashness loses.

SEE ALSO	RELATED SUBJECTS
Chastity 750	Conservative
Eggs 1826	Discretion
Property 4682	Excess
Thought 5397	Judgment

CENSORSHIP

621   She flays with indignation haughty
      The passages she thinks are naughty,
      But reads them *carefully* so that
      She'll know what to be angry at.   —*Edward Anthony*

622   Pontius Pilate was the first great censor and Jesus Christ the first
      great victim of censorship.   —*Ben Lindsey*

623   Why have you come into my show, austere Cato? Pray, did you
      walk in merely for the purpose of walking out?   —*Martial*

624   Censorship ends in logical completeness when nobody is allowed
      to read any books except the books nobody can read.
                                                —*G. B. Shaw*

625   Damn all expurgated books, the dirtiest book of all is the ex-
      purgated book.   —*Whitman*

RELATED SUBJECTS
Books
Criticism
Dictators
Liberty
Literature

CHANCE

631   Chance is a nickname of Providence.   —*De Chamfort*

632   Work and acquire, and thou hast chained the wheel of Chance.
                                                —*Emerson*

633   Chance fights ever on the side of the prudent.   —*Euripides*

634   Chance is perhaps the pseudonym of God when He did not want
      to sign.   —*Anatole France*

635   Chances rule men and not men chances.   —*Herodotus*

636   He is no wise man that will quit a certainty for an uncertainty.
                                                      —*Johnson*

637   The only certainty is that nothing is certain.   —*Pliny the Elder*

638   All chance, direction, which thou canst not see.   —*Pope*

639   Chance is a name for our ignorance.   —*Leslie Stephens*

640   He who trusts all things to chance, makes a lottery of his life.

641   A wise man turns chance into good fortune.

SEE ALSO   RELATED SUBJECTS
Action 16   Danger
Fight 2217   Fortune
                        Gambling
                        Judgment
                        Luck
                        Opportunity

CHANGE

651   He that will not apply new remedies must expect new evils.
                                                      —*Bacon*

652   The world is a scene of changes; to be constant in nature were
         inconstancy.   —*Cowley*

653   Matters change and morals change; men remain.   —*Galsworthy*

654   All change is not growth; as all movement is not forward.
                                                      —*Ellen Glasgow*

655   What I possess I would gladly retain
        Change amuses the mind, yet scarcely profits.   —*Goethe*

SEE ALSO   RELATED SUBJECTS
Fortune 2327   Caution
Luck 3776   Compromise
Mirror 3975   Habit
                        Revolution

CHARACTER

661   In all thy humors, whether grave or mellow,
        Thou'rt such a touchy, testy, pleasant fellow,
        Hast so much wit and mirth and spleen about thee,
        There is no living with thee, nor without thee.   —*Addison*

662   The tragedy of a man who has found himself out.—*J. M. Barrie*

663   No author ever drew a character consistent to human nature, but
         he was forced to ascribe to it many inconsistencies.
                                                      —*Bulwer-Lytton*

664 Character must be kept bright, as well as clean.   —*Chesterfield*

665 I am not concerned that I have no place,
     I am concerned how I may fit myself for one,
     I am not concerned that I am not known,
     I seek to be worthy to be known.   —*Confucius*

666 Every woman's man and every man's woman.
                                          —*Curio, of Julius Caesar*

667 Make the most of yourself, for that is all there is of you.
                                                        —*Emerson*

668 And what is a weed? A plant whose virtues have not been dis-
     covered.   —*Emerson*

669 A character is like an acrostic—read it forward, backward, or
     across, it still spells the same thing.   —*Emerson*

670 Character is that which can do without success.   —*Emerson*

671 A foolish consistency is the hobgoblin of little minds.—*Emerson*

672 You cannot dream yourself into a character; you must hammer and
     forge yourself one.   —*Froude*

673 Our opinion of people depends less upon what we see in them, than
     upon what they make us see in ourselves.   —*Sarah Grand*

674 The goal of evolution is self-conquest.   —*Elbert Hubbard*

675 If men could only know each other, they would never either idolize
     or hate.   —*Elbert Hubbard*

676 He is happy whose circumstances suit his temper but he is more
     excellent who can suit his temper to any circumstances.
                                                       —*David Hume*

677 To be capable of respect is almost as rare as to be worthy of it.
                                                         —*Joubert*

678 You'll never plumb the Oriental mind,
     And if you did, it isn't worth the toil.   —*Kipling*

679 Many men, suspected of being good fellows, have, when the evi-
     dence was summed up, proved an alibi.   —*R. G. Knowles*

680 It is often temperament which makes men brave and women chaste.
                                                —*La Rochefoucauld*

681 Even when the bird walks we see that he has wings.   —*Lemoine*

682 Character is like a tree and reputation like its shadow. The shadow
     is what we think of it; the tree is the real thing.   —*Lincoln*

683 Circumstances are the rulers of the weak; they are but the instru-
     ments of the wise.   —*Samuel Lover*

684   The measure of a man's real character is what he would do if he knew he would never be found out.   *—Macaulay*

685   You often ask me, Priscus, what sort of man I should be, if all of a sudden I became rich and powerful. Do you think that anybody can tell you what his future character will be? Tell me, if you became a lion, what sort of lion would you be?   *—Martial*

686   With red hair, a black face, a cloven foot, and blear eyes, you show the world a progidy, Zoilus, if you are an honest man.*—Martial*

687   You wish to appear, Cotta, a pretty man and a great man at one and the same time: but he who is a pretty man, Cotta, is a very small man.   *—Martial*

688   Your face is black, your hair like flame,
And one eye's damaged, one foot lame:
If, still, you're quite a decent chap—
Well, 'tis a feather in your cap.   *—Martial*

689   A handsome person, with perverted will,
Is a fine craft that's handled without skill.   *—Menander*

690   He who attends to his greater self becomes a great man, and he who attends to his smaller self becomes a small man.*—Mencius*

691   No one but yourself knows whether you are cowardly and cruel, or loyal and devout; others do not see you; they surmise you by uncertain conjectures; they perceive not so much your nature as your art.   *—Montaigne*

692   Everyone can play the mummer's part, and represent an honest personage on the stage; but inwardly, within his own bosom, where all is permitted us, where all is concealed, to keep a duel role there, that's the point.   *—Montaigne*

693   Few men have been admired by their own domestic servants.
   —Montaigne

694   Character is what you are in the dark.   *—Dwight L. Moody*

695   Some lives are like an ebbing tide in a harbor; the farther they go out, the more mud they expose.   *—Austin O'Malley*

696   All the world is queer save thee and me, and even thou art a little queer.   *—Robert Owen*

697   Character is much easier kept than recovered.   *—Thomas Paine*

698   Reputation is what men and women think of us; character is what God and the angels know of us.   *—Thomas Paine*

699   The fate of all extremes is such:
Men may be read, as well as books, too much.   *—Pope*

700   It matters not what you are thought to be, but what you are.
                                                —*Publilius Syrus*

701   A man never shows his own character so plainly as by the way he
      portrays another's.   —*J. P. Richter*

702   They say best men are moulded out of faults;
      And, for the most, become much more the better
      For being a little bad.   —*Shakespeare*

703   Our remedies oft in ourselves do lie,
      Which we ascribe to Heaven.   —*Shakespeare*

704   It is safest to be moderately base—to be flexible in shame, and to
      be always ready for what is generous, good, and just, when any-
      thing is to be gained by virtue.   —*Sidney Smith*

705   Put more trust in nobility of character than in an oath.   —*Solon*

706   The fox changes his fur, but not his habits.   —*Suetonius*

707   Fame is what you have taken,
          Character's what you give;
      When to this truth you waken,
          Then you begin to live.   —*Bayard Taylor*

708   Occasions do not make a man either strong or weak, but they show
      what he is.   —*Thomas à Kempis*

709   How can we expect a harvest of thought who have not had a seed-
      time of character?   —*Thoreau*

710   Everyone is a moon, and has a dark side which he never shows to
      anybody.   —*Mark Twain*

711   I am as bad as the worst, but thank God I am as good as the best.
                                                    —*Whitman*

712   Character is a by-product; it is produced in the great manufacture
      of daily duty.   —*Woodrow Wilson*

713   You can mold a mannerism, but you must chisel a character.

714   The strongest woman and the weakest man are about equally mean.

715   Little people do not wear well under either extremes of fortune.

716   Crows are never the whiter for washing themselves.

717   When wealth is lost, nothing is lost;
      When health is lost, something is lost;
      When character is lost, all is lost!

718   An ape is ne'er so like an ape
      As when he wears a doctor's cape.

719   When we can no longer blame things on liquor or war's reaction, we may begin to suspect that human nature itself is a little faulty.

720   Small people never learn to be indifferent; they either envy or pity.

SEE ALSO	RELATED SUBJECTS
Beauty, 358	Conscience
Children 767	Conviction
Laughter 3362	Courage
Morality 4092	Deeds
Solitude 5153	Duty
	Honor
	Purpose

CHARITY

721   He who confers a benefit on anyone loves him better than he is beloved.   *—Aristotle*

722   If you confer a benefit, never remember it; if you receive one, never forget it.   *—Chilon*

723   There is a hook in every benefit, that sticks in his jaws that takes the benefit, and draws him whither the benefactor will.
—John Donne

724   Take egotism out, and you would castrate the benefactors.
—Emerson

725   Alas for the rarity
Of Christian charity
Under the sun!   *—Thomas Hood*

726   In faith and hope the world will disagree,
But all mankind's concern is charity.   *—Pope*

727   To accept a benefit is to sell one's freedom.   *—Publilius Syrus*

728   Let him that hath done the good office conceal it; let him that hath received it disclose it.   *—Seneca*

729   He that feeds upon charity has a cold dinner and no supper.

730   Whatever is given to the poor, is laid out of the reach of fortune.

731   The charitable give out at the door and God puts in at the window.

732   Charity and pride have different aims, yet both feed the poor.

733   Charity begins at home, but should not end there.

734   Charity excuseth not cheating.

735   Benefits, like flowers, please most when they are fresh.

736   Charity begins at home and generally dies from lack of out-of-door exercise; sympathy travels abroad extensively.

737   A charitable man is like an apple tree—he gives his fruit and is
      silent; the philanthropist is like the hen.

                              RELATED SUBJECTS
                              Generosity
                              Gifts
                              Greed
                              Kindness
                              Pity
                              Selfishness

CHASTITY

741   She is chaste who was never asked the question.   —*Congreve*

742   Beneath this stone I lie, the famous woman who loosed her zone
      to one man only.   —*Greek Epigram*

743   A woman's chastity consists, like an onion, of a series of coats.
                                                    —*Hawthorne*

744   A chaste woman ought not to dye her hair yellow.   —*Menander*

745   An unattempted woman cannot boast of her chastity.—*Montaigne*

746   If she is chaste when there is no fear of detection, she is truly
      chaste; she who sins not because she dare not, does the sin.—*Ovid*

747   I will find you twenty lascivious turtles ere one chaste man.
                                                    —*Shakespeare*

748   Who doth desire that chaste his wife should be,
      First be he true, for truth doth truth deserve.—*Sir Philip Sidney*

749   I have been so misused by chaste men with one wife
      That I would live with satyrs all my life.   —*Anna Wickham*

750   If not chastely, at all events cautiously.

      SEE ALSO   RELATED SUBJECTS
      Credit 1201   Blushing
      Poetry 4524   Coquetry
                              Maid
                              Modesty
                              Virtue

CHEATING

751   The first and worst of all frauds is to cheat oneself.
                                                    —*Philip J. Bailey*

752   Don't steal; thou'lt never thus compete
      Successfully in business. Cheat.   —*Ambrose Bierce*

753   'Tis my opinion every man cheats in his way, and he is only honest
      who is not discovered.   —*Susannah Centlivre*

754   Prefer loss before unjust gain; for that brings grief but once; this forever.   *—Chilon*

755   Hope of ill gain is the beginning of loss.   *—Democritus*

756   Three things are men most likely to be cheated in, a horse, a wig, and a wife.   *—Franklin*

757   He who purposely cheats his friend, would cheat his God.   *—Lavater*

758   He that's cheated twice by the same man is an accomplice with the cheater.

759   He that will cheat at play
Will cheat you any way.

SEE ALSO
Charity 734
Gambling 2459

RELATED SUBJECTS
Competition
Crime
Deception
Gambling
Honesty

CHILDREN

761   I love little children, and it is not a slight thing when they, who are fresh from God, love us.   *—Dickens*

762   It is good to be children sometimes, and never better than at Christmas, when its mighty Founder was a child himself.   *—Dickens*

763   Childhood has no forebodings; but then, it is soothed by no memories of outlived sorrow.   *—George Eliot*

764   Infancy is the perpetual Messiah, which comes into the arms of fallen men, and pleads with them to return to paradise.   *—Emerson*

765   If Nature had arranged that husbands and wives should have children alternatively, there would never be more than *three* in a family.   *—Laurence Housman*

766   Th' worst feature of a new baby is its mother's singing.   *—Kin Hubbard*

767   The proper time to influence the character of a child is about a hundred years before he is born.   *—Dean Inge*

768   Children have more need of models than of critics.   *—Joubert*

769   There's nothing costs a man less than his son.   *—Juvenal*

770   'Tis unto children most respect is due.   *—Juvenal*

771   The childhood shows the man,
      As morning shows the day.   *Milton*

772   The only bird that gives the poor a real tumble is the stork.
                                                  —*Wilson Mizner*

773   One of the best things in the world to be is a boy; it requires no ex-
      perience, but needs some practice to be a good one.
                                          —*Charles Dudley Warner*

774   A boy has a natural genius for combining business with pleasure.
                                          —*Charles Dudley Warner*

775   Children begin by loving their parents; as they grow older they
      judge them; sometimes they forgive them.   —*Oscar Wilde*

776   The child is father of the man.   —*Wordsworth*

777   A man among children will be long a child, a child among men
      will be soon a man.

778   Many children, and little bread, is a painful pleasure.

779   Children are certain cares, but uncertain comforts.

780   Children increase the cares of life, but mitigate the remembrance
      of death.

781   Late children are early orphans.

SEE ALSO	RELATED SUBJECTS
Debt 1399	Family
Home 2906	Father
Vice 5644	Mother

CHRISTIANITY

791   Everyone in the world is Christ and they are all crucified.
                                              —*Sherwood Anderson*

792   A Christian is nothing but a sinful man who has put himself to
      school to Christ for the honest purpose of becoming better.
                                                  —*H. W. Beecher*

793   Christians and camels receive their burdens kneeling.
                                                  —*Ambrose Bierce*

794   Jesus Christ, the condescension of divinity, and the exaltation of
      humanity.   —*Phillips Brooks*

795   The Christian has greatly the advantage of the unbeliever, having
      everything to gain and nothing to lose.   —*Byron*

796   The difference between Socrates and Jesus Christ? The great Con-
      scious; the immeasurably great Unconscious.   —*Carlyle*

797   His Christianity was muscular.   —*Disraeli*

798 The Christian is like the ripening corn; the riper he grows the more lowly he bends his head. —*Guthrie*

799 He who shall introduce into public affairs the principles of primitive Christianity, will revolutionize the world. —*Franklin*

800 Every bird that upwards swings
Bears the Cross upon its wings. —*John M. Neale*

801 Take up the cross if thou the crown wouldst gain. —*St. Paulinus*

802 All history is incomprehensible without Christ. —*Rénan*

803 Whatever makes men good Christians, makes them good citizens.
—*Daniel Webster*

804 Scratch the Christian and you find the pagan—spoiled.
—*Israel Zangwill*

805 The greatest service that could be rendered the Christian peoples would be to convert them to Christianity.

SEE ALSO	RELATED SUBJECTS
Censorship 622	Atheism
Cowardice 1186	Belief
Hypocrisy 3037	Church
Injury 3143	God
Self-Denial 4984	Heaven
	Morality
	Prayer
	Religion

CHURCH

811 Where God hath a temple, the Devil will have a chapel.—*Burton*

812 The only place a new hat can be carried into with safety is a church, for there is plenty of room there. —*Leigh Hunt*

813 To be of no church is dangerous. —*Johnson*

814 Who builds a church to God, and not to fame,
Will never mark the marble with his name. —*Pope*

815 To the Church I once went,
But I grieved and I sorrowed;
For the season was Lent,
And the sermon was borrowed.

816 Church-work goes on slowly.

817 Many come to bring their clothes to church rather than themselves.

818 Bells call others, but themselves enter not into the Church.

819 The building of a "sky-scraper church" would seem to be a move in the right direction.

820   "Attend your Church," the parson cries:
      To church each fair one goes;
      The old go there to close their eyes,
      The young to eye their clothes.

821   This is God's House; but 'tis to be deplor'd,
      More come to see the house than serve its Lord.

SEE ALSO   RELATED SUBJECTS
Difficulty 1592   Christianity
                            God
                            Prayer
                            Preachers
                            Religion

CITIES

831   New York, the hussy, was taken in sin again!   —*Thomas Beer*

832   If you would be known, and not know, vegetate in a village; if
      you would know, and not be known, live in a city.—*C. C. Colton*

833   A community is like a ship; every one ought to be prepared to take
      the helm.   —*Ibsen*

834   Cities have always been the fireplaces of civilization, whence light
      and heat radiated out into the dark.   —*Theodore Parker*

835   What is the city but the people?   —*Shakespeare*

836   The thing generally raised on city land is taxes.
                                          —*Charles Dudley Warner*

837   A great city is that which has the greatest men and women.
                                                        —*Whitman*

838   Broadway is a main artery of New York life—the hardened artery.
                                                  —*Walter Winchell*

839   A great city, a great solitude.

890   The most dangerous savages live in cities.

SEE ALSO   RELATED SUBJECTS
Money 4041   Architecture
Soldiers 5144   People
World 6095   Society

CIVILIZATION

841   The origin of civilization is man's determination to do nothing for
      himself which he can get done for him.   —*H. C. Bailey*

842   Increased means and increased leisure are the two civilizers of man.
                                                        —*Disraeli*

843 The true test of civilization is, not the census, nor the size of cities, nor the crops, but the kind of man that the country turns out.
—Emerson

844 A sufficient and sure method of civilization is the influence of good women. *—Emerson*

845 A decent provision for the poor is the true test of civilization.
—Johnson

846 "Civilization totters," say the pessimists. "But it totters steadily onward," cheerfully respond the men of optimistic mind.

847 Civilization is just a slow process of learning to be kind.

848 Civilized nations are ones that simply can't endure wrongs or injustice except at home.

SEE ALSO
Art 282
Bed 401
Bores 532
Happiness 2790
Haste 2824
Vanity 5631
War 5745

RELATED SUBJECTS
America
Ancestors
Democracy
Dictators
Government
History
Kings
People
Reform
War
World

CLEANLINESS

851 When a man reproached him (Diogenes) for going into unclean places, he said, "The sun too penetrates into privies, but is not polluted by them." *—Diogenes Laertius*

852 Beauty will fade and perish, but personal cleanliness is practically undying, for it can be renewed whenever it discovers symptoms of decay. *—W. S. Gilbert*

853 Above all things, keep clean. It is not necessary to be a pig in order to raise one. *—Robert Ingersoll*

854 Dirt is not dirt, but only something in the wrong place.
—Lord Palmerston

855 Cleanliness is next to godliness.

856 Cleanliness is next to impossible.

857 One keep-clean is better than ten make-cleans.

RELATED SUBJECTS
Habits
Health

CLEVERNESS

861   Cleverness is serviceable for everything, sufficient for nothing.
—Amiel

862   It's clever, but is it art?   *—Kipling*

863   It is great cleverness to know how to conceal one's cleverness.
—La Rochefoucauld

864   Too clever is dumb.   *—Ogden Nash*

865   Clever people needn't be good; they can simulate.

See Also	Related Subjects
Genius 2485	Conversation
Women 5979	Epigrams
	Fools
	Ignorance
	Learning
	Speeches
	Words

CLOTHES

871   It is not only fine feathers that make fine birds.   *—Aesop*

872   *Garter:* an elastic band intended to keep a woman from coming out of her stockings and desolating the country.   *—Ambrose Bierce*

873   Trust not the heart of that man for whom old clothes are not venerable.   *—Carlyle*

874   'Tis the same to him who wears a shoe, as if the whole earth were covered with leather.   *—Emerson*

875   Any garment which is cut to fit you is much more becoming, even if it is not so splendid as a garment which has been cut to fit somebody not of your stature.   *—Edna Ferber*

876   A sweet disorder in the dress
Kindles in clothes a wantonness.   *—Robert Herrick*

877   The style's the man, so books avow;
The style's the woman, anyhow.   *—O. W. Holmes*

878   Young Lafe Bud says he allus hates t' git his hair cut cause it makes his hat look so old.   *—Kin Hubbard*

879   Legs are staple articles and will never go out of fashion while the world lasts.   *—Jarrett & Palmer*

880   Where's the man could ease a heart
Like a satin gown?   *—Dorothy Parker*

881 The wasting moth ne'er spoil'd my best array;
The cause was this, I wore it every day. —*Pope*

882 The fashion wears out more apparel than the man.—*Shakespeare*

883 Through tatter'd clothes small vices do appear;
Robes and furr'd gowns hide all. —*Shakespeare*

884 She wears her clothes as if they were thrown on with a pitchfork.
—*Swift*

885 Beware of all enterprises that require new clothes. —*Thoreau*

886 We are all Adam's children, but silk makes the difference.

887 Fond pride of dress is sure a very curse;
Ere fancy you consult, consult your purse.

888 Better go to heaven in rags than to hell in embroidery.

889 A fop of fashion is the mercer's friend, the tailor's fool, and his
own foe.

890 When dressed for the evening, the girls now-a-days
Scarce an atom of dress on them leave;
Nor blame them; for what is an evening dress
But a dress that is suited for Eve?

SEE ALSO   RELATED SUBJECTS
Church 817, 820   Conceit
God 2530   Extravagance
Poverty 4570   Modesty
Truth 5564   Vanity
Vanity 5619

COMPETITION

891 Anybody can win unless there happens to be a second entry.
—*George Ade*

892 The only competition worthy of a wise man is with himself.
—*Washington Allston*

893 Thou shalt not covet: but tradition
Approves all forms of competition. —*A. H. Clough*

894 It's them as take advantage that get advantage i' this world.
—*George Eliot*

895 There is great ability in knowing how to conceal one's ability.
—*La Rochefoucauld*

896 Do unto the other feller the way he'd like to do unto you an' do
it fust. —*E. N. Westcott*

897   Every advantage has its disadvantage.

SEE ALSO   RELATED SUBJECTS
Conversation 1015   Business
Success 5244   Difficulty
                                  Money
                                  Opportunity
                                  Work

COMPLAINT

901   Those who do not complain are never pitied.   *—Jane Austen*

902   If you know a better 'ole, go to it.   *—Bruce Bairnsfather*

903   I hate to be a kicker, I always long for peace,
       But the wheel that does the squeaking is the one that gets the
       grease.   *—Josh Billings*

904   It is a general error to suppose the loudest complainers for the
       public to be the most anxious for its welfare.   *—Burke*

905   Go not for every grief to the physician, nor for every quarrel to the
       lawyer, nor for every thirst to the pot.   *—George Herbert*

906   The usual fortune for complaint is to excite contempt more than
       pity.   *—Johnson*

907   Some people are always grumbling because roses have thorns. I am
       thankful that thorns have roses.   *—Alphonse Karr*

908   Striving to better, oft we mar what's well.   *—Shakespeare*

909   Cease to lament for that thou canst not help;
       And study help for that which thou lamentst.   *—Shakespeare*

910   Discontent is the first step in the progress of a man or a nation.
                                                           —Oscar Wilde

911   The complaint of the present times is the general complaint of all
       times.

SEE ALSO   RELATED SUBJECTS
Business 595   Content
Flattery 2244   Criticism
Gambling 2453   Disappointment
                                  Excuse
                                  Hardship
                                  Resignation
                                  Weather

COMPROMISE

921   Please all, and you will please none.   *—Aesop*

922 Compromise is but the sacrifice of one right or good in the hope of retaining another, too often ending in the loss of both.
—*Tryon Edwards*

923 If two people ride the same horse, one must ride behind.
—*Bishop Fowler*

924 It is the weak man who urges compromise—never the strong man.
—*Elbert Hubbard*

925 Who·seeks to please all men each way,
And not himself offend,
He may begin his work today,
But God knows where he'll end.　　　—*Rowlands*

926 'Tis not so deep as a well, nor so wide as a churchdoor; but 'tis enough, 'twill serve.　　　—*Shakespeare*

927 Your "If" is the only peacemaker; much virtue in "If."
—*Shakespeare*

928 A lean compromise is better than a fat lawsuit.

RELATED SUBJECTS
Decision
Diplomacy
Politics
Weakness

CONCEIT

931 Much outcry, little outcome.　　　—*Aesop*

932 Conceit is God's gift to little men.　　　—*Bruce Barton*

933 Anybody, providing he knows how to be amusing, has the right to talk about himself.　　　—*Baudelaire*

934 The world tolerates conceit from those who are successful, but not from anybody else.　　　—*John Blake*

935 I winna blaw about mysel,
As ill I like my faults to tell.　　　—*Burns*

936 The greatest of faults, I should say, is to be conscious of none.
—*Carlyle*

937 I've never any pity for conceited people, because I think they carry their comfort about with them.　　　—*George Eliot*

938 We reproach people for talking about themselves; but it is the subject they treat best.　　　—*Anatole France*

939 The average man plays to the gallery of his own self-esteem.
—*Elbert Hubbard*

940   Conceit is the finest armor a man can wear.—*Jerome K. Jerome*

941   Every man's affairs, however little, are important to himself.
                                                          —*Johnson*

942   And so we plough along, as the fly said to the ox.   —*Longfellow*

943   The empty vessel giveth a greater sound than the full barrel.
                                                          —*John Lyly*

944   You are pretty—we know it; and young—it's true; and rich—who
        can deny it? But when you praise yourself extravagantly, Fabula,
        you appear neither rich, nor pretty, nor young.   —*Martial*

945   If the world complains that I speak too much about myself, I com-
        plain that the world does not so much as think of itself at all.
                                                          —*Montaigne*

946   Conceit may puff a man up, but never prop him up.   —*Ruskin*

947   The worst cliques are those which consist of one man.—*G. B. Shaw*

948   Self-complacency is pleasure accompanied by the idea of oneself as
        cause.   —*Spinoza*

949   To love oneself is the beginning of a lifelong romance.
                                                          —*Oscar Wilde*

950   Self-praise is no recommendation.

951   If you love yourself over much, nobody else will love you at all.

952   He that is always right is always wrong.

953   No man can think well of himself who does not think well of
        others.

954   Great boast, small roast.

955   A boaster and a liar are cousins.

956   He has the greatest blind-side, who thinks he has none.

957   Egotism is the anesthesia that keeps people on living terms with
        themselves.

958   Great cry and little wool, as the Devil said when he sheared the
        hogs.

SEE ALSO	RELATED SUBJECTS
Actors 50	Flattery
Charity 724	Illusion
Conscience 967	Modesty
God 2537	Reputation
Honesty 2930	Selfishness
Success 5237	Vanity

CONSCIENCE

961   The disease of an evil conscience is beyond the practice of all the physicians of all the countries in the world.   *—Gladstone*

962   Conscience: an inner voice that warns us somebody is·looking.
         —Mencken

963   A New England conscience doesn't keep you from doing anything; it just keeps you from enjoying it.   *—Mendell*

964   Conscience has no more to do with gallantry than it has with politics.   *—Sheridan*

965   Conscience is, in most men, an anticipation of the opinion of others.
         —Taylor

966   Conscience and cowardice are really the same things.*—Oscar Wilde*

967   Conscience makes egotists of us all.   *—Oscar Wilde*

968   What a pity to be born a rascal and be handicapped by a conscience!

969   A guilty conscience flatters the good.

SEE ALSO	RELATED SUBJECTS
Conviction 1043	Character
Debt 1409	Conviction
Gratitude 2612	Help
Modesty 4001	Hypocrisy
	Idealism
	Remorse

CONSERVATIVE

971   It seems to me a barren thing, this conservatism—an unhappy crossbreed, the mule of politics that engenders nothing.   *—Disraeli*

972   Men are conservative when they are least vigorous, or when they are most luxurious.   *—Emerson*

973   The highest function of conservatism is to keep what progressiveness has accomplished.   *—R. H. Fulton*

974   The only difference between a rut and a grave is their dimensions.
         —Ellen Glasgow

975   A conservative is a man who is too cowardly to fight and too fat to run.   *—Elbert Hubbard*

976   A conservative is a man who will not look at the new moon, out of respect for that "ancient institution," the old one.
         —Douglas Jerrold

977   Those who first oppose a good work
      Seize it and make it their own,
      When the corner-stone is laid,
      And memorial tablets are erected.   *—Edgar Lee Masters*

978   No man can be a conservative until he has something to lose.
                                               —James P. Warburg

979   A true conservative is one who can't see any difference between
      radicalism and an idea.

980   Conservatives are but men who have learned to love the new order
      forced upon them by radicals.

981   Conservatism is a state of mind resulting from a good job.

982   The most hopeless conservative is the left-over progressive of an
      earlier generation.

983   There are men so conservative they believe nothing should be done
      for the first time.

SEE ALSO   RELATED SUBJECTS
Science 4942   Caution
                            Change
                            Discretion
                            Excess
                            Obstinacy
                            Reform

CONTEMPT

991   Wrongs are often forgiven; contempt never.   *—Chesterfield*

992   He despises men with tenderness.   *—Anatole France*

993   None but the contemptible are apprehensive of contempt.
                                               —La Rochefoucauld

994   If a man sets out to hate all the miserable creatures he meets, he
      will not have much energy left for anything else; whereas he can
      despise them, one and all, with the greatest ease.
                                               —Schopenhauer

SEE ALSO   RELATED SUBJECTS
Complaint 906   Admiration
Wealth 5797   Cynicism
                            Misanthrope
                            Opinion
                            Pessimism
                            Tolerance

CONTENT

1001 Content is the philosopher's stone, that turns all it touches into
      gold.   *—Franklin*

1002 There's many a life of sweet content
Whose virtue is environment.

—Walter Learned

1003 The secret of contentment is knowing how to enjoy what you
have, and to be able to lose all desire for things beyond your
reach. *—Lin Yutang*

1004 Naught's had, all's spent
Where our desire is got without content. *—Shakespeare*

1005 Our idea of a contented man is the one, if any, that enjoys the
scenery along the detour.

1006 They need much, whom nothing will content.

SEE ALSO   RELATED SUBJECTS
Beauty 347   Curiosity
Man 3825   Optimism
Property 4683   Pessimism
Wealth 5796   Resignation
     Worry

CONVERSATION

1011 In dinner talk it is perhaps allowable to fling on any faggot rather
than let the fire go out. *—J. M. Barrie*

1012 The true spirit of conversation consists in building on another
man's observation, not overturning it. *—Bulwer-Lytton*

1013 Never hold anyone by the button, or the hand, in order to be
heard out; for if people are unwilling to hear you, you had
better hold your tongue than them. *—Chesterfield*

1014 "My idea of an agreeable person," said Hugo Bohun, "is a person who agrees with me." *—Disraeli*

1015 Conversation is an art in which a man has all mankind for com-
petitors. *—Emerson*

1016 Next to the originator of a good sentence is the first quoter of it.
—Emerson

1017 The *faux pas* is repartee which has become accidentally entangled
with *hara-kiri*. *—Jack Goodman and Albert Rice*

1018 Monkeys, who very sensibly refrain from speech, lest they should
be set to earn their livings. *—Kenneth Grahame*

1019 Quotation is a good thing, there is a community of thought in it.
—Johnson

1020 The difference between chirping out of turn and a *faux pas* depends on what kind of a bar you're in. *—Wilson Mizner*

1021   One of the best rules in conversation is, never to say a thing which any of the company can reasonably wish had been left unsaid.   —*Swift*

1022   Dinner was made for eatin', not for talkin'.   —*Thackeray*

1023   War talk by men who have been in a war is always interesting; whereas moon talk by a poet who has not been in the moon is likely to be dull.   —*Mark Twain*

1024   Lettuce is like conversation; it must be fresh and crisp, so sparkling that you scarcely notice the bitter in it.
     —*Charles Dudley Warner*

1025   Talk to every woman as if you loved her, and to every man as if he bored you, and at the end of your first season you will have the reputation of possessing the most perfect social tact.
     —*Oscar Wilde*

1026   The secret of success in conversation is to be able to disagree without being disagreeable.

1027   He that converses not, knows nothing.

1028   Conversation teaches more than meditation.

1029   A single conversation across the table with a wise man is worth a month's study of books.

SEE ALSO
Conceit 933, 938
Money 4049

RELATED SUBJECTS
Bores
Speeches
Wit
Words

CONVICTION

1031   It is easier to fight for one's principles than to live up to them.
     —*Alfred Adler*

1032   Strong beliefs win strong men, and then make them stronger.
     —*Walter Bagehot*

1033   It does not take great men to do great things; it only takes consecrated men.   —*Phillips Brooks*

1034   Christians have burnt each other, quite persuaded
That all the Apostles would have done as they did.   —*Byron*

1035   Neutral men are the devil's allies.   —*E. H. Chapin*

1036   The downright fanatic is nearer to the heart of things than the cool and slippery disputant.   —*E. H. Chapin*

1037   No wild enthusiast ever yet could rest,
Till half mankind were, like himself, possess.   —*Cowper*

1038   We often excuse our own want of philanthropy by giving the
       name of fanaticism to the more ardent zeal of others.
                                                       —Longfellow

1039   The world belongs to the Enthusiast who keeps cool.
                                                     —William McFee

1040   This man will go far for he believes every word he says.
                                            —Mirabeau of Robespierre

1041   Fanaticism consists in redoubling your effort when you have for-
       gotten your aim.   *—Santayana*

1042   Principles have no real force except when one is well fed.
                                                       —Mark Twain

1043   Conviction is the Conscience of the Mind.
                                                —Mrs. Humphrey Ward

1044   Convictions are mortgages on the mind.

1045   A man of principles is generally as insufferable as a man of preju-
       dices; furthermore, he is more pretentious.

1046   Zeal is fit only for wise men, but is found mostly in fools.

                          RELATED SUBJECTS
                          Belief
                          Courage
                          Doubt
                          Idealism
                          Opinion
                          Truth

COOKS

1051   God sends meat, the devil sends cooks.   *—Charles VI*

1052   The art of cookery is the art of poisoning mankind, by rendering
       the appetite still importunate, when the wants of nature are
       supplied.   *—Fenelon*

1053   The cook cares not a bit for the toil, if the fowl be plump and
       fat.   *—Horace*

1054   He makes his cook his merit, and the world visits his dinners and
       not him.   *—Molière*

1055   The cook was a good cook, as cooks go; and as cooks go she went.
                                                        —H. H. Munro

1056   The receipts of cookery are swelled to a volume; but a good
       stomach excels them all.   *—William Penn*

1057   He is a sairy cook that mauna lick his ain fingers.

1058   Boil stones in butter, and you may sip the broth.

RELATED SUBJECTS
Eating
Eggs

COQUETRY

1061   Every line in her face is the line of least resistance.
—*Irvin S. Cobb*

1062   A coquette is a woman without any heart, who makes a fool of a
man that hasn't got any head.   —*Mme. Deluzy*

1063   There is one antidote only for coquetry, and that is true love.
—*Mme. Deluzy*

1064   The characteristic of coquettes is affectation governed by whim.
—*Fielding*

1065   An accomplished coquette excites the passions of others, in proportion as she feels none herself.   —*Hazlitt*

1066   A coquette is like a recruiting sergeant, always on the lookout for
fresh victims.   —*Douglas Jerrold*

1067   One can find women who have never had one love affair, but it is
rare indeed to find any who have had only one.
—*La Rochefoucauld*

1068   A coquette is a young lady of more beauty than sense, more ac-
complishments than learning, more charms of person than
graces of mind, more admirers than friends, more fools than
wise men for attendants.   —*Longfellow*

1069   Had we but world enough, and time,
This coyness, lady, were no crime.   —*Andrew Marvell*

1070   Still panting o'er a crowd to reign,
    More joy it gives to woman's breast
To make ten frigid coxcombs vain,
    Than one true, manly lover blest.   —*Pope*

1071   Have you not heard it said full oft,
A woman's nay doth stand for naught?   —*Shakespeare*

1072   "Yea," quoth he, "dost thou fall upon thy face?
Thou wilt fall backward when thou hast more wit."
—*Shakespeare*

1073   Mme. de Genlis, in order to avoid the scandal of coquetry, always yielded easily.   —*Talleyrand*

1074   Tenderness is the coquetry of age.

1075   An old coquette does not die of old age—she dies of anxiety.

SEE ALSO   RELATED SUBJECTS
Conscience 964   Blushing
Silence 5039   Chastity
                          Maid
                          Modesty
                          Sex

COURAGE

1081   His resolve is not to seem the bravest, but to be.   *—Aeschylus*

1082   It is easy to be brave from a safe distance.   *—Aesop*

1083   It is an error to suppose that courage means courage in every-
        thing.   *—Bulwer-Lytton*

1084   The courage we desire and prize is not the courage to die de-
        cently, but to live manfully.   *—Carlyle*

1085   It is better to have a lion at the head of an army of sheep, than
        a sheep at the head of an army of lions.   *—Defoe*

1086   Adventures are to the adventurous.   *—Disraeli*

1087   Here is he laid to whom for daring deed
        Nor friend nor foe could render worthy meed.   *—Ennius*

1088   Brave men were living before Agamemnon.   *—Horace*

1089   One man with courage makes a majority.   *—Andrew Jackson*

1090   No man can answer for his courage who has never been in danger.
                                                    —La Rochefoucauld

1091   The probability that we may fail in the struggle ought not to de-
        ter us from the support of a cause we believe to be just.
                                                                  —Lincoln

1092   If the heart be right, it matters not which way the head lies.
                                     —Sir Walter Raleigh, at the scaffold

1093   The blood more stirs
        To rouse a lion than to start a hare!   *—Shakespeare*

1094   Bravery never goes out of fashion.   *—Thackeray*

1095   Shipwrecked I; but be none scared by my ill-starred lot;
        Other ships sailed the sea with mine, and suffered not.
                                              —Theodorides, of Syracuse

1096   She'd fight a rattlesnake and give it the first two bites.
                                                —Harry Leon Wilson

1097   A courageous foe is better than a cowardly friend.

1098   Return with your shield or on it.

1099   The man who says he would give his last drop of blood for a
        lofty cause really means the first drop—no one but a fool would
        risk a hemorrhage.

SEE ALSO   RELATED SUBJECTS
Courtship 1174   Character
Defeat 1491   Conviction
Eating 1787   Cowardice
Pride 4660   Danger
Resignation 4868   Deeds
Teaching 5291   Soldiers

COURTESY

1101   To dispense with ceremony is the most delicate mode of con-
        ferring a compliment.   —*Bulwer-Lytton*

1102   One of the embarrassments of being a gentleman is that you are
        not permitted to be violent in asserting your rights.
                                        —*Nicholas Murray Butler*

1103   True politeness is perfect ease and freedom. It simply consists in
        treating others just as you love to be treated yourself.
                                                    —*Chesterfield*

1104   The manner of a vulgar man has freedom without ease; the man-
        ner of a gentleman, ease without freedom.   —*Chesterfield*

1105   No man can possibly improve in any company for which he has
        not respect enough to be under some degree of restraint.
                                                    —*Chesterfield*

1106   A man's own good breeding is the best security against other
        people's ill manners.   —*Chesterfield*

1107   Tact consists in knowing how far to go too far.—*Jean Cocteau*

1108   To remind a man of the good turns you have done him is very
        much like a reproach.   —*Demosthenes*

1109   Manner is all in all, whate'er is writ,
        The substitute for genius, sense, and wit.   —*Cowper*

1110   Life is not so short but that there is always time for courtesy.
                                                        —*Emerson*

1111   Good manners are made up of petty sacrifices.   —*Emerson*

1112   Manners are the happy ways of doing things. . . . If they are
        superficial, so are the dewdrops, which give such a depth to the
        morning meadow.   —*Emerson*

1113   We must be courteous to a man as we are to a picture, which we are willing to give the advantage of a good light.   *—Emerson*

1114   We cannot live pleasantly without living wisely and nobly and righteously.   *—Epicurus*

1115   Of what use are forms, seeing at times they are empty? Of the same use as barrels, which, at times, are empty too.
—A. W. & J. C. Hare

1116   If a person has no delicacy, he has you in his power.   *—Hazlitt*

1117   A gentleman is one who never hurts anyone's feelings unintentionally.   *—Oliver Herford*

1118   Apologizing—a very desperate habit—one that is rarely cured. Apology is only egotism wrong side out.   *—O. W. Holmes*

1119   The audience was swell. They were so polite, they covered their mouths when they yawned.   *—Bob Hope*

1120   He was so generally civil, that nobody thanked him for it.
—Johnson

1121   Politeness of the mind is to have delicate thoughts.
—La Rochefoucauld

1122   He who reflects on another man's want of breeding, shows he wants it as much himself.   *—Plutarch*

1123   Politeness is to human nature what warmth is to wax.
—Schopenhauer

1124   Good breeding consists in concealing how much we think of ourselves and how little we think of the other person.
—Mark Twain

1125   A courtesy much entreated is half recompensed.

1126   A civil denial is better than a rude grant.

1127   Courtesy on one side can never last long.

1128   Less of your courtesy and more of your purse.

1129   In courtesy, rather pay a penny too much than too little.

1130   Politeness travels on short fares.

1131   A favor ill-placed is great waste.

1132   There is something of the prostitute in all gallant men.

1133   The only way to treat a Prussian is to step on his toes until he apologizes.

1134   Good nature without prudence, is foolishness.

1135   A gentleman *invariably* follows a lady upstairs.
                        —From a well-known book on etiquette

SEE ALSO   RELATED SUBJECTS
Begging 430   Guests
                     Habit
                     Kindness
                     Vulgarity

COURTIER

1141   To laugh, to lie, to flatter to the face,
       Four ways in court to win men's grace.   *—Roger Ascham*

1142   Young courtiers be beggars in their age.   *—Alexander Barclay*

1143   Falsehood and dissimulation are certainly to be found at courts;
       but where are they not to be found? Cottages have them, as
       well as courts, only with worse manners.   *—Chesterfield*

1144   To make a fine gentleman several trades are required, but chiefly
       a barber.   *—Goldsmith*

1145   There is a pleasure in affecting affectation.   *—Lamb*

1146   Some people resemble ballads which are only sung for a certain
       time.   *—La Rochefoucauld*

1147   Affectation endeavors to correct natural defects, and has always
       the laudable aim of pleasing, though always misses it.*—Locke*

1148   Court-virtues bear, like gems, the highest rate,
       Born where Heaven's influence scarce can penetrate.   *—Pope*

1149   The two maxims of any great man at court are, always to keep
       his countenance and never to keep his word.   *—Swift*

1150   A court is an assemblage of noble and distinguished beggars.
                                                     —Talleyrand

1151   O, happy they that never saw the court,
       Nor ever knew great men but by report.   *—John Webster*

1152   All charming people, I fancy, are spoiled. It is the secret of their
       attraction.   *—Oscar Wilde*

1153   A nod from a lord is a breakfast for a fool.

                     RELATED SUBJECTS
                     Ancestors
                     Kings

COURTSHIP

1161   Romances paint at full length people's wooings,
       But only give a bust of marriages:
       But no one cares for matrimonial cooings.   *—Byron*

1162   Single gentlemen who would be double.   *—Byron*

1163   If you cannot inspire a woman with love of yourself, fill her above the brim with love of herself; all that runs over will be yours.   *—C. C. Colton*

1164   The surest way to hit a woman's heart is to take aim kneeling.   *—Douglas Jerrold*

1165   Follow a shadow, it still flies you;
    Seem to fly it, it will pursue:
So court a mistress, who denies you;
    Let her alone, she will court you.   *—Jonson*

1166   If I speak to thee in friendship's name,
    Thou think'st I speak too coldly;
If I mention love's devoted flame,
    Thou say'st I speak too boldly.   *—Thomas Moore*

1167   Men seldom make passes
At girls who wear glasses.   *—Dorothy Parker*

1168   By the time you swear you're his, shivering and sighing,
And he vows his passion is infinite, undying—
Lady, make a note of this:
One of you is lying.   *—Dorothy Parker*

1169   She is a woman, therefore may be woo'd;
She is a woman, therefore may be won.   *—Shakespeare*

1170   Who wooed in haste and means to wed at leisure. *—Shakespeare*

1171   That man that hath a tongue, I say, is no man,
If with his tongue he cannot win a woman.   *—Shakespeare*

1172   Courtship consists in a number of quiet attentions, not so pointed as to alarm, nor so vague as not to be understood.   *—Sterne*

1173   In courtship a man pursues a woman until she catches him.

1174   Faint heart never won fair lady.

1175   He that would the daughter win, must with the mother first begin.

1176   Happy's the wooing that's not long in doing.

1177   Courting and wooing, brings dallying and doing.

1178   Woman begins by resisting man's advances and ends by blocking his retreat.

1179   Sustained gallantry is almost inconceivable.

1180   In the old days the young fellow who went courting turned down
        the gas. Now he steps on it.

RELATED SUBJECTS
Coquetry
Husband
Jealousy
Maid
Wife

COWARDICE

1181   Cowards do not count in battle; they are there, but not in it.
                                                            —*Euripides*

1182   Fannius, as he was fleeing from the enemy, put himself to death.
        Isn't this, I ask, madness—to die for fear of dying?—*Martial*

1183   When the blandishments of life are gone,
        The coward creeps to death—the brave lives on.   —*Martial*

1184   All enchantments die; only cowards die with them.
                                                    —*Charles Morgan*

1185   A coward like this deserves to—have his life prolonged.
                                                            —*Seneca*

1186   Not every man is so great a coward as he thinks he is—nor yet
        so good a Christian.   —*Stevenson*

1187   You do well to weep like a woman for what you could not de-
        fend like a man.   —*Sultana Zoraya*

1188   The first in banquets, but the last in fight.

1189   Cowards run the greatest danger of any men in a battle.

1190   Many would be cowards if they had courage enough.

1191   A coward's fear may make a coward valiant.

1192   A coward is a man in whom the instinct of self-preservation acts
        normally.

1193   Ned would liken himself to Achilles of old.
            I hope he'll admit of a single correction;
        In his heels lay Achilles' danger we're told,
            Whilst Ned in his heels finds his only protection.

SEE ALSO   RELATED SUBJECTS
Conscience 966   Courage
                           Danger
                           Duty
                           Hero
                           Weakness

CREDIT

1201 Credit is like chastity, they can both stand temptation better than
suspicion.   —*Josh Billings*

1202 A person who can't pay, gets another person who can't pay, to
guarantee that he can pay.   —*Dickens*

1203 However gradual may be the growth of confidence, that of credit
requires still more time to arrive at maturity.   —*Disraeli*

1204 Creditors have better memories than debtors; they are a super-
stitious sect, great observers of set days and times.—*Franklin*

1205 If a feller screwed up his face when he asked fer credit like he
does when he's asked t' settle, he wouldn't git it.
—*Kin Hubbard*

1206 A creditor is worse than a master; for a master owns only your
person, a creditor owns your dignity, and can belabor that.
—*Victor Hugo*

1207 Blest paper-credit! last and best supply!
That lends corruption lighter wings to fly!   —*Pope*

1208 Thy credit wary keep, 'tis quickly gone;
Being got by many actions, lost by one.   —*T. Randolph*

1209 Credit is like a looking-glass, which when once sullied by a
breath, may be wiped clear again; but if once cracked can never
be repaired.   —*Scott*

1210 Who quick be to borrow and slow be to pay,
Their credit is naught, go they never so gay.—*Thomas Tusser*

1211 He getteth a great deal of credit, who payeth but a small debt.

1212 More credit may be thrown down in a moment, than can be built
up in an age.

1213 In God we trust—all others pay cash.

SEE ALSO	RELATED SUBJECTS
Virtue 5692	Business
	Debt
	Economy

CRIME

1221 Society prepares the crime; the criminal commits it.—*V. Alfieri*

1222 Crimes are not to be measured by the issue of events, but by the
bad intentions of men.   —*Cicero*

1223 He who sells what isn't his'n,
Must buy it back or go to prison.   —*Daniel Drew*

1224 Successful crimes alone are justified.   *—Dryden*

1225 It is worse than a crime; it is a blunder.   *—Fouché*

1226 Crimes sometimes shock us too much; vices almost always too little.   *—A. W. & J. C. Hare*

1227 The police are fully able to meet and compete with all criminals!
      —Mayor Hylan

1228 What man have you ever seen who was contented with one crime only?   *—Juvenal*

1229 If poverty is the mother of crimes, want of sense is the father of them.   *—La Bruyère*

1230 We easily forget crimes that are known only to ourselves.
      —La Rochefoucauld

1231 Those who are themselves incapable of great crimes, are ever backward to suspect others.   *—La Rochefoucauld*

1232 The reason there are so many imbeciles among imprisoned criminals is that an imbecile is so foolish even a detective can detect him.   *—Austin O'Malley*

1233 Much as he is opposed to law-breaking, he is not bigoted about it.
      —Damon Runyon

1234 A criminal is a person with predatory instincts who has not sufficient capital to form a corporation.   *—Howard Scott*

1235 Successful and fortunate crime is called virtue.   *—Seneca*

1236 When superficiality is not a virtue, it is worse than a crime.

1237 The greater the man, the greater the crime.

1238 A nation is no better than its charlatans.

1239 A little stealing is a dangerous part,
      But stealing largely is a noble art;
      'Tis mean to rob a henroost, or a hen,
      But stealing thousands makes us gentlemen.

1240 The informer is the worst rogue of the two.

1241 It is wit to pick a lock, and steal a horse, but wisdom to let it alone.

SEE ALSO   RELATED SUBJECTS
Blushing 474   Guilt
                     Hanging
                     Law
                     Punishment
                     Vice

CRITICISM

1251 It is ridiculous for any man to criticize the works of another if he has not distinguished himself by his own performances.
 —Addison

1252 Silence is sometimes the severest criticism. *—Charles Buxton*

1253 It is much easier to be critical than to be correct. *—Disraeli*

1254 The most noble criticism is that in which the critic is not the antagonist so much as the rival of the author. *—Disraeli*

1255 You know who critics are?—the men who have failed in literature and art. *—Disraeli*

1256 The good critic relates the adventures of his soul among works of art. *—Anatole France*

1257 The stones that critics hurl with harsh intent
A man may use to build his monument. *—Arthur Guiterman*

1258 Criticism, as it was first instituted by Aristotle, was meant as a standard of judging well. *—Johnson*

1259 Few persons have sufficient wisdom to prefer censure, which is useful to them, to praise, which deceives them.
 —La Rochefoucauld

1260 If we were without faults, we should not take so much pleasure in remarking them in others. *—La Rochefoucauld*

1261 The proper function of a critic is to save the tale from the artist who created it. *—D. H. Lawrence*

1262 The strength of criticism lies only in the weakness of the thing criticised. *—Longfellow*

1263 Critics are sentinels in the grand army of letters, stationed at the corners of newspapers and reviews to challenge every new author. *—Longfellow*

1264 Nature fits all her children with something to do,
He who would write and can't write, can surely review.
 —Lowell

1265 Ten censure wrong, for one that writes amiss. *—Pope*

1266 Criticism often takes from the tree caterpillars and blossoms together. *—J. P. Richter*

1267 A woman's flattery may inflate a man's head a little; but her criticism goes straight to his heart, and contracts it so that it can never again hold quite as much love for her. *—Rowland*

1268 Court not the critic's smile, nor dread his frown. *—Scott*

1269 Pay no attention to what critics say. There has never been set up a statue in honor of a critic. *—Sibelius*

1270 Censure is the tax a man pays to the public for being eminent. *—Swift*

1271 Criticism comes easier than craftsmanship. *—Zeuxis*

1272 A literary critic is a person who finds meaning in literature that the author didn't know was there.

1273 A book reviewer is usually a "barker" before the door of a publisher's circus.

SEE ALSO   RELATED SUBJECTS
Insults 3161, 3163, 3175   Actors
Books
Censorship
Literature
Understanding

CURIOSITY

1281 Curiosity
Does, no less than devotion, pilgrims make. *—Cowley*

1282 Creatures whose mainspring is curiosity—enjoy the accumulating of facts, far more than the pausing at times to reflect on those facts. *—Clarence Day*

1283 Curiosity is little more than another name for hope.
—A. W. & J. C. Hare

1284 The over curious are not over wise. *—Massinger*

1285 You know what a woman's curiosity is. Almost as great as a man's! *—Oscar Wilde*

1286 To go beneath the surface argues the curious—not the profound.

RELATED SUBJECTS
Discretion
Gossip
Knowledge

CYNICISM

1291 Cynicism is intellectual dandyism. *—George Meredith*

1292 Be wisely worldly, be not worldly wise. *—Francis Quarles*

1293 I hate cynicism a great deal worse than I do the devil; unless, perhaps, the two were the same thing. *—Stevenson*

1294 What is a cynic? A man who knows the price of everything, and the value of nothing. *—Oscar Wilde*

1295   Cynic: a sentimentalist on guard.

SEE ALSO	RELATED SUBJECTS
Honesty 2916	Belief
Kings 3280	Epigrams
Sincerity 5073	Philosophy
Wit 5947	Wit

D

DANGER

1301   In counsel it is good to see dangers; but in execution, not to see them unless they be very great.   —*Bacon*

1302   Who rides a tiger cannot dismount.   —*Chinese Proverb*

1303   The absent danger greater still appears.
Less fears he who is near the thing he fears.   —*Samuel Daniel*

1304   See what perils do environ
Those who meddle with hot iron.   —*Galsworthy*

1305   In great straits and when hope is small, the boldest counsels are the safest.   —*Livy*

1306   The danger past and God forgotten.

1307   Who seeks adventures finds blows.

1308   A fallen lighthouse is more dangerous than a reef.

SEE ALSO	RELATED SUBJECTS
Action 31	Courage
Age 158	Cowardice
Begging 421	Hero
Cowardice 1189	Soldiers
Knowledge 3336	War
Sincerity 5071	

DAY

1311   The first hour of the morning is the rudder of the day.
  —*H. W. Beecher*

1312   There are many persons who look on Sunday as a sponge to wipe out the sins of the week.   —*H. W. Beecher*

1313   He seems
To have seen better days, as who has not
Who has seen yesterday?   —*Byron*

1314   The public only takes up yesterday as a stick to beat today.
  —*Jean Cocteau*

1315   Finish every day and be done with it. You have done what you
        could. Some blunders and absurdities no doubt crept in; forget
        them as soon as you can.   —*Emerson*

1316   Sunday is the golden clasp that binds together the volume of the
        week.   —*Longfellow*

1317   With each returning night we're born again
        And nought of all our former life retain.
        Today—estranged from all past joy and strife—
        Today is radiant with new opening life.   —*Palladas*

1318   A bad day never hath a good night.

SEE ALSO	RELATED SUBJECTS
Happiness 2761	Light
Laughter 3370	Sun
Optimism 4273	Time
Time 5408	
Weather 5806	
Worry 6111	

DEATH

1321   The sole equality on earth is death.   —*Philip J. Bailey*

1322   To himself every one is an immortal; he may know that he is
        going to die, but he can never know that he is dead.
                                                        —*Samuel Butler*

1323   Heaven gives its favorites—early death.   —*Byron*

1324   Death, so called, is a thing which makes men weep,
        And yet a third of life is passed in sleep.   —*Byron*

1325   Death comes not to the living soul,
        Nor age to the loving heart.   —*Phoebe Cary*

1326   He who fears death has already lost the life he covets.
                                                        —*Cato the Censor*

1327   Far happier are the dead, methinks, than they
        Who look for death, and fear it every day.   —*Cowper*

1328   I shall ask leave to desist, when I am interrupted by so great an
        experiment as dying.   —*Sir William D'Avenant*

1329   Death is a law, not a punishment.   —*Jean-Baptiste Dubos*

1330   I die well paid, whilst my expiring breath,
        Smiles o'er the tombs of foes made kin by death.
                                                        —*Dutch Epigram*

1331   Nay! Let not Lycus be forgotten. He
        Died of sore gout. Much marvel 'twas to me,
        Who here still limped on crutch-borne feet and slow,
        Could in one night to distant Hades go! —*Diogenes Laertius*

1332   Worldly faces never look so worldly as at a funeral.

—George Eliot

1333   Death is never at a loss for occasions.   *—Greek epigram*

1334   For mortals vanished from the day's sweet light
I shed no tear:
Rather I mourn for those who day and night
Live in death's fear.   *—Greek epigram*

1335   "Tell me, good dog, whose tomb you guard so well?"
"The Cynic's." "True; but who that cynic tell?"
"Diogenes, of fair Sinape's race."
"What? He that in a tub was wont to dwell?"
"Yes: but the stars are now his dwelling-place."

—Greek epigram

1336   No useless sepulchre I crave:
Nature gives all her sons a grave.   *—Horace*

1337   This goin' ware glory waits ye haint one agreeable feetur.

—Lowell

1338   God cheats men into living on by hiding
How blest it is to die.   *—Lucan*

1339   All our knowledge merely helps us to die a more painful death
than the animals that know nothing.   *—Maeterlinck*

1340   A man's dying is more the survivors' affair than his own.

—Thomas Mann

1341   Death, like generation, is a secret of Nature. *—Marcus Aurelius*

1342   Light may Earth's crumbling sand be laid on thee
That dogs may dig thy bones up easily.   *—Martial*

1343   Rest lightly on her, earth, for she
Trod never heavily on thee.   *—Martial*

1344   Death hath a thousand doors to let out life.   *—Massinger*

1345   Bound to die? Were I a gymnast 'twould be the same?
Why mind then if by gout I drink myself dead-lame?
Either way be carried? So, wine—let lamps be lit!
While life still laughs, we'll make a merry night of it!

—Nicarchus

1346   Much talking man, in earth thou soon wilt lie;
Be still, and living think what 'tis to die.   *—Palladas*

1347   As Caesar was at supper the discourse was of death—which sort
was the best, "That," said he, "which is unexpected."

—Plutarch

1348   But thouands die without or this or that,
        Die, and endow a college or a cat.   —*Pope*

1349   "All things mortal are";
        And o'er this on tomorrow's hearth,
        Muse: "Even maids divinely fair
        Must, like flowers, resolve to earth."   —*Rufinus*

1350   Death is more universal than life; everyone dies but not everyone
            lives.   —*A. Sachs*

1351   Death without dread of death is welcome death.   —*Seneca*

1352   Death ne'er can fail the man who wills to die.   —*Seneca*

1353   Death's the discharge of our debt of sorrow.   —*Seneca*

1354   Death? 'Tis one of life's duties.   —*Seneca*

1355   Golden lads and girls all must,
        As chimney-sweepers, come to dust.   —*Shakespeare*

1356   I know of nobody that has a mind to die this year.
                                                                —*Shakespeare*

1357   Death,
        The undiscover'd country, from whose bourne
        No traveller returns.   —*Shakespeare*

1358   This fell sergeant, death,
        Is strict in his arrest.   —*Shakespeare*

1359   Just death, kind umpire of men's miseries.   —*Shakespeare*

1360   Nothing in his life
        Became him like the leaving it.   —*Shakespeare*

1361   He that dies pays all debts.   —*Shakespeare*

1362   We owe God a death . . . he that dies this year is quit for the
            next.   —*Shakespeare*

1363   Death's a debt; his mandamus binds all alike—no bail, no de-
            murrer.   —*Sheridan*

1364   Death is the ugly fact which Nature has to hide, and she hides
            it well.   —*Alexander Smith*

1365   Strange an astrologer should die without one wonder in the sky.
                                                                —*Swift*

1366   God's fingers touch'd him, and he slept.   —*Tennyson*

1367   No life that breathes with human breath
        Has ever truly longed for death.   —*Tennyson*

1368   She ne'er was really charming till she died.   —*Terence*

1369 The reports of my death are greatly exaggerated. *—Mark Twain*

1370 Here's Death, twitching my ear:
"Live," says he, "for I'm coming."   *—Vergil*

1371 Two we were, and the heart was one;
    Which now being dead, dead I must be,
    Or seem alive as lifelessly
As in the choir the painted stone, Death!   *—Villon*

1372 If death did not exist today, it would be necessary to invent it.
—Voltaire

1373 It is an infamy to die and not be missed.   *—Carlos Wilcox*

1374 I wouldn't live forever,
    I wouldn't if I could:
But I needn't fret about it,
    For I couldn't if I would.

1375 On death, though wit is oft displayed,
No epigram could e'er be made;
Poets stop short, and lose their breath,
When coming to the point of death!

1376 When we pray for death we really desire a fuller life.

1377 Death has a subtle charm in youth which it loses in old age.

1378 Old men go to death; but death comes to young men.

1379 When you die, your trumpeter will be buried.

1380 He that died half a year ago is as dead as Adam.

1381 He hath liv'd ill that knows not how to die well.

1382 If death be terrible, the fault is not in death, but thee.

SEE ALSO	RELATED SUBJECTS
Action 23	Doctors
Beauty 351	Epitaphs
Cowardice 1182	Life
Love 3714	Sickness
Taxes 5282	
Theatre 5361	
Youth 6205	

DEBT

1391 Give, and you may keep your friend if you lose your money;
lend, and the chances are that you lose your friend if ever you
get back your money.   *—Bulwer-Lytton*

1392 Youth is in danger until it learns to look upon debts as furies.
—Bulwer-Lytton

1393   Dear Furius, you may rest assured,
My country house is well secured.
How? With good timber, stone, and plaster,
From wind, and rain, and all disaster?
Ah, no! but by a certain skin,
Which is encased in painted tin,
It is secured for "money lent,"
To a cursed son of Ten-per-Cent.
          —*Catullus*

1394   It is better to give than to lend, and it costs about the same.
          —*Sir Philip Gibbs*

1395   We are always much better pleased to see those whom we have
obliged, than those who have obliged us.   —*La Rochefoucauld*

1396   You are buying everything now, Castor. It will end in your selling everything.   —*Martial*

1397   You are not in debt, Sextus. I assure you, Sextus, you are not in
debt, for a man is. in debt, Sextus, only if he can pay.
          —*Martial*

1398   Because you made me a loan of one hundred and fifty thousand
sesterces out of all the wealth on which your heavy money-
chest shuts tight, you fancy yourself, Telesinus, a great friend.
You a great friend because you give! I, rather, because I pay
back.   —*Martial*

1399   Debts are nowadays like children, begot with pleasure, but
brought forth with pain.   —*Molière*

1400   A small debt produces a debtor; a large one, an enemy.
          —*Publilius Syrus*

1401   Believe me, 'tis a godlike thing to lend; to owe is a heroic virtue.
          —*Rabelais*

1402   Debts and lies are generally mixed together.   —*Rabelais*

1403   You know it is not my Interest to pay the Principal; nor is it my
Principle to pay the Interest.   —*Sheridan*

1404   Most men remember obligations, but are not often likely to be
grateful; the proud are made sour by the remembrance and the
vain silent.   —*Simms*

1405   The holy passion of Friendship is of so sweet and steady and loyal
and enduring a nature that it will last through a whole lifetime, if not asked to lend money.   —*Mark Twain*

1406   When some men discharge an obligation you can hear the report
for miles around.   —*Mark Twain*

1407 God bless pawnbrokers!
They are quiet men. —*Marguerite Wilkinson*

1408 Jack ran so long, and ran so fast,
No wonder he ran out at last;
He ran in debt—and then, to pay,
He distanced all, and ran away.

1409 Mortgage: a house with a guilty conscience.

1410 I have discovered the philosopher's stone, that turns everything
into gold: it is, "Pay as you go."

1411 It is better to pay, and have but little left, than to have much,
and be always in debt.

1412 Debt is the worst poverty.

1413 He who oweth is all in the wrong.

1414 He begs at them that borrowed at him.

1415 He that lends, gives.

1416 The moment you make a man feel the weight of an obligation,
he will become your enemy.

1417 You say you nothing owe, and so I say;
He only owes, who something has to pay.

See Also	Related Subjects
Ancestors 224	Borrowing
Death 1361, 1363	Credit
Time 5426	Economy
Worry 6122	Extravagance

DECENCY

1421 Want of decency is want of sense. —*Wentworth Dillon*

1422 Decency is the least of all laws, but yet it is the law which is
most strictly observed. —*La Rochefoucauld*

1423 Respectable means rich, and decent means poor. I should die if I
heard my father called decent. —*T. L. Peacock*

1424 Decency is Indecency's Conspiracy of Silence. —*G. B. Shaw*

1425 No man has been thoroughly decent to more than one woman.

Related Subjects
Character
Courtesy
Kindness
Wickedness

DECEPTION

1431 The worst deluded are the self-deluded.   —*C. N. Bovee*

1432 We are never deceived; we deceive ourselves.   —*Goethe*

1433 Deceive not thy physician, confessor, nor lawyer.

—*George Herbert*

1434 The best happiness a woman can boast is that of being most carefully deceived.   —*George James*

1435 It is a double pleasure to deceive the deceiver.   —*La Fontaine*

1436 You can fool some of the people all of the time, and all of the people some of the time, but you cannot fool all of the people all of the time.   —*Lincoln*

1437 Are you astonished, Aulus, that our friend Fabullinus is so frequently deceived? A good man has always something to learn in regard to fraud.   —*Martial*

1438 You were constantly, Matho, a guest at my villa at Tivoli. Now you buy it. I have deceived you: I have merely sold you what was already your own.   —*Martial*

1439 Oh, what a tangled web we weave,
When first we practise to deceive.   —*Scott*

1440 Cunning is a short blanket—if you pull it over your face, you expose your feet.

1441 Deceit is in haste, but honesty can wait a fair leisure.

1442 By art and deceit men live half a year; and by deceit and art the other half.

1443 You can't fool all of the people all of the time—but it isn't necessary.

1444 A man would rather be deceived than convinced that the opinion he formed of a person at first sight was incorrect.

SEE ALSO   RELATED SUBJECTS
Business 562   Facts
Enemies 1833   Flattery
                      Frankness
                      Hypocrisy
                      Lies
                      Truth

DECISION

1451 But it is said and ever shall,
Between two stools lieth the fall.   —*John Gower*

1452   It does not take much strength to do things, but it requires great
       strength to decide on what to do.   *—Elbert Hubbard*

1453   The measure of choosing well, is, whether a man likes and finds
       good in what he has chosen.   *—Lamb*

1454   Decide not rashly. The decision made
       Can never be recalled.   *—Longfellow*

1455   Deliberate as often as you please, but when you decide it is once
       for all.   *—Publilius Syrus*

1456   Men must be decided on what they will not do, and then they are
       able to act with vigor in what they ought to do.

RELATED SUBJECTS
Aim
Opinion
Purpose

DEEDS

1461   Conspiracies no sooner should be formed than executed.
       —Addison

1462   The beginning, as the proverb says, is half the whole.
       —Aristotle

1463   Whatever is worth doing at all, is worth doing well.
       —Chesterfield

1464   The distance is nothing; it is only the first step that costs.
       —Mme. Du Deffand

1465   If thou wouldst not be known to do anything, never do it.
       —Emerson

1466   Our chief want in life is somebody who shall make us do what
       we can.   *—Emerson*

1467   A bad beginning makes a bad ending.   *—Euripides*

1468   He who has put a good finish to his undertaking is said to have
       placed a golden crown to the whole.   *—Eustachius*

1469   His conduct still right, with his argument wrong.   *—Goldsmith*

1470   A noble deed is a step toward God.   *—J. G. Holland*

1471   A good lather is half the shave.   *—William Hone*

1472   He has half the deed done, who has made a beginning. *—Horace*

1473   There are thousands willing to do great things for one willing to
       do a small thing.   *—George Macdonald*

1474 A wrong-doer is often a man that has left something undone, not always he that has done something.   —*Marcus Aurelius*

1475 Between the great things that we *cannot* do and the small things we *will* not do, the danger is that we shall do nothing.
—*Adolph Monod*

1476 To do two things at once is to do neither.   —*Publilius Syrus*

1477 While we deliberate about beginning, it is already too late to begin.   —*Quintilian*

1478 Doing is the great thing. For if, resolutely, people do what is right, in time they come to like doing it.   —*Ruskin*

1479 He who considers too much will perform little.   —*Schiller*

1480 The attempt and not the deed
Confounds us.   —*Shakespeare*

1481 If to do were easy as to know what were good to do, chapels had been churches, and poor men's cottages princes' palaces.
—*Shakespeare*

1482 One good deed, dying tongueless,
Slaughters a thousand waiting upon that.   —*Shakespeare*

1483 'Tis strange what a man may do and a woman yet think him an angel.   —*Thackeray*

1484 The first faults are theirs that commit them; the second theirs that permit them.

1485 Better do it than wish it done.

1486 He who commences many things finishes but few.

SEE ALSO   RELATED SUBJECTS
Aim 183   Action
Duty 1753   Courage
Faith 2083   Example
Prayer 4602   Purpose
Women 5974   Work
Words 6048

DEFEAT

1491 To yield to the stronger is valor's second prize.   —*Martial*

1492 There are some defeats more triumphant than victories.
—*Montaigne*

1493 Another victory like this will send me back without a man to Epirus.   —*Pyrrhus*

1494   Defeat isn't bitter if you don't swallow it.

SEE ALSO   RELATED SUBJECTS
Time 5419   Enemies
Truth 5551   Failure
War 5735   Hero
                       War

DELAY

1501   He slept beneath the moon,
        He basked beneath the sun;
        He lived a life of going-to-do
        And died with nothing done.   —*James Albery*

1502   By the street of By-and-By, one arrives at the house of Never.
                                                —*Cervantes*

1503   It's but little good you'll do, a-watering the last year's crop.
                                                —*George Eliot*

1504   Delay in vengeance gives a heavier blow.   —*John Ford*

1505   When a man's life is at stake, no delay is too long.   —*Juvenal*

1506   Delay is ever fatal to those who are prepared.   —*Lucan*

1507   procrastination is the
        art of keeping
        up with yesterday.   —*Don Marquis*

1508   Delay is a great procuress.   —*Ovid*

1509   Never do to-day what you can
        Put off till to-morrow.   —*W. B. Rands*

1510   Delays increase desires, and sometimes extinguish them.

1511   Procrastination is a relief.

SEE ALSO   RELATED SUBJECTS
Duty 1754   Caution
Justice 3247   Haste
Thought 5397   Opportunity
Wisdom 5898

DEMOCRACY

1521   I'm one that like to find
        Myself of the Common Kind.   —*Antiphilus, of Byzantium*

1522   You can never have a revolution in order to establish a democ-
        racy. You must have a democracy in order to have a revolution.
                                                —*Chesterton*

1523   Every man is wanted, and no man is wanted much. —*Emerson*

1524   Democracy is based upon the conviction that there are extraordinary possibilities in ordinary people.   —*H. E. Fosdick*

1525   Democracy has not failed; the intelligence of the race has failed before the problems the race has raised.   —*Robert M. Hutchins*

1526   Democ'acy gives every man
         The right to be his own oppressor.   —*Lowell*

1527   The only way in which to fit a people for self-government is to entrust them with self-government.   —*Macaulay*

1528   Like a barber's chair, that fits all buttocks.   —*Shakespeare*

1529   It is easier for a republican form of government to be applauded than realized.   —*Tacitus*

SEE ALSO   RELATED SUBJECTS
Labor 3354   America
Vulgarity 5715   Dictators
                             Government
                             History
                             Liberty
                             Politics
                             Revolution

DESIRE

1531   We should aim rather at leveling down our desires than leveling up our means.   —*Aristotle*

1532   He who desires but acts not, breeds pestilence.   —*Blake*

1533   The thirst of desire is never filled, nor fully satisfied.   —*Cicero*

1534   Nothing troubles you for which you do not yearn.   —*Cicero*

1535   It is not the greatness of a man's means that makes him independent, so much as the smallness of his wants.   —*Cobbett*

1536   A man's desire is for the woman, but the woman's desire is rarely other than for the desire of the man.   —*Coleridge*

1537   Where desire doth bear the sway,
         The heart must rule, the head obey.   —*Francis Davison*

1538   Socrates said, "Those who want fewest things are nearest to the gods."   —*Diogenes Laertius*

1539   By annihilating the desires, you annihilate the mind. Every man without passions has within him no principle of action, no motive to act.   —*Helvetius*

1540   We live in our desires rather than in our achievements.
                                                           —*George Moore*

1541 Each man has his own desires; all do not possess the same inclinations.   —*Persius*

1542 We desire nothing so much as what we ought not to have.
—*Publilius Syrus*

1543 Is it not strange that desire should so many years outlive performance?   —*Shakespeare*

1544 There are two tragedies in life.
One is not to get your heart's desire.
The other is to get it.   —*G. B. Shaw*

1545 The stoical scheme of supplying our wants by lopping off our
desires, is like cutting off our feet when we want shoes.
—*Swift*

1546 Discontents arise from our desires oftener than from our wants.

1547 Shameless craving must have shameful nay.

1548 If your desires be endless, your cares will be so too.

1549 By persistently desiring the unattainable, one weakens oneself
without attaining anything.

SEE ALSO	RELATED SUBJECTS
Belief 445	Discretion
Content 1004	Excess
Delay 1510	Greed
Drinking 1732	Passion
Love 3677	Sex
Vice 5647	Temperance
Virtue 5671	

DESPAIR

1551 When we are flat on our backs there is no way to look but up.
—*Roger W. Babson*

1552 Let me not know that all is lost,
Though lost it be—leave me not tied
To this despair, this corpse-like bride.   —*Browning*

1553 Our last and best defense, despair;
Despair, by which the gallant'st feats
Have been achiev'd in greatest straits.   —*Samuel Butler*

1554 Despair is the damp of hell, as joy is the serenity of heaven.
—*John Donne*

1555 Despair is a great incentive to honorable death.
—*Quintus Curtius Rufus*

1556 He that stands upon a slippery place,
Makes nice of no vile hold to stay him up.   —*Shakespeare*

1557   What matters it to a blind man that his father could see?

SEE ALSO   RELATED SUBJECTS
Doubt 1694   Failure
Excess 1982   Fear
Happiness 2765   Grief
Philosophy 4439   Hope
                         Worry

DEVIL

1561   When dining with the devil, one must use a long spoon.
                                                    —*Bismarck*

1562   The Devil was sick—the Devil a monk would be,
        The Devil was well—the Devil a monk was he.   —*Rabelais*

1563   The prince of darkness is a gentleman.   —*Shakespeare*

1564   As good eat the devil as the broth he is boiled in.

SEE ALSO   RELATED SUBJECTS
Atheism 329   God
Church 811   Saint
Conviction 1035   Sin
Cynicism 1293   Temptation
Drinking 1724   Wickedness
Lawyers 3423
Misanthrope 3981

DICTATORS

1571   Dictatorship is like a great beech tree. nice to look at, but nothing
        grows under it.   —*Stanley Baldwin*

1572   What millions died—that Caesar might be great!
                                            —*Thomas Campbell*

1573   When the Hun is poor and down
        He's the humblest man in town;
        But once he climbs and holds the rod
        He smites his fellow-man—and God.
                        —*Joseph Cats (Written around 1600)*

1574   Who is all-powerful should fear everything.   —*Corneille*

1575   When liberty becomes license, dictatorship is near.
                                            —*Will Durant*

1576   Many he needs must fear whom many fear.   —*Horace*

1577   It is useless for the sheep to pass resolutions in favor of vege-
        tarianism, while the wolf remains of a different opinion.
                                            —*Dean Inge*

1578 In a state of anarchy power is the measure of right. —*Lucan*

1579 Dictators always look good until the last ten minutes.
—*Jan Masaryk*

1580 Anarchy is the sure consequence of tyranny; or no power that is not limited by laws can ever be protected by them. —*Milton*

1581 In times of anarchy one may seem a despot in order to be a savior.
—*Mirabeau*

1582 Every anarchist is a baffled dictator. —*Mussolini*

1583 Dr. Goebbels and Virginio Gayda are joint holders of the running broad jump to conclusions. —*N. Y. Times*

1584 He must fear many whom many fear. —*Publilius Syrus*

1585 Excessive power seeks power beyond its power. —*Seneca*

1586 A very fair spot but there is no way down from it.
—*Solon, of dictatorship*

1587 Virginio Gayda is about the only newspaperman we know of who can write the way a peke barks. —*Frank Sullivan*

1588 Despotism may govern without faith, but liberty cannot.
—*De Tocqueville*

1589 Hitler's word is as good as his Bund.

1590 Mussolini is a man possible only in a country that has no appreciation of real acting.

SEE ALSO
Liberty 3508
Peace 4355

RELATED SUBJECTS
Democracy
Government
Liberty
Politics

DIFFICULTY

1591 Never trust the advice of a man in difficulties. —*Aesop*

1592 Depressions may bring people closer to the church—but so do funerals. —*Clarence Darrow*

1593 The difficulty in life is the choice. —*George Moore*

1594 Difficulty is the excuse history never accepts. —*Samuel Grafton*

1595 He who accounts all things easy will have many difficulties.
—*Lao-Tsze*

1596 The occasion is piled high with difficulty, and we must rise high with the occasion. —*Lincoln*

1597   Look for a tough wedge for a tough log.   —*Publilius Syrus*

SEE ALSO   RELATED SUBJECTS
Resignation 4864   Hardship
                          Optimism
                          Troubles

DIGNITY

1601   The superior man is slow in his words and earnest in his conduct.
                                                                —*Confucius*

1602   Perhaps the only true dignity of man is his capacity to despise
        himself.   —*Santayana*

1603   It is easier to grow in dignity than to make a start.   —*Seneca*

1604   The eagle does not catch flies.

SEE ALSO   RELATED SUBJECTS
Credit 1206   Character
Farming 2146   Courtesy
Rank 4762   Vulgarity

DIPLOMACY

1611   International arbitration may be defined as the substitution of
        many burning questions for a smouldering one.
                                                        —*Ambrose Bierce*

1612   American diplomacy is easy on the brain but hell on the feet.
                                                        —*Charles G. Dawes*

1613   Diplomacy is to do and say
        The nastiest thing in the nicest way.   —*Isaac Goldberg*

1614   There are three species of creature who when they seem coming
        are going,
        When they seem going they come:
        Diplomats, women, and crabs.   —*John Hay*

1615   Men, like bullets, go farthest when they are smoothest.
                                                        —*J. P. Richter*

1616   An ambassador is an honest man sent to lie abroad for the com-
        monwealth.   —*Sir Henry Wotton*

1617   It is fortunate that diplomats generally have long noses, since
        usually they cannot see beyond them.

SEE ALSO   RELATED SUBJECTS
America 202   Courtesy
                          Discretion
                          Government
                          Politics

DISAPPOINTMENT

1621 Man must be disappointed with the lesser things of life before he can comprehend the full value of the greater.
—*Bulwer-Lytton*

1622 The best-laid schemes o' mice an' men
Gang aft agley,
An' lea'e us nought but grief an' pain,
For promis'd joy!
—*Burns*

1623 The disappointment of manhood succeeds the delusion of youth.
—*Disraeli*

1624 What we anticipate seldom occurs; what we least expected generally happens.
—*Disraeli*

1625 Nothing is so good as it seems beforehand. —*George Eliot*

1626 How disappointment tracks the steps of hope. —*L. E. Landon*

1627 Disappointment should always be taken as a stimulant, and never viewed as a discouragement.
—*C. B. Newcomb*

1628 Blessed is he who expects nothing, for he shall never be disappointed.
—*Pope*

1629 Mean spirits under disappointment, like small beer in a thunderstorm, always turn sour.
—*John Randolph*

1630 For of all sad words of tongue or pen,
The saddest are these: "It might have been!" —*Whittier*

SEE ALSO	RELATED SUBJECTS
Eating 1776	Defeat
News 4175	Difficulty
Philosophy 4432	Faith
Virtue 5685	Grief
Women 6035	

DISCRETION

1631 I have never been hurt by anything I didn't say.
—*Calvin Coolidge*

1632 For good and evil in our actions meet;
Wicked is not much worse than indiscreet. —*John Donne*

1633 A lover without indiscretion is no lover at all. —*Thomas Hardy*

1634 Know when to speak—for many times it brings
Danger, to give the best advice to kings. —*Robert Herrick*

1635 He knows not when to be silent who knows not when to speak.
—*Publilius Syrus*

1636   Wise men say nothing in dangerous times.   —*John Selden*

1637   Have more than thou showest,
       Speak less than thou knowest.   —*Shakespeare*

1638   Thy friend has a friend, and thy friend's friend has a friend;
       be discreet.   —*Talmud*

1639   Questions are never indiscreet: answers sometimes are.
                                                       —*Oscar Wilde*

1640   And I oft have heard defended—
       Little said is soonest mended.   —*Wither*

1641   The age of discretion is the age of impotence.

1642   Those who live in stone houses should not throw glass.

1643   Once man demanded virtue in woman; now all he expects is that
       she be discreet.

1644   Much that well may be thought cannot wisely be said.

1645   He that hears much, and speaks not all, shall be welcome both in
       bower and hall.

       SEE ALSO   RELATED SUBJECTS
       Friend 2397   Caution
       Letters 3481   Decision
                             Judgment
                             Wisdom

DOCTORS

1651   Pray, dear Doctor, alter your rule; and prescribe only for your
       enemies.   —*Topham Beauclerk*

1652   And Nathan, being sick, trusted not in the Lord, but sent for a
       physician—and Nathan was gathered unto his fathers.
                                                       —*Bible*

1653   Physicians mend or end us,
       Secundum artem; but although we sneer
       In health—when ill we call them to attend us,
       Without the least propensity to jeer.   —*Byron*

1654   A good surgeon operates with his hand, not with his heart.
                                                       —*Dumas*

1655   It's no trifle at her time of life to part with a doctor who knows
       her constitution.   —*George Eliot*

1656   Joy and Temperance and Repose
       Slam the door on the doctor's nose.   —*Longfellow*

1657   Till lately Diaulus was a doctor; now he is an undertaker. What he does as an undertaker, he had already done as a doctor.
        —Martial

1658   The Doctor—detected, while he stole
A patient's favorite drinking bowl,
Had still his answer pat enough:
"You fool! You shouldn't touch the stuff!"   *—Martial*

1659   You are now a gladiator; you were formerly an oculist. You did as an ophthalmic surgeon what you now do as a gladiator.
        —Martial

1660   When I was ill, you came to me,
Doctor, and with great urgency
A hundred students brought with you
A most instructive case to view.
The hundred finger'd me with hands
Chill'd by the blasts of northern lands:
Fever at outset had I none—
I have it, Sir, now you have done.   *—Martial*

1661   Agelaus chanced, operating on a man, to kill.
"Lucky wretch!" he cried: "Might have limped for life, but for my skill."   *—Nicarchus*

1662   The physician who killed me,
Neither bled, purged or pilled me,
Nor counted my pulse, but it comes to the same,
In the height of my fever I thought of his name.   *—Nicarchus*

1663   Yesterday the Zeus of stone from the doctor had a call:
Though he's Zeus and though he's stone, yet today's his funeral.
        —Nicarchus

1664   The patient surely had been lame for life,
So Scalpel, pitying, killed him with his knife.   *—Nicarchus*

1665   Surgery is by far the worst snob among the handicrafts.
        —Austin O'Malley

1666   The alienist is not a joke:
He finds you cracked, and leaves you broke.   *—Keith Preston*

1667   I had rather follow you to your grave than see you owe your life to any but a regular-bred physician.   *—Sheridan*

1668   The best doctors in the world are Doctor Diet, Doctor Quiet, and Doctor Merryman.   *—Swift*

1669   At Highgate by salubrious air,
    Had thriven butchers, bakers;
But since a doctor settled there,
    None thrive but undertakers.

1670 Diagnosis: a preface to an autopsy.

1671 Physicians of the highest rank
(To pay their fees, we need a bank),
Combine all wisdom, art and skill,
Science and sense, in Calomel.

1672 If the doctor cures, the sun sees it; but if he kills, the earth
hides it.

1673 That patient is not like to recover who makes the doctor his heir.

1674 God cures and the doctor takes the fee.

1675 If anybody comes to I,
I physics, bleeds and sweats 'em;
If after that they choose to die,
Why, what care I? I. Lettsom.

SEE ALSO   RELATED SUBJECTS
Lawyers 3424   Body
Temperance 5329   Health
                           Medicine
                           Sickness

DOGS

1681 The more I see of dogs the less I think of men.
—*Arsène Houssaye*

1682 Whoever beats dogs loves not man.   —*Arsène Houssaye*

1683 When a man's dog turns against him it is time for his wife to
pack her trunk and go home to mamma.   —*Mark Twain*

1684 They say a reasonable number of fleas is good fer a dog—keeps
him from broodin' over bein' a dog.   —*E. N. Westcott*

SEE ALSO   RELATED SUBJECTS
Fidelity 2195   Cat
Gratitude 2611   Nature
Religion 4810

DOUBT

1691 More persons, on the whole, are humbugged by believing in nothing, than by believing too much.   —*P. T. Barnum*

1692 I've stood upon Achilles' tomb,
And heard Troy doubted: time will doubt of Rome.   —*Byron*

1693 Just think of the tragedy of teaching children not to doubt.
—*Clarence Darrow*

1694 Uncertain ways unsafest are,
And doubt a greater mischief than despair.   —*Sir John Denham*

1695   Scepticism is the first step on the road to philosophy.   *—Diderot*

1696   For right is right, since God is God,
    And right the day must win;
To doubt would be disloyalty,
    To falter would be sin.   *—F. W. Faber*

1697   Incredulity robs us of many pleasures, and gives us nothing in
return.   *—Lowell*

1698   He who dallies is a dastard, he who doubts is damned.
—George McDuffle

1699   I respect faith, but doubt is what gets you an education.
—Wilson Mizner

1700   O Lord—if there is a Lord; save my soul—if I have a soul.
Amen.   *—Rénan*

1701   Our doubts are traitors,
And make us lose the good we oft might win,
By fearing to attempt.   *—Shakespeare*

1702   There lives more faith in honest doubt,
Believe me, than in half the creeds.   *—Tennyson*

1703   Doubt makes the mountain which faith can move.

SEE ALSO   RELATED SUBJECTS
Advice 126   Caution
Reason 4784   Conviction
                 Cynicism
                 Knowledge
                 Trust

DRINKING

1711   To be bowed by grief is folly;
Naught is gained by melancholy;
Better than the pain of thinking,
Is to steep the sense in drinking.   *—Alcaeus*

1712   Man being reasonable must get drunk;
The best of life is but intoxication;
Glory, the grape, love, gold—in these are sunk
The hopes of all men and of every nation.   *—Byron*

1713   What's drinking?
A mere pause from thinking!   *—Byron*

1714   I drink when I have occasion, and sometimes when I have no
occasion.   *—Cervantes*

1715   Be kind, O Bacchus, take this empty pot
       Offered to thee by Xenophon, the sot,
       Who, giving this, gives all that he has got.   —*Eratosthenes*

1716   O Strangers! By Anacreon's tomb who pass,
       Shed o'er it wine, in life he lov'd his glass.   —*Greek epigram*

1717   Licker talks mighty loud w'en it gits loose from de jug.
                                                  —*Joel Chandler Harris*

1718   One drink is plenty;
       Two drinks too many,
       And three not half enough.   —*W. Knox Haynes*

1719   Teetot'lers seem to die the same as others,
       So what's the use of knocking off the beer?   —*A. P. Herbert*

1720   Bacchus drowns within the bowl
       Troubles that corrode the soul.   —*Horace*

1721   First the man takes a drink; then the drink takes a drink; then
            the drink takes the man.   —*Japanese proverb*

1722   As for the Brandy, "Nothing extenuate;"
       And the water, "Put naught in in malice."   —*Douglas Jerrold*

1723   Claret is the liquor for boys,
       Port for men; but he who aspires to be a hero must drink brandy.
                                                                  —*Johnson*

1724   There is a devil in every berry of the grape.   —*Koran*

1725   You make any number of promises when you have been drinking
            all evening. Next morning you won't keep one. Drink in the
            morning, Pollio.   —*Martial*

1726   It is a mistake to think that Acerra reeks of yesterday's liquor:
       Acerra always drinks till next morning.   —*Martial*

1727   Candy
       Is dandy
       But liquor
       Is quicker.   —*Ogden Nash*

1728   Not drunk is he who from the floor
       Can rise alone and still drink more;
       But drunk is he, who prostrate lies,
       Without the power to drink or rise.   —*T. L. Peacock*

1729   Nose, Nose, Nose, Nose!
       And who gave thee that jolly red nose?
       Cinnamon and Ginger, Nutmegs and Cloves,
       And that gave me my jolly red nose.   —*Ravenscroft*

1730   The sot Loserus is drunk twice a day,
       Bibinus only once; now of these say,
       Which may a man·the greatest drunkard call?
       Bibinus still, for he's drunk once for all.   —*Scaliger*

1731   Drunkenness does not create vice; it merely brings it into view.
                                                          —*Seneca*

1732   It (drink) provokes the desire, but takes away the performance.
                                                          —*Shakespeare*

1733   O God! that men should put an enemy in their mouths to steal
       away their brains!   —*Shakespeare*

1734   A bumper of good liquor
       Will end a contest quicker
       Than justice, judge, or vicar.   —*Sheridan*

1735   He who drinks one glass a day,
       Will live to die some other way.   —*Stanlicus*

1736   I cannot eat but little meat,
          My stomach is not good;
       But sure I think that I can drink
          With him that wears a hood.   —*John Still*

1737   Better belly burst than good liquor be lost.   —*Swift*

1738   There are two things that will be believed of any man whatso-
       ever, and one of them is that he has taken to drink.
                                                          —*Tarkington*

1739   The first glass for myself; the second for my friends; the third
       for good humor; and the fourth for mine enemies.
                                                          —*W. Temple*

1740   'Tis clear, since Brandy kill'd Tom's scolding wife,
       That drinking rids us of the cares of life.

1741   A drunkard is like a whiskey-bottle, all neck and belly and no
       head.

1742   A soft drink turneth away company.

1743   He is not drunk gratis, who pays his reason for his shot.

1744   When your companions get drunk and fight, take up your hat
       and wish them good night.

1745   Drunkenness is a pair of spectacles to see the devil and all his
       works.

1746   A drink is shorter than a tale.

1747   Of all meat in the world, drink goes down the best.

1748   If you'd know when you've enough
        Of the punch and the claret cup
        It's time to quit the blessed stuff
        When you fall down and can't get up.

SEE ALSO   RELATED SUBJECTS
Excess 1979   Eating
Writers 6138   Excess
                         Temperance
                         Wine

DUTY

1751   The reward of one duty done is the power to fulfill another.
                                                    —*George Eliot*

1752   I don't translate my own convenience into other people's duties.
                                                    —*George Eliot*

1753   So nigh is grandeur to our dust,
            So near is God to man,
        When Duty whispers low, Thou must,
            The youth replies, I can!   —*Emerson*

1754   You have a disagreeable duty to do at twelve o'clock. Do not
        blacken nine and ten and eleven and all between with the color
        of twelve.   —*George Macdonald*

1755   When you have a number of disagreeable duties to perform
        always do the most disagreeable first.   —*Josiah Quincy*

1756   I fancy that it is just as hard to do your duty when men are
        sneering at you as when they are shooting at you.
                                                —*Woodrow Wilson*

1757   Life has no moral purpose; no one is born with a duty to anyone
        else.

1758   Duty leads a few to virtue and the rest to discontent.

1759   Men do not love to perform their duties; for every newly created
        duty there are new laws to enforce them.

1760   Best way to get rid of your duties is to discharge them.

SEE ALSO   RELATED SUBJECTS
Aim 198   Conscience
Character 712   Courage
Death 1354   Example
Happiness 2766, 2783   Martyr
Nature 4144   Morality
Vanity 5619   Self-Denial

E

EATING

1761 What most moved him was a certain meal on beans.
—*Browning*

1762 All human history attests
That happiness for man—the hungry sinner—
Since Eve ate apples, much depends on dinner!   —*Byron*

1763 The belly carries the legs, and not the legs the belly.
—*Cervantes*

1764 A man must eat though every tree were a gallows.
—*C. M. Clarke*

1765 To eat is human; to digest, divine.   —*C. T. Copeland*

1766 He fasts enough who eats with reason.   —*A. J. Cronin*

1767 A man once asked Diogenes what was the proper time for supper, and he made answer, "If you are a rich man, whenever you please; and if you are a poor man, whenever you can."
—*Diogenes Laertius*

1768 When I demanded of my friend what viands he preferred,
He quoth: "A large cold bottle, and a small hot bird!"
—*Eugene Field*

1769 Fools make feasts, and wise men eat them.   —*Franklin*

1770 A full belly makes a dull brain.   —*Franklin*

1771 It isn't so much what's on the table that matters, as what's on the chairs.   —*W. S. Gilbert*

1772 By suppers more have been killed than Galen ever cured.
—*George Herbert*

1773 Among the great whom Heaven has made to shine,
How few have learned the art of arts—to dine!
—*O. W. Holmes*

1774 "Better is a dinner of herbs where love is, than a stalled ox and hatred therewith."—Bitter is a dinner of herbs where love is. Give me a stalled ox and hatred therewith. —*Anthony Hope*

1775 The chief pleasure in eating does not consist in costly seasoning or exquisite flavor but in yourself.   —*Horace*

1776 When a man is invited to dinner, he is disappointed if he does not get something good.   —*Johnson*

1777   i have noticed that when chickens quit quarrelling over their food
they often find that there is enough for all of them i wonder
if it might not be the same way with the human race
—Don Marquis

1778   Our friend Caecilianus does not dine without a wild-boar. What a
charming companion at the dinner-table!   *—Martial*

1779   When the crowd of your admirers is shouting, "Bravo! Hear,
hear!" it is not you, Pomponius, but your dinner that is elo-
quent.   *—Martial*

1780   You say that the hare is not cooked, Rufus, and you call for your
whip. You would rather give the cook a cut than the hare.
—Martial

1781   When I was young I had no dial but appetite,
The very best and truest of all time-pieces.
When that said "Eat," I ate—if I could get it.   *—Menander*

1782   Oh, better, no doubt, is a dinner of herbs,
When season'd by love, which no rancor disturbs,
And sweeten'd by all that is sweetest in life,
Than turbot, bisque, ortolans, eaten with strife.
—Owen Meredith

1783   The more the merrier; the fewer, the better fare.
—John Palgrave

1784   The difference between a rich man and a poor man, is this—the
former eats when he pleases, and the latter when he can get it.
—Sir Walter Raleigh

1785   A dinner lubricates business.   *—William Scott*

1786   Serenely full, the epicure would say,
Fate cannot harm me—I have dined today.   *—Sidney Smith*

1787   He was a bold man that first eat an oyster.   *—Swift*

1788   When the belly is full, the bones would be at rest.   *—Swift*

1789   He who eats with most pleasure is he who least requires sauce.
—Xenophon

1790   When the belly is full the mind is amongst the maids.

1791   The epicure puts his purse into his belly.

1792   There are more gluttons than drunkards in hell.

1793   The discovery of a new dish does more for the happiness of man
than the discovery of a star.

1794   He sups ill, who eats up all at dinner.

1795 At a round table there's no dispute of place.

1796 Eat-well is drink-well's brother.

1797 If it were not for the belly, the back might wear gold.

1798 The belly robs the back.

SEE ALSO   RELATED SUBJECTS
Conversation 1022   Cooks
Wealth 5773   Drinking

ECONOMY

1801 Not to be covetous, is money; not to be a purchaser, is a revenue.
—*Cicero*

1802 Men do not realize how great a revenue economy is. —*Cicero*

1803 Beware of little expenses; a small leak will sink a great ship.
—*Franklin*

1804 A man often pays dear for a small frugality. —*Emerson*

1805 At the beginning of the cask and at the end take thy fill; but be saving in the middle; for at the bottom saving comes too late.
—*Hesiod*

1806 Th' feller that brags 'bout how cheap he heats his home allus sees th' first robin. —*Kin Hubbard*

1807 Without economy none can be rich, and with it few can be poor.
—*Johnson*

1808 Bassus bought a Tyrian cloak of the best color for a hundred. He made a good bargain. "Did he get it very cheap?" you ask. Very cheap indeed, for he will never pay for it. —*Martial*

1809 If you keep a thing seven years, you are sure to find a use for it.
—*Scott*

1810 Economy is too late at the bottom of the purse. —*Seneca*

1811 The regard one shows economy, is like that we show an old aunt, who is to leave us something at last. —*William Shenstone*

1812 Solvency is entirely a matter of temperament and not of income.
—*Logan Pearsall Smith*

1813 They take their pride in making their dinner cost much; I take my pride in making my dinner cost little. —*Thoreau*

1814 Take care to be an economist in prosperity; there is no fear of your not being one in adversity. —*Zimmerman*

1815 He that considers in prosperity, will be less afflicted in adversity.

1816   Spend not, where you may save; spare not, where you must spend.

1817   To make your candles last for aye,
          Ye wives and maids give ear-o!
       To put them out's the only way,
          Says honest John Boldero.

1818   Many have been ruin'd by buying good pennyworths.

1819   Good bargains are pick-pockets.

SEE ALSO   RELATED SUBJECTS
Greed 2660   Business
Love 3735   Extravagance
Selfishness 4994   Money
Truth 5581   Poverty
                            Wealth

EGGS

1821   A hen is only an egg's way of making another egg.
                                                    —*Samuel Butler*

1822   All the goodness of a good egg cannot make up for the badness
       of a bad one.   —*Charles A. Dana*

1823   There is always a best way of doing everything, if it be to boil
       an egg.   —*Emerson*

1824   It is very hard to shave an egg.   —*George Herbert*

1825   Omelettes are not made without breaking eggs. —*Robespierre*

1826   Put all your eggs in one basket, and—watch the basket.
                                                    —*Mark Twain*

SEE ALSO   RELATED SUBJECTS
Honesty 2915, 2926   Cooks
Price 4647   Eating

ENEMIES

1831   You shall judge of a man by his foes as well as by his friends.
                                                    —*Joseph Conrad*

1832   If you have no enemies, you are apt to be in the same predica-
       ment in regard to friends.   —*Elbert Hubbard*

1833   Let us not talk ill of our enemies.
       They, only, never deceive us.   —*Arsène Houssaye*

1834   He makes no friends who never made a foe.   —*Tennyson*

1835   It is an unhappy lot which finds no enemies.

1836   If we are bound to forgive an enemy, we are not bound to trust
       him.

1837   When your enemy flies, build him a golden bridge.

1838   A reconciled friend is a double enemy.

SEE ALSO
Advertising 73
Death 1330
Drinking 1733
Love 3694
Weakness 5751
Women 6006

RELATED SUBJECTS
Friend
Hate
Insults
War

ENGLAND

1841   An Englishman is a man who lives on an island in the North Sea governed by Scotsmen.   *—Philip Guedalla*

1842   Things they don't understand always cause a sensation among the English.   *—Alfred De Musset*

1843   There are only two classes in good society in England: the equestrian classes and the neurotic classes.   *—G. B. Shaw*

1844   A famine in England begins at the horse-manger.

SEE ALSO
Ancestors 223

EPIGRAMS

1851   A proverb is a short sentence based on long experience.   *—Cervantes*

1852   What is an epigram? a dwarfish whole,
Its body brevity, and wit its soul.   *—Coleridge*

1853   An epigram is but a feeble thing
With straw in tail, stuck there by way of sting.   *—Cowper*

1854   Let no one weep for me, or celebrate my funeral with mourning; for I still live, as I pass to and fro through the mouths of men.   *—Ennius*

1855   Three things must epigrams, like bees, have all,
A sting, and honey, and a body small.   *—Latin distich*

1856   An epigram is a gag that's played Carnegie Hall.*—Oscar Levant*

1857   He misses what is meant by epigram
Who thinks it only frivolous flim-flam.   *—Martial*

1858   No amount of misfortune will satisfy the man who is not satisfied with reading a hundred epigrams.   *—Martial*

1859   In Marsus and the accomplished Pedo, a single epigram often occupies a couple of pages. Things are not long, if they contain nothing which you can take away. As for yourself, Cosconius, you write long couplets.   *—Martial*

1860   You ask me to read you my epigrams, Afer. No, thank you—you
       want to read me yours, not to hear mine.   *—Martial*

1861   You complain, Velox, that my epigrams are too long. You make
       yours shorter, for you write nothing.   *—Martial*

1862   An epigram is a half truth so stated as to irritate the person who
       believes the other half.   *—Mathews*

1863   No choice maxims—we Stoics don't practice that kind of window-
       dressing.   *—Seneca*

1864   No epigram contains the whole truth.   *—C. W. Thompson*

1865   It is more trouble to make a maxim than it is to do right.
                                                       —Mark Twain

1866   Somewhere in the world there is an epigram for every dilemma.
                                                       —H. W. Van Loon

1867   An epigram often flashes light into regions where reason shines
       but dimly.   *—E. P. Whipple*

1868   An epigram should be, if right,
       Short, simple, pointed, keen, and bright—
         A lively little thing!
       Like wasp with taper body, bound
       By lines—not many—neat and round;
         All ending in a sting.

1869   Take a portion of wit,
       And fashion it fit,
       Like a needle, with point and with eye:
       A *point* that can wound,
       An *eye* to look round,
       And at *folly* or *vice* let it fly.

See Also	Related Subjects
Books 511	Conversation
Death 1375	Fools
Hanging 2751	Insults
	Jokes
	Wisdom
	Wit

EPITAPHS

1871   Slumbereth Timocrates within this grave,
       For Ares spares the coward, not the brave.
                                    —Anacreon, to a slain warrior

1872   Beneath this stone my wife doth lie:
       Now she's at rest, and so am I!
                                                       —Boileau

1873   At rest here Saon, Dicon's son, of Acanthos, lies.
      It is sleep from Heaven; say not that a good man dies.

                                                  —Callimachus

1874   Pay me no tears; nor for my passing grieve:
      I linger on the lips of men—and live.   *—Ennius*

1875

The Body
of
Benjamin Franklin, Printer
(Like the cover of an old book,
Its contents torn out,
And stript of its lettering and gilding,)
Lies food for worms.
Yet the work itself shall not be lost,
For it will (as he believed) appear once more,
In a new
And more beautiful edition,
Corrected and amended
by
The Author.

                                                  —Franklin

1876   Here lies Nolly Goldsmith, for shortness called Noll,
      Who wrote like an angel, but talk'd like poor Poll.   *—Garrick*

1877   No heap of dust is Erasippus' grave,
      Nor funeral stone, but all the wild sea wave,
      As wide and far as e'er thine eye can see.   *—Glaucus*

1878   Here lies Anacreon: then, stranger, pour
      Freely thy wine—I'm thirsty as of yore.   *—Greek epitaph*

1879   My country and my name inquire not: I
      Wish all who pass my tomb like me to die.   *—Greek epitaph*

1880   Here ended my sad life, my tomb you see,
      Ask not my name—on all my curses be!   *—Greek epitaph*

1881   Here lies the Christian, judge, and poet Peter,
      Who broke the laws of God, and man, and metre.
          —John Gibson Lockhart on Lord Peter Robertson

1882   Here lapped in hallowed slumber Saon lies,
      Asleep, not dead; a good man never dies.   *—Saon of Acanthus*

1883   Here lie I, Timon; who alive, all living men did hate:
      Pass by, and curse thy fill; but pass and stay not here thy gait.
                                  —Shakespeare

1884   Beneath this stone there lies a skull,
       Which when it breath'd, was monstrous dull,
       But now 'tis dead and doom'd to rot,
       This skull's as wise (pray is it not?)
       As Shakespeare's, Newton's, Prior's, Gay's,
       The wits, the sages of their days.
                     —*Epitaph in the Poet's Corner, Westminster Abbey*

1885   Here lies William Trollope,
       Who made these stones roll up;
       When death took his soul up,
       His body filled this hole up.   —*On the architect, Trollope*

1886   Hoe hoe who lyes here
       'Tis I the goode erle of Devonsheere
       With Kate my wyfe to mee full dere
       Wee lyved togeather fyfty-fyve yeare
       That wee spent wee had
       That wee left wee lost
       That wee gave wee have.
                     —*On a tomb in Twerton churchyard, dated* 1419

1887   Peace to his hashes.   —*On a celebrated cook*

1888   Cease to lament his change, ye just,
       He's only gone from dust to dust.
                                            —*On a coal heaver*

1889   Finis
       Maginnis   —*Irish epitaph*

1890   Here lies
                     Pierre Cabochard, grocer.
                     His inconsolate widow
              dedicates this monument to his memory,
              and continues the same business at
              the old stand, 167 Rue Mouffetard.
                     —*In Pere-la-Chaise Cemetery, Paris*

1891   Here lies Poor Charlotte,
       Who died no harlot,
       But in her virginity,
           Though just turned nineteen,
       Which within this vicinity
           Is hard to be found and seen.
                     —*St. George's churchyard, Somerset*

1892   Here lies Du Vall: Reader, if male, thou art,
       Look to thy purse: if female, to thy heart.
                     —*On the tombstone of the 17th century highwayman, Duval*

1893   Since I am so quickly done for,
I wonder what I was begun for.
—On an infant only three months old

1894   Here lie my two children dear,
One in Ireland, and the other here.
—In an Oswego, N. Y., cemetery

1895   Here lies my wife in earthly mould,
Who when she lived, did nought but scold;
Peace wake her not, for now she's still,
She had, but now I have my will.

1896   Here lies my wife, a sad slattern and a shrew,
If I said I regretted her I should lie too.

1897   Here lies my poor wife, without bed or blanket,
But dead as a door-nail, and God be thankit.

1898   Here I lie at the church door,
Here I lie because I am poor;
When I rise at the Judgment Day,
I shall be as warm as they.

1899   Here lies the body of Mary Ford,
Whose soul, we trust, is with the Lord;
But if for hell she's changed this life,
'Tis better than being John Ford's wife.

1900   Erected to the memory of
      John Phillips
      Accidently shot,
As a mark of affection by his Brother.

1901   I laid my wife beneath this stone
For her repose and for my own.

1902   He lived one hundred and five
      Sanguine and strong;
A hundred to five
      You live not so long.

1903   Here lies the body of Jonathan Ground,
Who was lost at sea and never found.

1904   Misplacing—mistaking—
Misquoting—misdating;
Men, manners, things, and facts all.
Here lies Sir Nathaniel Wraxall.

1905   Here lies Joan Kitchin; when her life was spent,
She kicked up her heels, and away she went.

1906   Here lies two babbies, as dead as nits,
Who died in agonising fits;
They were too good to live with we,
So God did take to live with He.

1907   Here I lies, and no wonder I'm dead,
For the wheel of a wagon went over my head.

1908   She's gone and cannot come to we,
But we shall shortly go to she.

1909   See how God works His wonders now and then—
Here lies a lawyer and an honest man.

1910   Near to this stone John Barnet lies,
There's no man frets, nor no man cries,
Where he's gone, or how he fares,
There's no man knows, nor no man cares.

1911   Here lie the remains of John Hall, grocer. The world is not
worth a fig, and I have good reason for saying so.

1912   This stone was raised by Sarah's lord,
Not Sarah's virtues to record,
For they're well-known to all the town,
But it was *raised* to keep her *down*.

1913   To all my friends I bid adieu,
A more sudden death you never knew.
As I was leading the old mare to drink,
She kicked, and killed me quicker'n a wink.

1914   Here lies the body of Lady O'Looney,
Great niece of Burke, commonly
Called the Sublime.
   She was
Bland, passionate, and deeply religious.
Also she painted in water-colours,
And sent several pictures to the Exhibition.
She was first cousin to Lady Jones,
And of such is the kingdom of heaven.

1915   Here lies the body of W. W.,
Who never more will trouble you, trouble you.

1916   Lelio is buried here;
He was born, he lived, he died.

1917   Friend, in your epitaphs I'm grieved
   So very much is said:
One-half will never be believed,
   The other never read.

1918   Here lies I and my three daughters,
       Kill'd by drinking the Cheltenham waters;
       If we had stuck to our Epsom salts,
       We'd not been a lying in these here vaults.

1919   Ah, cruel Death! why so unkind,
       To take her, and leave me behind.
       Better to have taken both or neither,
       It would have been more kind to the survivor!

1920   I lost the comfort of my life,
       Death came and took my wife;
       And now I don't know what to do,
       Lest death should come, and take me too.

1921   Here lies the carcass of a cursèd sinner
       Doomed to be roasted for the Devil's dinner.

1922   Here lies I, Martin Elmrod;
       Have mercy on my soul, gude God,
       As I would have gin I were God,
       And thou wert Martin Elmrod.

1923   John Carnegie lies here,
         Descended from Adam and Eve;
       If any can boast of a pedigree higher,
         He will willingly give them leave.

1924   Beneath this stone, in hopes of Zion,
       Is laid the landlord of the Lion.
       Resigned unto the Heavenly will,
       His son keeps on the business still.

1925   My time was come! My days were spent!
       I was called away—and away I went!!!

1926   Mammy and I together lived
         Just two years and a half;
       She went first—I followed next,
         The cow before the calf.

1927   Here lies I
       Kill'd by a sky-
       Rocket in the eye.

1928   Here lies the bones of Margaret Gwynn,
       Who was so very pure within,
       She cracked her outer shell of sin
       And hatched herself a Seraphin.

1929 Here lies Pat Steele.
That's very true:
Who was he? What was he?
What's that to you?

ERROR

1931 I would rather err with Plato than think rightly with these
(Pythagoreans).   —*Cicero*

1932 Perhaps it is a good thing to have an unsound hobby ridden hard;
for it is sooner ridden to death.   —*Dickens*

1933 Errors, like straws, upon the surface flow;
He who would search for pearls must dive below.   —*Dryden*

1934 Freedom is not worth having if it does not connote freedom to
err.   —*Mahatma Gandhi*

1935 Error of opinion may be tolerated where reason is left free to
combat it.   —*Jefferson*

1936 Error is none the better for being common, nor truth the worse
for having lain neglected.   —*John Locke*

1937 It takes less time to do a thing right than it does to explain why
you did it wrong.   —*Longfellow*

1938 The wrong way always seems the more reasonable.
—*George Moore*

1939 Men err from selfishness; women because they are weak.
—*Mme. de Stael*

1940 An expert is a person who avoids the small errors as he sweeps on
to the grand fallacy.   —*Benjamin Stolberg*

1941 Men are apt to prefer a prosperous error to an afflicted truth.
—*Jeremy Taylor*

1942 The history of human opinion is scarcely anything more than the
history of human errors.   —*Voltaire*

EXAMPLE   109

EVIL

1951 It is some compensation for great evils that they enforce great lessons.   *—C. N. Bovée*

1952 God makes all things good; man meddles with them and they become evil.   *—Rousseau*

1953 Men's evil manners live in brass; their virtues we write in water.   *—Shakespeare*

1954 There's small choice in rotten apples.   *—Shakespeare*

1955 If evils come not, then our fears are vain;
And, if they do, fear but augments the pain.

1956 Real and imaginary evils have the same effect on the human mind.

1957 No choice amongst stinking fish.

SEE ALSO	RELATED SUBJECTS
Marriage 3876	Crime
Women 5993	Devil
	Good
	Sin
	Wickedness

EXAMPLE

1961 For behavior, men learn it, as they take diseases, one of another.   *—Bacon*

1962 It is not enough to be an upright man, we must be seen to be one; society does not exist on moral ideas only.   *—Balzac*

1963 We are far more liable to catch the vices than the virtues of our associates.   *—Diderot*

1964 The rotten apple spoils his companion.   *—Franklin*

1965 You can preach a better sermon with your life than with your lips.   *—Goldsmith*

1966 People seldom improve when they have no model but themselves to copy after.   *—Goldsmith*

1967 We can do more good by being good, than in any other way.   *—Rowland Hill*

1968 Rules make the learner's path long, examples make it short and successful.   *—Seneca*

1969 Things bad begun make strong themselves by ill.*—Shakespeare*

1970   Few things are harder to put up with than the annoyance of a
       good example.   —*Mark Twain*

SEE ALSO   RELATED SUBJECTS
Action 12   Conviction
Children 768   Deeds
Courtesy 1105   Teaching

EXCESS

1971   Nor too much wealth nor wit come to thee,
       So much of either may undo thee.   —*Bishop Corbet*

1972   Thus each extreme to equal danger tends,
       Plenty, as well as Want, can sep'rate friends.   —*Cowley*

1973   There is moderation even in excess.   —*Disraeli*

1974   Too much plenty makes mouth dainty.   —*Franklin*

1975   Wild oats will get sown some time, and one of the arts of life is
       to sow them at the right time.   —*Richard Le Gallienne*

1976   But just disease to luxury succeeds.
       And ev'ry death its own avenger breeds.   —*Pope*

1977   They never taste who always drink;
       They always talk who never think.   —*Matthew Prior*

1978   A bellyfull is a bellyfull.   —*Rabelais*

1979   'Tis not the drinking that is to be blamed, but the excess.
                                                    —*John Selden*

1980   The superfluous, a very necessary thing.   —*Voltaire*

1981   The excesses of old men incline toward perversion.

1982   Dissipation: stupidity in despair.

SEE ALSO   RELATED SUBJECTS
Greed 2661   Conservative
                            Discretion
                            Extravagance
                            Temperance

EXCUSE

1991   Excellence is the perfect excuse.
       Do it well, and it matters little what.   —*Emerson*

1992   Never mind what I told you—you do as *I* tell you.
                                                    —*W. C. Fields*

1993   Don't make excuses—make good.   —*Elbert Hubbard*

1994   Contests allow no excuses, no more do friendships.   —*Ibycus*

1995   He who excuses himself accuses himself.   *—Gabriel Meurier*

SEE ALSO   RELATED SUBJECTS
Difficulty 1594   Error
Error 1937   Failure
Failure 2068   Sin

EXPERIENCE

2001   A proof that experience is of no use, is that the end of one love does not prevent us from beginning another.   *—Paul Bourget*

2002   Experience is the child of thought, and thought is the child of action.   *—Disraeli*

2003   Only so much do I know, as I have lived.   *—Emerson*

2004   Skill to do comes of doing.   *—Emerson*

2005   Experience keeps a dear school, but fools will learn in no other.   *—Franklin*

2006   After the event, even a fool is wise.   *—Homer*

2007   The spectacles of experience; through them you will see clearly a second time.   *—Ibsen*

2008   I had six honest serving men—
They taught me all I knew:
Their names were Where and What and When—and
Why and How and Who.   *—Kipling*

2009   Experience is the only prophecy of wise men.   *—Lamartine*

2010   One thorn of experience is worth a whole wilderness of warning.   *—Lowell*

2011   No one knows what he can do till he tries.   *—Publilius Syrus*

2012   I had rather have a fool to make me merry than experience to make me sad.   *—Shakespeare*

013   He cannot be a perfect man, not being tried and tutored in the world.
Experience is by industry achieved, and perfected by the swift course of time.   *—Shakespeare*

2014   He jests at scars, that never felt a wound.   *—Shakespeare*

2015   Everything happens to everybody sooner or later if there is time enough.   *—G. B. Shaw*

2016   And others' follies teach us not,
Nor much their wisdom teaches;
And most, of sterling worth, is what
Our own experience preaches.   *—Tennyson*

2017 No man was ever so completely skilled in the conduct of life, as not to receive new information from age and experience.
—*Terence*

2018 Experience is of no ethical value. It is merely the name men give to their mistakes.   —*Oscar Wilde*

2019 Experience teaches us at the expense of our illusions.

2020 Experience makes a man wiser but leaves a woman a complete ruin.

2021 Experience finds a woman stupid and leaves her dumbfounded.

2022 Experiences are mortgages on life.

2023 Experience: flirting with fate.

2024 Experience is one thing you can't get for nothing.

See Also	Related Subjects
Art 311	Action
Conversation 1023	Fate
Hope 2957	Knowledge
Law 3394	Life
Virtue 5672	Understanding

EXTRAVAGANCE

2031 Beggar'd by fools, whom still he found too late,
He had his jest, but they had his estate.   —*Dryden*

2032 A princely mind will undo a private family.   —*Lord Halifax*

2033 The prodigal robs his heir, the miser himself.

2034 "I'll follow thy fortune," a termagant cries,
    Whose extravagance caus'd all the evil;
"That were some consolation," the husband replies,
    "For my fortune has gone to the devil."

2035 Don't waste too many stones on one bird.

See Also	Related Subjects
Clothes 887	Borrowing
Eating 1794	Conservative
Wife 5873	Debt
	Economy
	Temperance
	Value

EYES

2041 The eyes of the dead are closed gently; we also have to open gently the eyes of the living.   —*Jean Cocteau*

2042 I have a good eye, uncle; I can see a church by daylight.
—*Shakespeare*

2043 The dearest things in the world are our neighbor's eyes; they cost everybody more than anything else in housekeeping.
—*Sydney Smith*

2044 The buyer needs a hundred eyes, the seller not one.

SEE ALSO
Hunger 2999
Obstinacy 4216
Women 6032
Work 6064

RELATED SUBJECT
Light

F

FACTS

2051 Facts that are not frankly faced have a habit of stabbing us in the back. —*Harold Bowden*

2052 No facts to me are sacred; none are profane. —*Emerson*

2053 He wasn't exactly hostile to facts, but he was apathetic about them. —*Wolcott Gibbs, of Alexander Woollcott*

2054 Facts do not cease to exist because they are ignored.
—*Aldous Huxley*

2055 Facts are apt to alarm us more than the most dangerous principles. —*Junius*

2056 Don't tell me of facts, I never believe facts; you know Canning said nothing was so fallacious as facts, except figures.
—*Sydney Smith*

2057 Two and two continue to make four, in spite of the whine of the amateur for three, or the cry of the critic for five.—*Whistler*

2058 There are men who can think no deeper than a fact. —*Voltaire*

SEE ALSO
Death 1364
Politics 4481
Teaching 5294

RELATED SUBJECTS
Deeds
Doubt
Experience
Ideas
Illusion
Knowledge

FAILURE

2061   They fail, and they alone, who have not striven.—*T. B. Aldrich*

2062   He that is down needs fear no fall,
He that is low, no pride.   *—Bunyan*

2063   Our greatest glory is not in never falling but in rising every time
we fall.   *—Confucius*

2064   There is only one real failure possible; and that is, not to be true
to the best one knows.   *—Canon Farrar*

2065   A failure is a man who has blundered but is not able to cash in
the experience.   *—Elbert Hubbard*

2066   There is the greatest practical benefit in making a few failures
early in life.   *—T. H. Huxley*

2067   There is not a fiercer hell than the failure in a great object.
      —Keats

2068   We have forty million reasons for failure, but not a single excuse.
      —Kipling

2069   Never give a man up until he has failed at something he likes.
      —Lewis E. Lawes

2070   Not failure, but low aim, is crime.   *—Lowell*

2071   Some falls are means the happier to rise.   *—Shakespeare*

2072   No good thing is failure and no evil thing success.

SEE ALSO   RELATED SUBJECTS
Courage 1091   Defeat
Criticism 1255   Disappointment
Democracy 1525   Excuse
Optimism 4279   Success
                    Work

FAITH

2081   He hath denied the faith, and is worse than an infidel.   *—Bible*

2082   Faith is the substance of things hoped for; the evidence of things
not seen.   *—Bible*

2083   Faith without works is dead.   *—Bible*

2084   Faith is the pencil of the soul that pictures heavenly things.
      T. Burbridge

2085   But Faith, fanatic Faith, once wedded fast
To some dear falsehood, hugs it to the last.   *—Moore*

2086   If a man have a strong faith he can indulge in the luxury of
scepticism.   *—Nietzsche*

2087 Love asks faith, and faith asks firmness.

SEE ALSO
Dictators 1588
Fear 2174

RELATED SUBJECTS
Atheism
Belief
Conviction
Hope
Idealism
Martyr
Religion
Trust

FAME

2091 It is not the places that grace men, but men the places.
—*Agesilaus*

2092 You canna expect to be baith grand and comfortable.
—*J. M. Barrie*

2093 The extremes of glory and of shame,
Like east and west, become the same:
No Indian prince has to his palace
More followers than a thief to the gallows. —*Butler*

2094 Nothing is more annoying than a low man raised to a high
position. —*Claudian*

2095 Fame is a fickle food
Upon a shifting plate. —*Emily Dickinson*

2096 What's fame, afther all, me la-ad? 'Tis as apt to be what some
wan writes on ye'er tombstone. —*F. P. Dunne*

2097 I hate the man who builds his name
On ruins of another's fame. —*John Gay*

2098 Herein the only royal road to fame and fortune lies:
Put not your trust in vinegar—molasses catches flies!
—*Eugene Field*

2099 Popularity? It is glory's small change. —*Victor Hugo*

2100 After a feller gits famous it don't take long fer some one t' bob
up that used t' set by him at school. —*Kin Hubbard*

2101 Fame, like a wayward girl, will still be coy
To those who woo her with too slavish knees. —*Keats*

2102 The world more often rewards the appearance of merit than
merit itself. —*La Rochefoucauld*

2103 If fame is only to come after death, I am in no hurry for it.
—*Martial*

2104   Glory arrives too late when it comes only to one's ashes.
                                                        —*Martial*

2105   How prudently we proud men compete for nameless graves, while
        now and then some starveling of Fate forgets himself into
        immortality.   —*Wendell Phillips*

2106   Nor Fame I slight, nor for her favors call;
        She comes unlooked for, if she comes at all.   —*Pope*

2107   Unblemish'd let me live or die unknown;
        Oh, grant an honest fame or grant me none!   —*Pope*

2108   Fame does not always light at random: sometimes she chooses
        her man.   —*Seneca*

2109   Fame is the perfume of heroic deeds.   —*Socrates*

2110   Greater things are believed of those who are absent.   —*Tacitus*

2111   Fame is but the breath of the people, and that often unwholesome.

2112   The man who wakes up and finds himself famous hasn't been
        asleep.

2113   Desire of glory is the last garment that even wise men put off.

SEE ALSO   RELATED SUBJECTS
Character 707   Fortune
Criticism 1270   Greatness
Tears 5311   History
                      Reputation
                      Society
                      Success

FAMILY

2121   Accidents will occur in the best regulated families.   —*Dickens*

2122   Distant relatives er th' best kind, an' th' further th' better.
                                                        —*Kin Hubbard*

2123   Never praise a sister to a sister, in the hope of your compliments
        reaching the proper ears.   —*Kipling*

2124   Don't get married unless you want to start raising a family, and
        don't start raising a family unless you want to get married.
                                                        —*R. A. Lyman*

2125   A daughter is an embarrassing and ticklish possession.—*Menander*

2126   A family is but too often a commonwealth of malignants.—*Pope*

2127   A family enjoying the unspeakable peace and freedom of being
        orphans.   —*G. B. Shaw*

2128　All happy families resemble one another; every unhappy family is unhappy in its own fashion. —*Tolstoi*

2129　He that has no fools, knaves, or beggars in his family, was begot by a flash of lightning.

2130　He that hath a wife and children must not sit with his fingers in his mouth.

2131　He that is poor all his kindred scorn him, he that is rich all are kin to him.

2132　It is a poor family that hath neither a whore nor a thief in it.

2133　A great many prominent family trees were started by grafting.

SEE ALSO　　　　　RELATED SUBJECTS
Friend 2376, 2377　Children
Wealth 5764　　　　Father
　　　　　　　　　　　Home
　　　　　　　　　　　Mother

FARMING

2141　If you tickle the earth with a hoe she laughs with a harvest. —*Douglas Jerrold*

2142　A cow is a very good animal in the field; but we turn her out of a garden. —*Johnson*

2143　There is no ancient gentlemen but gardeners . . . they hold up Adam's profession. —*Shakespeare*

2144　The farmer works the soil,
The agriculturist works the farmer. —*E. F. Ware*

2145　What a man needs in gardening is a cast-iron back, with a hinge in it. —*Charles Dudley Warner*

2146　No race can prosper till it learns that there is as much dignity in tilling a field as in writing a poem. —*Booker T. Washington*

2147　He that hires one garden eats birds; he that hires more than one will be eaten by the birds.

2148　All is not butter that comes from the cow.

SEE ALSO　　　　RELATED SUBJECTS
Delay 1503　　　　Labor
Work 6053　　　　 Nature

FATE

2151　Fate is unpenetrated causes. —*Emerson*

2152　That which God writes on thy forehead, thou wilt come to it. —*Koran*

2153   It's no good crying over spilt milk, because all the forces of the universe were bent on spilling it.   —*Somerset Maugham*

2154   There is no such thing as accident; it is fate misnamed.
                                                                                                    —*Napoleon*

2155   Heaven know its time; the bullet has its billet.   —*Scott*

2156   There's a divinity that shapes our ends
Rough-hew them how we will.   —*Shakespeare*

2157   What fates impose, that men must needs abide;
It boots not to resist both wind and tide.   —*Shakespeare*

2158   Hanging and wiving goes by destiny.   —*Shakespeare*

2159   Destiny leads the willing, but drags the unwilling.

2160   The inevitable is the great tragedian, never the humorist.

SEE ALSO   RELATED SUBJECTS
Eating 1786   Chance
Experience 2023   Luck
Future 2434   Opportunity
Marriage 3907   Future

FATHER

2161   Diogenes struck the father when the son swore.   —*Burton*

2162   The child whom many fathers share
Hath seldom known a father's care.   —*John Gay*

2163   It is impossible to please all the world and one's father.
                                                                                                    —*La Fontaine*

2164   It is a wise father that knows his own child.   —*Shakespeare*

2165   It is a wise child that knows its own father.

2166   Nearly every man is a firm believer in heredity until his son makes a fool of himself.

2167   The worst misfortune that can happen to an ordinary man is to have an extraordinary father.

RELATED SUBJECTS
Children
Family
Home
Mother

FEAR

2171   Cruelty and fear shake hands together.   —*Balzac*

2172   All is to be feared where all is to be lost.   —*Byron*

2173 If a man harbors any sort of fear, it percolates through all his thinking, damages his personality, makes him landlord to a ghost. —*Lloyd Douglas*

2174 Fear clogs; Faith liberates. —*Elbert Hubbard*

2175 The only thing we have to fear—is fear itself. —*Franklin D. Roosevelt*

2176 When our actions do not,
Our fears do make us traitors. —*Shakespeare*

2177 To him who is in fear everything rustles. —*Sophocles*

2178 Two things ought to be the object of our fear, the envy of friends, and the hatred of enemies.

2179 Fear can keep a man out of danger, but courage only can support him in it.

2180 He that's afraid to do good would do ill if he durst.

2181 They that worship God merely from fear,
Would worship the devil too, if he appear.

SEE ALSO
Dictators 1576, 1584
Hope 2958

RELATED SUBJECTS
Conscience
Cowardice
Danger
Troubles
Worry

FIDELITY

2191 What men call gallantry, and gods adultery,
Is much more common where the climate's sultry. —*Byron*

2192 A good man it is not mine to see.
Could I see a man possessed of constancy, that would satisfy me. —*Confucius*

2193 How happy could I be with either,
Were t'other dear charmer away! —*John Gay*

2194 Women deceive the lover, never the friend. —*Mercier*

2195 There are two kinds of fidelity—that of dogs and that of cats; and you, gentlemen, have the fidelity of cats who never leave the house. —*Napoleon*

2196 Inconstancy is but a name to fright poor lovers from a better choice. —*John Rutter*

2197 You never so much want to be happy with a woman as when you know that you're ceasing to care for her.—*Arthur Schnitzler*

2198   O Heaven! were man
       But constant, he were perfect: that one error
       Fills him with faults.   —*Shakespeare*

2199   When my love swears that she is made of truth,
       I do believe her, though I know she lies.   —*Shakespeare*

2200   There is nothing in this world constant but inconstancy.—*Swift*

2201   The only difference between a caprice and a lifelong passion is
       that the caprice lasts a little longer.   —*Oscar Wilde*

2202   Let's be gay while we may
       And seize love with laughter;
       I'll be true as long as you
       But not a moment after.

2203   Infidelity in woman is a masculine trait.

2204   Constancy in the woman whom we have ceased to love is a very
       negative virtue—also very irritating.

2205   Devotion: love in cold storage.

2206   Call your husband cuckold in jest, and he'll never suspect you.

2207   Absence makes the heart grow fonder—of somebody else.

2208   Nokes went, he thought, to Stiles' wife to bed,
       Nor knew his own was laid there in her stead:
       Civilians! is the child he then begot,
       To be allow'd legitimate, or not?   —*After Martial*

SEE ALSO   RELATED SUBJECTS
Chastity 748   Faith
                            Marriage

FIGHT

2211   Who only in his cups will fight, is like
       A clock that must be oiled well ere it strike.   —*Bancroft*

2212   "Thrice is he armed that has his quarrel just"—
       But four times he who gets the blow in fust.   —*Josh Billings*

2213   For those that fly may fight again,
       Which he can never do that's slain.   —*Samuel Butler*

2214   When I got through with him, he was all covered wit' blood—
       my blood.   —*Jimmy Durante*

2215   You should never wear your best trousers when you go out to
       fight for freedom and truth.   —*Ibsen*

2216   Thrusting my nose firmly between his teeth, I threw him heavily
       to the ground on top of me.   —*Mark Twain*

2217   Never hit a man unless he is down; in a combat it is a sign of utter idiocy to leave anything to chance.

SEE ALSO	RELATED SUBJECTS
Books 503	Courage
Conviction 1031	Deeds
Drinking 1744	Enemies
Pride 4659	Soldiers
Women 5965	War

FIRE

2221   Fire is the best of servants; but what a master!   *—Carlyle*

2222   Three removes are as bad as a fire.   *—Franklin*

2223   Fire is the most tolerable third party.   *—Thoreau*

SEE ALSO	RELATED SUBJECT
Love 3707, 3725, 3758	Light

FISH

2231   A hook's well lost to catch a salmon.

2232   Still he fisheth that catcheth one.

2233   It is good fish, if it were but caught.

SEE ALSO	RELATED SUBJECTS
Evil 1957	Cooks
Guests 2717	Eating
Heaven 2861	
Purpose 4730	

FLATTERY

2241   And wrinkles (the damned democrats) won't flatter.   *—Byron*

2242   Imitation is the sincerest flattery.   *—C. C. Colton*

2243   You know what a fan letter is—it's just an inky raspberry.
—Bob Hope

2244   Th' chronic grumbler is a church social compared t' th' feller that agrees with everything you say.   *—Kin Hubbard*

2245   Madam, before you flatter a man so grossly to his face, you should consider whether your flattery is worth his having.
—Johnson

2246   Men are not flattered by being shown that there has been a difference of purpose between the Almighty and them.*—Lincoln*

2247   The voice of flattery affects us after it has ceased, just as after a concert men find some agreeable air ringing in their ears to the exclusion of all serious business.   *—Seneca*

2248   But when I tell him he hates flatterers,
He says he does, being then most flattered.   *—Shakespeare*

2249   Flattery is like friendship in show, but not in fruit.   *—Socrates*

2250   None are more taken in by flattery than the proud, who wish to be
the first and are not.   *—Spinoza*

2251   'Tis an old maxim in the schools,
That flattery's the food of fools;
Yet now and then your men of wit
Will condescend to take a bit.   *—Swift*

2252   If we did not flatter ourselves, nobody else could.

2253   He that is open to flattery is fenced against admonition.

2254   He that rewards flattery, begs it.

2255   Flatterers haunt not cottages.

2256   Flattery never comes up to the expectancy of conceit.

2257   A flatterer: one who extremely exaggerates in his opinion of your
qualities so that it may come nearer to your opinion of them.

SEE ALSO	RELATED SUBJECTS
Advice 100	Conceit
America 206	Modesty
Criticism 1267	Praise
Fortune 2329	Vanity
Prejudice 4632	

FOOLS

2261   A good folly is worth what you pay for it.   *—George Ade*

2262   A prosperous fool is a grievous burden.   *—Aeschylus*

2263   If others had not been foolish, we should be so.   *—Blake*

2264   "Stop thief," Dame Nature cried to Death,
As Willy drew his latest breath,
"How shall I make a fool again?
My choicest model thou hast ta'en."
Burns, on William Graham of Morsknowe

2265   Four thousand people cross London Bridge every day, mostly
fools.   *—Carlyle*

2266   The most artful part in a play is the fool's.   *—Cervantes*

2267   Young men think old men are fools;
But old men know young men are fools.   *—George Chapman*

2268   Nobody can describe a fool to the life, without much patient self-
inspection.   *—Frank M. Colby*

2269 I love fools' experiments. I am always making them. —*Darwin*

2270 Fools may our scorn, not envy raise,
For envy is a kind of praise. —*John Gay*

2271 The folly of others is ever most ridiculous to those who are themselves most foolish. —*Goldsmith*

2272 Almost all absurdity of conduct arises from the imitation of those
whom we can not resemble. —*Johnson*

2273 The silliest woman can manage a clever man; but it needs a very
clever woman to manage a fool! —*Kipling*

2274 Who lives without folly is not so wise as he thinks.
—*La Rochefoucauld*

2275 Sometimes there are accidents in our lives the skillful extrication
from which demands a little folly. —*La Rochefoucauld*

2276 A fellow who is always declaring he's no fool, usually has his sus-
picions. —*Wilson Mizner*

2277 The world of fools has such a store
That he who would not see an ass
Must bide at home, and bolt his door,
And break his looking-glass. —*La Monnaye*

2278 For fools rush in where angels fear to tread. —*Pope*

2279 Folly is the direct pursuit of Happiness and Beauty.
—*G. B. Shaw*

2280 Let a fool hold his tongue and he will pass for a sage.
—*Publilius Syrus*

2281 Always the dulness of the fool is the whetstone of the wits.
—*Shakespeare*

2282 The fool doth think he is wise, but the wise man knows himself
to be a fool. —*Shakespeare*

2283 Give me the young man who has brains enough to make a fool of
himself. —*Stevenson*

2284 Accept a proverb out of Wisdom's schools—
"Barbers first learn to shave by shaving fools." —*John Wolcot*

2285 A flea-bitten fool made this foolish remark
As he blew out the light: "They can't see in the dark."

2286 Fools are the witticisms of nature.

2287 What makes folly so impossible is that no amount of improve-
ment perfects it.

2288   Every fool can find faults that a great many wise men can't remedy.

2289   Natural folly is bad enough; but learned folly is intolerable.

2290   The most exquisite folly is made of wisdom too fine spun.

2291   If fools went not to market, bad wares would not be sold.

2292   Unless a fool knows Latin he is never a great fool.

2293   No one is a fool always, every one sometimes.

2294   He is na the fool that the fool is, but he that wi' the fool deals.

2295   If wise men play the fool, they do it with a vengeance.

2296   He who is born a fool is never cured.

2297   Who drives an ass and leads a whore,
       Hath pain and sorrow evermore.

2298   The road to ruin is always in good repair; the travellers pay the expense of it.

SEE ALSO   RELATED SUBJECTS
Admiration 62, 67   Nonsense
Atheism 321   Wisdom
Conviction 1046
Marriage 3846
Poetry 4541
Silence 5047

FORGETTING

2301   Life cannot go on without much forgetting.   *—Balzac*

2302   A retentive memory may be a good thing, but the ability to forget is the true token of greatness.   *—Elbert Hubbard*

2303   Nobuddy ever fergits where he buried a hatchet.*—Kin Hubbard*

2304   Were it not better to forget
       Than but remember and regret?   *—L. E. Landon*

2305   The world does not require so much to be informed as reminded.
                                             —Hannah More

2306   Blessed are the forgetful; for they get the better even of their blunders.   *—Nietzsche*

2307   Women and elephants never forget an injury.   *—Saki*

2308   We bury love;
       Forgetfulness grows over it like grass:
       That is a thing to weep for, not the dead.   *—Alexander Smith*

2309   The remedy for wrongs is to forget them.   —*Publilius Syrus*

2310   Forgetting of a wrong is a mild revenge.

SEE ALSO   RELATED SUBJECT
Crimes 1230   Memory
Insults 3170
Love 3736

FORGIVENESS

2311   "I can forgive, but I cannot forget," is only another way of say-
       ing, "I cannot forgive."   —*H. W. Beecher*

2312   Forgiveness to the injured doth belong,
       But they ne'er pardon who have done the wrong.   —*Dryden*

2313   God will pardon me: that's his business.   —*Heine*

2314   Reversing your treatment of the man you have wronged is better
       than asking his forgiveness.   —*Elbert Hubbard*

2315   We never ask God to forgive anybody except where we haven't.
                                            —*Elbert Hubbard*

2316   To forgive all is as inhuman as to forgive none.   —*Seneca*

SEE ALSO   RELATED SUBJECTS
Business 590   Kindness
Children 775   Mercy
Contempt 991   Morality
Sacrifice 4903   Prejudice
Sex 5011   Revenge
Understanding 5594

FORTUNE

2321   If a man look sharply and attentively, he shall see Fortune; for
       though she is blind, she is not invisible.   —*Bacon*

2322   Fortune is like the market, where many times, if you can stay a
       little, the price will fall.   —*Bacon*

2323   I am not in Fortune's power:
       He that is down can fall no lower.   —*Samuel Butler*

2324   Extremes of fortune are true wisdom's test;
       And he's of men most wise who bears them best.   —*Cumberland*

2325   Reflect upon your present blessings of which every man has
       many; not on your past misfortunes, of which all men have
       some.   —*Dickens*

2326   It is better to be bold than too circumspect, because fortune is of
       a sex which likes not a tardy wooer and repulses all who are
       not ardent.   —*Machiavelli*

2327   Fortune does not change men; it unmasks them.—*Mme. Necker*

2328   Fortune is like glass—the brighter the glitter, the more easily
       broken.   ·—*Publilius Syrus*

2329   When Fortune flatters, she does it to betray.   —*Publilius Syrus*

2330   It is more easy to get a favor from fortune than to keep it.
                                                       —*Publilius Syrus*

2331   Fortune dreads the brave, and is only terrible to the coward.
                                                              —*Seneca*

2332   Fortune brings in some boats that are not steer'd.—*Shakespeare*

2333   Fortune can take from us nothing but what she gave us.

RELATED SUBJECTS
Chance
Failure
Fame
Luck
Success

FRANCE

2341   The thirst for truth is not a French passion.   —*Amiel*

2342   France, fam'd in all great arts, in none supreme.
                                                       —*Matthew Arnold*

2343   Frenchmen are like gunpowder, each by itself smutty and con-
       temptible; but mass them together, they are terrible indeed!
                                                           —*Coleridge*

2344   The French have taste in all they do,
           Which we are quite without;
       For Nature, that to them gave *goût,*
           To us gave only gout.   —*Erskine*

2345   France is an absolute monarchy tempered by songs.
                                                       —*French proverb*

2346   Never go to France
           Unless you know the lingo,
       If you do, like me,
           You will repent, by jingo.   —*Thomas Hood*

2347   A Frenchman loves his mother—in the abstract.
                                                       —*H. S. Merriman*

2348   Have the French for friends, but not for neighbors.
                                                       —*Emperor Nicephorus*

FRANKNESS

2351 The young man turned to him with a disarming candor which instantly put him on his guard. —*Saki*

2352 Candor and generosity, unless tempered by due moderation, lead to ruin. —*Tacitus*

2353 I think it good plain English, without fraud,
To call a spade a spade, a bawd a bawd. —*John Taylor*

2354 The person that always says just what he thinks at last gets just what he deserves.

2355 Frankness, aside from the pain it causes, is always in bad taste.

SEE ALSO   RELATED SUBJECTS
Facts 2052   Deception
Secret 4966   Honesty

FRIEND

2361 "Stay" is a charming word in a friend's vocabulary.
—*Bronson Alcott*

2362 My friends! There are no friends. —*Aristotle*

2363 It is good discretion not to make too much of any man at the first; because one cannot hold out that proportion. —*Bacon*

2364 Every man should keep a fair-sized cemetery in which to bury the faults of his friends. —*H. W. Beecher*

2365 This man was poor, mean of estate, a slave;
Did no one bear him love?
Oh yes, in one friend's heart he reigned supreme,
All other men above. —*Bianor*

2366 Friendship is a word, the very sight of which in print makes the heart warm. —*Augustine Birrell*

2367 Our friends see the best in us, and by that very fact call forth the best from us. —*Black*

2368 Thy friendship oft has made my heart to ache:
Do be my enemy—for friendship's sake. —*Blake*

2369 To all my friends I leave kind thoughts.
—*From the Will of John Brougham, Comedian*

2370 Whatever the number of a man's friends, there will be times in his life when he has one too few; but if he has only one enemy, he is lucky indeed if he has not one too many.
—*Bulwer-Lytton*

2371 Friendship is Love without his wings. —*Byron*

2372 No more thy pains for others' welfare spend,
      Nor think by service to attach a friend:
      All are ungrateful—love goes slighted still—
      Nor merely so, but is repaid by ill;
      Witness myself, whose bitterest foe is he,
      Who never had a friend on earth but me.   —*Catullus*

2373 Most people enjoy the inferiority of their best friends.
                                                     —*Chesterfield*

2374 Acquaintance many, and conquaintance few,
      But for inquaintance I know only two—
      The friend I've wept with, and the maid I woo.   —*Coleridge*

2375 Love is flower-like;
      Friendship is like a sheltering tree.   —*Coleridge*

2376 Fate makes our relatives, choice makes our friends.
                                                     —*Jacques Delille*

2377 Friends—those relations that one makes for oneself.—*Deschamps*

2378 Friendship consists in forgetting what one gives, and remembering
      what one receives.   —*Dumas the Younger*

2379 When friendships are real, they are not glass threads or frost
      work, but the solidest things we can know.   —*Emerson*

2380 The only way to have a friend is to be one.   —*Emerson*

2381 Tell me with whom thou art found, and I will tell thee who
      thou art.   —*Goethe*

2382 He who does not feel his friends to be the world to him, does
      not deserve that the world should hear of him.   —*Goethe*

2383 Friendship is a disinterested commerce between equals; love, an
      abject intercourse between tyrants and slaves.   —*Goldsmith*

2384 True friends appear less mov'd than counterfeit;
      As men that truly grieve at funerals
      Are not so loud, as those that cry for hire.   —*Horace*

2385 Friendship lives on its income, love devours its capital.
                                                     —*Arsène Houssaye*

2386 A man, sir, should keep his friendship in constant repair.
                                                     —*Johnson*

2387 A friend may be often found and lost, but an old friend can
      never be found, and nature has provided that he cannot easily
      be lost.   —*Johnson*

2388 To suspect a friend is worse than to be deceived by him.
                                                     —*La Rochefoucauld*

2389 Friendship is only a reciprocal conciliation of interests, and an exchange of good offices; it is a species of commerce out of which self-love always expects to gain something.
—*La Rochefoucauld*

2390 If you want to make a dangerous man your friend, let him do you a favor. —*Lewis E. Lawes*

2391 I said, "I will go out and look for mine enemies," and that day I found no friends. Again, I said, "I will go out and look for my friends," and that day I found no enemies.
—*Gertrude R. Lewis*

2392 Women, like princes, find few real friends. —*Lord Lyttelton*

2393 You have friends, Paullus, just like your pictures and vases, all antique originals. —*Martial*

2394 To no man make yourself a boon companion:
Your joy will be less, but less will be your grief. —*Martial*

2395 Regulus, Hermagoras says that we must not please everybody. Choose out of the many whom you would please. —*Martial*

2396 Friends are like melons. Shall I tell you why?
To find one good, you must a hundred try. —*Claude Mermet*

2397 The best way to keep your friends is not to give them away.
—*Wilson Mizner*

2398 Friendship is a creature formed for a companionship, not for a herd. —*Montaigne*

2399 Men use care in purchasing a horse, and are neglectful in choosing friends. —*John Muir*

2400 We should thank God that He did not give us the power of hearing through walls; otherwise there would be no such thing as friendship. —*Austin O'Malley*

2401 A home-made friend wears longer than one you buy in the market.
—*Austin O'Malley*

2402 Friends made fast seldom remain fast. —*Austin O'Malley*

2403 Strangers he gulls, but friends make fun of him. —*Phaedrus*

2404 True friendship's laws are by this rule express'd:
Welcome the coming, speed the parting guest. —*Pope*

2405 Treat your friend as if he might become an enemy.
—*Publilius Syrus*

2406 Friendship, one soul in two bodies. —*Pythagoras*

2407   That friendship will not continue to the end which is begun for
      an end.   *—Francis Quarles*

2408   Old friends are best. King James used to call for his old shoes;
      they were easiest for his feet.   *—John Selden*

2409   We need new friends; some of us are cannibals who have eaten
      their old friends up; others must have ever-renewed audiences
      before whom to re-enact an ideal version of their lives.
                                      —Logan Pearsall Smith

2410   An acquaintance that begins with a compliment is sure to develop
      into a real friendship.   *—Oscar Wilde*

2411   So long as we love we serve; so long as we are loved by others I
      would almost say that we are indispensable; and no man is
      useless while he has a friend.   *—Stevenson*

2412   Defend me from my friends; I can defend myself from my
      enemies.   *—Voltaire*

2413   Friendship is the only cement that will ever hold the world to-
      gether.   *—Woodrow Wilson*

2414   We need the friendship of a man in great trials; of a woman in
      the affairs of everyday life.

2415   He's a friend at a sneeze; the most you can get of him is a God
      bless you.

2416   It is best not to try to get the best of your best friend.

2417   One cannot depend on woman's friendship for she gives every-
      thing to love.

2418   Besides mutual admiration, the first requisite for Platonic friend-
      ship is a subtle trace of disdain.

2419   A friend is one who knows your faults yet loves you in spite of
      your virtues.

2420   Happy is he whose friends were born before him.

2421   Go slowly to the entertainments of thy friends, but quickly to
      their misfortunes.

2422   Friendship increases in visiting friends, but more in visiting them
      seldom.

2423   Few there are that will endure a true friend.

2424   A friend that you buy, will be bought from you.

2425   A man may see his friend need, but winna see him bleed.

2426   A true friend should be like a privy, open in necessity.

2427   Keep good company, and you shall be of the number.

2428   Have but few friends, though much acquaintance.

SEE ALSO   RELATED SUBJECTS
Advertising 77   Enemies
Age 142   Guests
Borrowing 548   Neighbor
Courtship 1166
Debt 1405
Laughter 3369
Love 3719
Persuasion 4413
Power 4581

FUTURE

2431   Shallow men speak of the past; wise men of the present; and
      fools of the future.   *—Mme. du Deffand*

2432   The future is a convenient place for dreams.   *—Anatole France*

2433   A single breaker may recede; but the tide is evidently coming in.
                                              —Macaulay

2434   What will be, is.   *—Austin O'Malley*

2435   Let us be such as help the life of the future.   *—Zoroaster*

2436   It isn't enough to safeguard posterity; we must also provide a
      posterity to safeguard.

SEE ALSO   RELATED SUBJECTS
Learning 3444   Fate
Society 5132   Fortune
                        Life
                        Prophecy

G

GAMBLING

2441   For most men (till by losing rendered sager)
      Will back their own opinions by a wager.   *—Byron*

2442   As much is lost by a card too many as a card too few.
                                              —Cervantes

2443   Death and the dice level all distinctions.   *—Samuel Foote*

2444   Cards were at first for benefits designed,
      Sent to amuse, not to enslave the mind.   *—Garrick*

2445   Could fools to keep their own contrive,
       On what, on whom could gamesters thrive?   —*John Gay*

2446   The strength of Monaco is the weakness of the world.
                                                       —*Herbert A. Gibbons*

2447   That picture raffles will conduce to nourish
       Design, or cause good coloring to flourish,
       Admits of logic-chopping and wise-sawing,
       For surely lotteries encourage drawing.   —*Thomas Hood*

2448   Gambling is a disease of barbarians superficially civilized.
                                                              —*Dean Inge*

2449   I never hear the rattling of dice that it does not sound to me
       like the funeral bell of the whole family.   —*Douglas Jerrold*

2450   If he plays, being young and unskilful,
       For shekels of silver or gold,
       Take his money, my son, praising Allah:
       The kid was ordained to be sold.   —*Kipling*

2451   It may be that the race is not always to the swift, nor the battle
       to the strong—but that's the way to bet.   —*Damon Runyon*

2452   Nothing between human beings is one to three. In fact, I long ago
       come to the conclusion that all life is six to five against.
                                                         —*Damon Runyon*

2453   I must complain the cards are ill shuffled till I have a good hand.
                                                                —*Swift*

2454   There are two times in a man's life when he should not speculate:
       when he can't afford it and when he can.   —*Mark Twain*

2455   Horse sense is what keeps horses from betting on what people will
       do.

2456   A feather in hand is better than a bird in the air.

2457   The best throw with the dice, is to throw them away.

2458   Gentlemen, the Queen!
       She gazed at us serene,
       She filled his flush,
       Amidst the hush—
       And gathered in the green.

2459   Many can pack the cards that cannot play.

GENEROSITY

2461   He that's liberal to all alike, may do a good by chance,
       But never out of judgment.   —*Beaumont and Fletcher*

2462   Liberality consists rather in giving reasonably than much.
                                                        —*La Bruyère*

2463   What is called liberality is often merely the vanity of giving.
                                                    —*La Rochefoucauld*

2464   Many men have been capable of doing a wise thing, more a cun-
       ning thing, but very few a generous thing.   —*Pope*

2465   He who refuses nothing, Atticilla, will soon have nothing to
       refuse.   —*Martial*

2466   You ask but small favors of your great friends, yet your great
       friends refuse you even small favors. That you may feel less
       ashamed, Matho, ask great favors.   —*Martial*

2467   Boards of public charity were invented by the Devil to prevent
       real individual charity.   —*Austin O'Malley*

2468   Feel for others—in your pocket.   —*C. H. Spurgeon*

2469   Philanthropy seems to me to have become simply the refuge of
       people who wish to annoy their fellow-creatures.—*Oscar Wilde*

2470   Generosity consists not in the sum given, but the manner in which
       it is bestowed.

SEE ALSO   RELATED SUBJECTS
Frankness 2352   Gifts
                      Help
                      Kindness
                      Selfishness

GENIUS

2471   Genius, that power which dazzles mortal eyes,
       Is oft but perseverance in disguise.   —*Henry W. Austin*

2472   If a man can have only one kind of sense, let him have common
       sense. If he has that and uncommon sense too, he is not far
       from genius.   —*H. W. Beecher*

2473   Genius is only patience.   —*Buffon*

2474   Talent may be in time forgiven, but genius never!   —*Byron*

2475   A force as of madness in the hands of reason has done all that
       was ever done in the world.   —*Carlyle*

2476   Great wits are sure to madness near allied,
       And thin partitions do their bounds divide.   —*Dryden*

2477   Genius is one per cent inspiration and ninety-nine per cent per-
       spiration.   —*Thomas A. Edison*

2478   Every man of genius sees the world at a different angle from his
       fellows, and there is his tragedy.   —*Havelock Ellis*

2479   In every work of genius we recognize our own rejected thoughts.
                                                      —*Emerson*

2480   The measure of a master is his success in bringing all men round
       to his opinion twenty years later.   —*Emerson*

2481   Great geniuses have the shortest biographies. —*Emerson*

2482   Men of genius do not excel in any profession because they labor
       in it, but they labor in it because they excel. —*Hazlitt*

2483   The man whom God wills to slay in the struggle of life He first
       individualizes.   —*Ibsen*

2484   A man of genius has been seldom ruined but by himself.—*Johnson*

2485   Something more than cleverness is needed to confer immortality
       on books. A work which is destined to live must have genius.
                                                      —*Martial*

2486   That man is thought a dangerous knave,
       Or zealot plotting crime,
       Who for advancement of his kind
       Is wiser than his time.   —*Milnes*

2487   He continued to be an infant long after he ceased to be a prodigy.
                                                      —*Robert Moses*

2488   One science only will one genius fit;
       So vast is art, so narrow human wit.   —*Pope*

2489   A great pilot can sail even when his canvas is rent. —*Seneca*

2490   It is with rivers as it is with people: the greatest are not always
       the most agreeable nor the best to live with.—*Henry Van Dyke*

2491   He drifts along as his lost Genius becks,
       A wreck of Fate, and fated source of wrecks.

2492   Talent does things tolerably well; genius does them intolerably
       better.

SEE ALSO   RELATED SUBJECTS
Literature 3621   Fame
Stupidity 5227   Greatness
Work 6064   Talent
                    Wisdom

GIFTS

2501 One can know nothing of giving aught that is worthy to give unless one also knows how to take.   *—Havelock Ellis*

2502 The only gift is a portion of thyself.   *—Emerson*

2503 It is better to deserve without receiving, than to receive without deserving.   *—Robert Ingersoll*

2504 It takes all the fun out of a bracelet if you have to buy it yourself.   *—Peggy Joyce*

2505 Presents, I often say, endear absents.   *—Lamb*

2506 For the will and not the gift makes the giver.   *—Lessing*

2507 However much a man gives, there is more that he withholds.   *—Martial*

2508 You may send poetry to the rich; to poor men give substantial presents.   *—Martial*

2509 Since in the house there's not a sou,
   There's but one thing to try.
I'll sell the gifts I've had of you,
   Dear Regulus. Come, buy!   *—Martial*

2510 You shameless fellow, Cinna, whatever you ask for you say, "Oh, it's a mere nothing." Well if it is a mere nothing that you ask for, Cinna, it is a mere nothing that I refuse.   *—Martial*

2511 The greatest favor that you can do for me, Cinna, if I ask anything of you, is to give it me; the next, Cinna, to refuse it at once. I love one who gives, Cinna; I do not hate one who refuses; but you, Cinna, neither give nor refuse.   *—Martial*

2512 Athenagoras says he is sorry that he has not sent me the presents which he usually sends in the middle of December. I shall see, Faustinus, whether Athenagoras is sorry. Certainly he has made me sorry.   *—Martial*

2513 Rich gifts wax poor when givers prove unkind.   *—Shakespeare*

2514 We like the gift when we the giver prize.   *—Sheffield*

2515 You must be fit to give before you can be fit to receive.   *—James Stephens*

2516 A man's gift makes room for him.

2517   The exchange of Christmas presents ought to be reciprocal rather than retaliatory.

2518   I send thee this sweet perfume, a fragrance to the fragrant, as one would offer wine to the god of wine.

SEE ALSO   RELATED SUBJECTS
Friend 2378   Generosity
Love 3734   Gratitude
Marriage 3841
Wealth 5784

GOD

2521   What men call accident is God's own part.   —*Gamaliel Bailey*

2522   God, as some cynic has said, is always on the side which has the best football coach.   —*Heywood Broun*

2523   If Alexander wishes to be a god, let him set up as a god.
                                                    —*Greek epigram*

2524   God will not look you over for medals, degrees or diplomas, but for scars.   —*Elbert Hubbard*

2525   An honest God is the noblest work of man.   —*Robert Ingersoll*

2526   Sir, my concern is not whether God is on our side; my great concern is to be on God's side, for God is always right.—*Lincoln*

2527   Though the mills of God grind slowly,
        Yet they grind exceeding small;
        Though with patience he stands waiting,
        With exactness grinds he all.   —*Longfellow*

2528   You've got to git up airly
        Ef you want to take in God.   —*Lowell*

2529   Man is certainly stark mad; he cannot make a worm, and yet he will be making gods by dozens.   —*Montaigne*

2530   You are not obliged to put on evening clothes to meet God.
                                                    —*Austin O'Malley*

2531   There are many scapegoats for our sins, but the most popular is Providence.   —*Mark Twain*

2532   If there were no God, it would have been necessary to invent Him.   —*Voltaire*

2533   Men have always made their gods in their own images—the Greeks like the Greeks, the Ethiopians like the Ethiopians.
                                                    —*Xenophanes*

2534　A God alone can comprehend a God.　　　　　　　*—Young*

2535　Every day God makes silk purses out of sows' ears.

2536　To most of us it would be very convenient if God were a rascal.

2537　A perfect God is the creation of a conceited man.

2538　I believe in the incomprehensibility of God.

2539　It is not so much God who created Man in His own Image, as every one of us who creates unto himself a God in his own Image.

2540　God is good to the Irish, but no one else is; not even the Irish.

See Also	Related Subjects
Art 286	Atheism
Chance 634	Church
Credit 1213	Devil
Danger 1306	Evil
Death 1362	Morality
Fear 2181	Preachers
Judgment 3228	Sin
Kings 3273	
Man 3806	
Soldiers 5149	
War 5725	
Wealth 5793	

GOOD

2541　It is as hard for the good to suspect evil, as it is for the bad to suspect good.　　　　　　　　　　　　*—Cicero*

2542　Look round the habitable world: how few
Know their own good, or knowing it, pursue.　　*—Dryden*

2543　The greatest pleasure I know is to do a good action by stealth, and have it found out by accident.　　　　　*—Lamb*

2544　There is no man so good, who, were he to submit all thoughts and actions to the laws, would not deserve hanging ten times in his life.　　　　　　　　　　*—Montaigne*

2545　A man ought to do as well as a horse;
I wish all men did as well.　　　　　　　　*—E. P. Roe*

2546　How far that little candle throws his beams!
So shines a good deed in a naughty world.　*—Shakespeare*

2547　If you wish the pick of men and women, take a good bachelor and a good wife.　　　　　　　　　　*—Stevenson*

2548　Mistrust first impulses, they are always good.　*—Talleyrand*

2549 Good intentions are, at least, the seed of good actions; and every
one ought to sow them, and leave it to the soil and the seasons
whether he or any other gather the fruit.   —*William Temple*

2550 Goodness is the only investment that never fails.   —*Thoreau*

2551 Gude fowk are scarce, tak' care o' ane.

2552 If they say you are good, ask yourself if it be true.

2553 Some men are good because they do not dare to be otherwise.

SEE ALSO   RELATED SUBJECTS
Advice 95   Character
Beauty 349, 359   Evil
Literature 3627   Kindness
                            Morality

GOSSIP

2561 Dead scandals form good subjects for dissection.   —*Byron*

2562 In the case of scandal, as in that of robbery, the receiver is
always thought as bad as the thief.   —*Chesterfield*

2563 She has a nice sense of rumor.   —*John H. Cutler*

2564 Talk of unusual swell of waist
In maid of honor loosely laced.   —*Matthew Green*

2565 There is so much good in the worst of us,
And so much bad in the best of us,
That it hardly behooves any of us
To talk about the rest of us.   —*Edward Hoch*

2566 What people say behind your back is your standing in the community.   —*E. W. Howe*

2567 Gossip is vice enjoyed vicariously.   —*Elbert Hubbard*

2568 Never tell evil of a man, if you do not know it for certainty, and
if you know it for a certainty, then ask yourself, "Why should
I tell it?"   —*Lavater*

2569 The only thing worse than being talked about is not being talked
about.   —*Oscar Wilde*

2570 People like to tell tales. If I take the rap for what they tell me,
they'll tell a lot.   —*Walter Winchell*

2571 Busy souls have no time to be busybodies.

2572 It is a matter of peculiar coincidence that great men have made
history; great women have merely created gossip.

2573 Scandal is the press agent of old age.

2574   Half the world knows how the other half ought to live.

SEE ALSO   RELATED SUBJECTS
History 2896   Curiosity
News 4171   Facts
Slave 5086   News

GOVERNMENT

2581   Why, O Catullus, why
        Do you delay to die?
        See Struma Nonius there
        Sits in the Curule Chair!
        Vatinius, too, that wretch forsworn,
        The Consul's office makes a butt for scorn!
        When such men are in power
        Why should you live an hour?   *—Catullus*

2582   Every form of government tends to perish by excess of its basic
        principle.   *—Will Durant*

2583   Republics end through luxury; monarchies through poverty.
                                                          —Montesquieu

2584   Government, like dress, is the badge of lost innocence.
                                                         —Thomas Paine

2585   For forms of government let fools contest.
        That which is best administered is best.   *—Pope*

2586   How a minority,
        Reaching majority,
        Seizing authority,
        Hates a minority.   *—L. H. Robbins*

2587   Every state that shines is on its decline.   *—Rousseau*

2588   Society is well governed when the people obey the magistrates,
        and the magistrates obey the law.   *—Solon*

2589   The long word comes only from *parler,* to speak,
          As best etymologists trace;
        So you see all is *parle* and nothing is *meant;*
          Too often the truth of the case.   *—On Parliament*

2590   Some say that popular government is still only a theory, and it
        must be admitted that no one has yet found a government that
        is popular.

2591   Congress seems to favor a stable Government, judging from the
        amount of stalling it does.

2592   Almost any system of government will work if the people will.

2593 One thing is inevitable: if government continues to fall down the people will rise up.

SEE ALSO   RELATED SUBJECTS
Pleasure 4455   Democracy
Thought 5380   Dictators
                                  Kings
                                  Law
                                  People
                                  Politics
                                  Revolution

GRATITUDE

2601 Gratitude is a burden, and every burden is made to be shaken off.
—*Diderot*

2602 Gratitude is a fruit of great cultivation; you do not find it among gross people.
—*Johnson*

2603 A man is very apt to complain of the ingratitude of those who have risen far above him.
—*Johnson*

2604 The gratitude of most men is but a secret desire of receiving greater benefits.
—*La Rochefoucauld*

2605 The man who is ungrateful is often less to blame than his benefactor.
—*La Rochefoucauld*

2606 Too great haste to repay an obligation is a kind of ingratitude.
—*La Rochefoucauld*

2507 Every time I fill a vacant office, I make ten malcontents and one ingrate.
—*Louix XIV*

2608 A benefit cited by way of reproach is equivalent to an injury.
—*Racine*

2609 Evermore thanks, the exchequer of the poor.   —*Shakespeare*

2610 Into the well which supplies thee with water, cast no stones.
—*Talmud*

2611 If you pick up a starving dog and make him prosperous, he will not bite you. This is the principal difference between a dog and a man.
—*Mark Twain*

2612 Gratitude is the conscience of memory.

2613 He that requites a benefit pays a great deal.

2614 We see more clearly what others fail to do for us than what they actually do.

SEE ALSO   RELATED SUBJECTS
Begging 423   Debt
Debt 1404   Forgetting
Friend 2378   Praise

GRAVITY

2621　Gravity is only the bark of wisdom's tree, but it preserves it.
　　　　　　　　　　　　　　　　　　　　—Confucius

2622　Gravity is the ballast of the soul, which keeps the mind steady.
　　　　　　　　　　　　　　　　　　　　—Thomas Fuller

2623　Gravity is a trick of the body devised to conceal deficiencies of
　　　　the mind.　　　　　　　　　　*—La Rochefoucauld*

2624　Gravity is the "safety zone" of stupidity.

RELATED SUBJECT
Conviction

GREATNESS

2631　The great of old!
　　　　The dead but sceptred sovereigns who still rule
　　　　Our spirits from their urns!　　　　　　*—Byron*

2632　The world cannot live at the level of its great men.
　　　　　　　　　　　　　　　　　　　　—James G. Frazer

2633　In short, whoever you may be,
　　　　To this conclusion you'll agree,
　　　　When everyone is somebodee,
　　　　Then no one's anybody!　　　　　　*—W. S. Gilbert*

2634　Greatness is so often a courteous synonym for great success.
　　　　　　　　　　　　　　　　　　　　—Philip Guedalla

2635　In ways to greatness, think on this,
　　　　That slippery all ambition is.　　　　　　*—Herrick*

2636　Great men are rarely isolated mountain peaks; they are the sum-
　　　　mits of ranges.　　　　　　　　*—T. W. Higginson*

2637　Great minds have purposes, others have wishes
　　　　　　　　　　　　　　　　　　　　—Washington Irving

2638　Great men lose somewhat of their greatness by being near us;
　　　　ordinary men gain much.　　　　　　*—Landor*

2639　Great men are meteors designed to burn so that the earth may
　　　　be lighted.　　　　　　　　　　*—Napoleon*

2640　Pathetic attitudes are not in keeping with greatness.—*Nietzsche*

2641　The great are only great because we are on our knees. Let us
　　　　rise!　　　　　　　　　　　　*—Proudhon*

2642　There's hope a great man's memory may outlive his life half a
　　　　year.　　　　　　　　　　　　*—Shakespeare*

2643   Not that the heavens the little can make great,
       But many a man has lived an age too late.   —R. H. Stoddard

2644   Ah vanity of vanities!
       How wayward the decrees of fate are,
       How very weak the very wise,
       How very small the very great are.   —Thackeray

2645   Great men undertake great things because they are great; fools,
       because they think them easy.   —Vauvenargues

2646   The prevailin' weakness of most public men is to slop over. G.
       Washington never slopt over.   —Artemus Ward

2647   We cry loudly for a man of vision and when we get one we call
       him a visionary.

2648   Serve a great man, and you will know what sorrow is.

SEE ALSO   RELATED SUBJECTS
Conviction 1033   Dignity
Crime 1237   Fame
Criticism 1270   Honor
Forgetting 2302   Power
Taste 5275   Reputation
Virtue 5683

GREED

2651   He would skin a flint.   —John Berthelson

2652   So for a good old-gentlemanly vice
       I think I must take up with avarice.   —Byron

2653   If you would abolish avarice, you must abolish its mother, luxury.
                                                            —Cicero

2654   Avarice and happiness never saw each other, how then should
       they become acquainted?   —Franklin

2655   Avarice, sphincter of the heart.   —Matthew Green

2656   The covetous man is ever in want.   —Horace

2657   Avarice, the spur of industry.   —David Hume

2658   He is one of those wise philanthropists who in a time of famine
       would vote for nothing but a supply of toothpicks.
                                                     —Douglas Jerrold

2659   The miser and the pig are of no use till death.   —La Mothe

2660   Avarice is more opposed to economy than liberality is.
                                                     —La Rochefoucauld

2661   Excess of wealth is cause of covetousness.   —Marlowe

2662 Tongilius in fever? I know what he's at:
On the dainties his toadies will send he'd be fat . . .
He must have a hot bath, every doctor's agreed.
Why, you idiots, it isn't a fever: it's greed! —*Martial*

2663 The most pitiful human ailment is a birdseed heart.
—*Wilson Mizner*

2664 It is not necessity but abundance which produces avarice.
—*Montaigne*

2665 If you were to give him the whole of Great Britain and Ireland
for an estate, he would ask the Isle of Man for a potato garden.
—*Lord North*

2666 To greed, all nature is insufficient. —*Seneca*

2667 You yourself
Are much condemn'd to have an itching palm. —*Shakespeare*

2668 Covetous men's chests are rich, not they.

2669 A gross belly does not produce a refined mind.

2670 Gold and silver were mingled with dirt, till avarice parted them.

2671 No one bull-dog yet could eat
Any other bull-dog's meat;
If you have a good-sized bone,
Let the other dog alone.

SEE ALSO	RELATED SUBJECTS
Aim 190	Desire
Modesty 4009	Jealousy
	Money

GRIEF

2681 It is foolish to pluck out one's hair for sorrow, as if grief could
be assuaged by baldness. —*Bion*

2682 You cannot prevent the birds of sorrow from flying over your
head, but you can prevent them from building nests in your
hair. —*Chinese proverb*

2683 A sorrow's crown of sorrow
Is remembering happier things. —*Dante*

2684 The hues of bliss more brightly glow,
Chastis'd by sabler tints of woe. —*Thomas Gray*

2685 Dionysius of Tarsus. Sixty. Married not.
And O that his father had but chosen the same lot.
—*Greek epigram*

2686 Do not mourn the dead with the belly. —*Homer*

2687   Hired mourners at a funeral say and do
        A little more than they whose grief is true.   —*Horace*

2688   There are sufferings which sympathy may not make lighter.
                                                            —*Lamennais*

2689   What we call mourning for our dead is perhaps not so much
        grief at not being able to call them back as it is grief at not
        being able to want to do so.   —*Thomas Mann*

2690   Poor mortals we who crave to have it so—
        Our grief to be deathless when we are dead.
                                                    —*Perses, of Thebes*

2691   Happiness is beneficial for the body but it is grief that develops
        the powers of the mind.   —*Marcel Proust*

2692   We are healed of a suffering only by experiencing it to the full.
                                                        —*Marcel Proust*

2693   Ah, why should we wear black for the guests of God?—*Ruskin*

2694   Every one can master a grief but he that has it.   —*Shakespeare*

2695   He that lacks time to mourn, lacks time to mend:
        Eternity mourns that. 'Tis an ill cure
        For life's worst ills, to have no time to feel them.—*Shakespeare*

2696   It is remarkable with what Christian fortitude and resignation
        we can bear the suffering of other folks.   —*Swift*

2697   If misery loves company, misery has company enough.—*Thoreau*

2698   Sorrow may be a good thing for a woman's heart, but it is a poor
        cosmetic for her face.

2699   Sadness is always the legacy of the past; regrets are pains of the
        memory.

2700   Bitter indeed must be the cup that a smile will not sweeten.

SEE ALSO	RELATED SUBJECTS
Drinking 1711	Death
Inheritance 3136	Despair
Knowledge 3323	Remorse
Marriage 3852	Tears
Time 5415	Troubles
	Worry

GUESTS

2701   People are either born hosts or born guests.   —*Max Beerbohm*

2702   Many a man who thinks to found a home discovers that he has
        merely opened a tavern for his friends.   —*Norman Douglas*

2703   Ye diners-out from whom we guard our spoons.   *—Macaulay*

2704   The guest at the lower end of the middle couch, with three hairs on his bald head and his scalp streaked with pigment, who is digging in his big mouth with a toothpick, is a fraud, Aefulanus. He has no teeth.   *—Martial*

2705   Annius has some two hundred tables, and servants for every table. Dishes run hither and thither, and plates fly about. Such entertainments as these keep to yourselves, ye pompous—I am displeased with a supper that walks.   *—Martial*

2706   Though you gladly dine at other people's houses, Cantharus, you indulge yourself there in clamor, complaints and threats . . . I advise you: a man cannot be both independent and a glutton.
   —Martial

2707   Two miles divide us, which, if I my door
Am once again to reach, amount to four . . .
Two miles to see you, that I do not mind;
Four *not* to see you, all too much I find.   *—Martial*

2708   You invite me, Gallicus, to eat a wild boar. Instead you place before me a home-fed pig. I am a wild-boar-home-fed-pig, Gallicus, if you can deceive me.   *—Martial*

2709   You invite no one, Cotta, except those whom you meet at the bath; and the bath alone supplies you with guests. I used to wonder why you had never asked me, Cotta. I know now: my appearance in a state of nature was unpleasing in your eyes.
   —Martial

2710   Last night I had invited you—after some fifty glasses, I suppose, had been despatched—to sup with me today. You immediately thought your fortune was made, and took note of my unsober words, with a precedent but too dangerous. I hate a boon companion whose memory is good, Procillus.   *—Martial*

2711   Nobody lodges in your house unless he be rich and childless. No one, Sosibianus, lets lodgings more profitably.   *—Martial*

2712   Varus did lately me to supper call,
The table sumptuous was, the supper small;
Loaden it was with weight of gold, not meat;
Much to be seen was served, little to eat;
Varus, our mouths, not our eyes, to feast we're here;
Take hence thy plate, or fill with better cheer.   *—Martial*

2713   I'm annoyed, my Lupercus; for ages your friend
Uninvited to dinner you've kept.
I shall take my revenge. You may beg, coax, and send—
"Well? And what will you do?" Why, accept.   *—Martial*

2714   The perfumes at your board last night
  Were exquisite, I won't deny it,
 But we were starved, we were, outright,
  For meat, we could no how come by it.

 The height of farce it is, I ween,
  To be so perfumed and anointed,
 And when one's appetite's most keen,
  To have it thus most disappointed.   *—Martial*

2715   You ask me to dinner and say there will be
 Three hundred at table, all strangers to me,
 And because I refuse you're surprised and make moan.
 Why Fabullus, I don't relish dining alone. *—Martial*

2716   Philo declares he never dines at home,
  And that is no exaggeration:
 He has no place whereat to dine in Rome,
  Unless he hooks an invitation.   *—Martial*

2717   Fish and guests smell at three days old.

2718   Unbidden guests are welcomest when they are gone.

2719   It is a sin against hospitality, to open your doors, and shut up
  your countenance.

SEE ALSO   RELATED SUBJECTS
Deception 1438   Drinking
Drinking 1742   Eating
Eating 1771, 1776   Friend
Friend 2404   Home
        Inns

GUILT

2721   Guilt has very quick ears to an accusation. *—Fielding*

2722   Successful guilt is the bane of society. *—Publilius Syrus*

2723   So full of artless jealousy is guilt,
 It spills itself in fearing to be spilt. *—Shakespeare*

2724   There is no refuge from confession but suicide; and suicide is
  confession.   *—Daniel Webster*

2725   Thy hands are washed, but, O, the water's spilt,
 That laboured to have washed thy guilt:
 The flood, if any be that can suffice
 Must have its fountain in thine eyes.

H

HABIT

2731 Chaos often breeds life, when order breeds habit.—*Henry Adams*

2732 Habit with him was all the test of truth;
"It must be right, I've done it from my youth."   —*Crabbe*

2733 The wise man does no wrong in changing his habits with the times.   —*Dionysius Cato*

2734 Each year, one vicious habit rooted out, in time ought to make the worst man good.   —*Franklin*

2735 Mankind are apt to be strongly prejudiced in favour of whatever is countenanced by antiquity, enforced by authority, and recommended by custom.   —*Hall*

2736 The secret of managing a man is to let him have his way in little things. He will change his life when he won't change his bootmaker.   —*John Oliver Hobbs*

2737 Custom meets us at the cradle and leaves us only at the tomb.   —*Robert Ingersoll*

2738 We are never so ridiculous from the habits we have as from those we affect to have.   —*La Rochefoucauld*

2739 Habit is a cable; we weave a thread of it every day, and at last we cannot break it.   —*Horace Mann*

2740 Celibates replace sentiment by habits.   —*George Moore*

2741 Fixed as a habit or some darling sin.   —*Oldham*

2742 Resist beginnings: it is too late to employ medicine when the evil has grown strong by inveterate habit.   —*Ovid*

2743 They that live in a trading street are not disturbed at the passage of carts.   —*Steele*

2744 Habit is habit and not to be flung out of the window by any man, but coaxed downstairs a step at a time.   —*Mark Twain*

2745   Nothing so needs reforming as other people's habits.

—*Mark Twain*

2746   Custom governs the world; it is the tyrant of our feeling and our manners, and rules us with the imperious hand of a despot.

2747   Man is a creature of habit; God made him first—he is his second creator.

SEE ALSO   RELATED SUBJECT
Anger 245   Change
Character 706
Liberty 3498
Politics 4504
Vice 5655
Youth 6206

HANGING

2751   His whole life is an epigram smart, smooth and neatly penned,
Plaited quite neat to catch applause, with a hangnoose at the end.
—*Blake*

2752   'Tis ill talking of halters in the house of a man that was hanged.
—*Cervantes*

2753   I think I will not hang myself to-day.   —*Chesterton*

2754   Ay, we must all hang together, else we shall all hang separately.
—*Franklin*

2755   He that hath one of his family hanged, may not say to his neighbor, "Hang up this fish."

2756   A hangman is a good trade, he doth his work by daylight.

2757   He rises o'er early that is hang'd ere noon.

2758   The thief is sorry he is to be hanged, not that he is a thief.

SEE ALSO   RELATED SUBJECTS
Fate 2158   Crime
Lies 3546   Justice
                   Punishment

HAPPINESS

2761   The long days are no happier than the short ones.
—*Philip J. Bailey*

2762   Happiness sneaks in through a door you didn't know you left open.   —*John Barrymore*

2763   If you ever find happiness by hunting for it, you will find it, as the old woman did her lost spectacles, safe on her own nose all the time.   —*Josh Billings*

2764 All who joy would win
Must share it—happiness was born a twin.   —*Byron*

2765 Gayety is often the reckless ripple over depths of despair.
—*E. H. Chapin*

2766 I am more and more impressed with the duty of finding happiness.   —*George Eliot*

2767 Human felicity is produc'd not so much by great pieces of good
fortune that seldom happen, as by little advantages that occur
every day.   —*Franklin*

2768 But mortal bliss will never come sincere;
Pleasure may lead, but grief brings up the rear.
—*Greek epigram*

2769 There is even a happiness
That makes the heart afraid.   —*Thomas Hood*

2770 Have you not sometimes seen happiness?
Yes, the happiness of others.   —*Arsène Houssaye*

2771 He who can conceal his joys, is greater than he who can hide
his griefs.   —*Lavaᵢer*

2772 Happiness, to some elation, is to others, mere stagnation.
—*Amy Lowell*

2773 To be happy is only to have freed one's soul from the unrest of
unhappiness.   —*Maeterlinck*

2774 Happiness is rarely absent; it is we that know not of its presence.
—*Maeterlinck*

2775 Who would have known of Hector, if Troy had been happy?
—*Ovid*

2776 Many people enjoy nothing of their happiness, but the fear of
losing it.   —*Rivarol*

2777 One is only happy before he is happy.   —*Rousseau*

2778 A merry heart goes all the day,
Your sad tires in a mile-a.   —*Shakespeare*

2779 A lifetime of happiness! No man alive could bear it: it would be
hell on earth.   —*G. B. Shaw*

2780 The secret of being miserable is to have leisure to bother about
whether you are happy or not.   —*G. B. Shaw*

2781 Eat with the Rich, but go to the play with the Poor, who are
capable of Joy.   —*Logan Pearsall Smith*

2782 The world is so full of a number of things,
I'm sure we should all be as happy as kings.   *—Stevenson*

2783 To me there is no duty we so much underrate as the duty of
being happy.   *—Stevenson*

2784 Joy is not in things; it is in us.   *—Wagner*

2785 Happiness is no laughing matter.   *—Richard Whately*

2786 Woman's happiness begins with her first love and ends about then.

2787 One must be perfectly stupid to be perfectly unhappy.

2788 Happiness is tranquil—pleasure riotous; happiness is apologetic—
pleasure blatant.

2789 A man of gladness seldom falls into madness.

2790 One of the indictments of civilization is that happiness and intelligence are so rarely found in the same person.

SEE ALSO   RELATED SUBJECTS
Business 588   Content
Deception 1434   Grief
History 2891
Illusion 3111
Inn 3152
Love 3664
Marriage 3862
Success 5249

HARDSHIP

2791 Prosperity is the blessing of the Old Testament; adversity is the
blessing of the New.   *—Bacon*

2792 Calamity is man's true touchstone.   *—Beaumont and Fletcher*

2793 A cobweb is as good as the mightiest cable when there is no
strain upon it.   *—H. W. Beecher*

2794 If thou faint in the day of adversity, thy strength is small.
—Bible

2795 Adversity is the first path to truth.   *—Byron*

2796 Calamity is the perfect glass wherein we truly see and know
ourselves.   *—Sir William D'Avenant*

2797 Bad times have a scientific value. These are occasions a good
learner would not miss.   *—Emerson*

2798 The times are not so bad as they seem; they couldn't be.
—Jay Franklin

2799   Half a calamity is better than a whole one.—*Lawrence of Arabia*

2800   In the adversity of our best friends we often find something that is not exactly displeasing.   —*La Rochefoucauld*

2801   Adversity reminds men of religion.   —*Livy*

2802   No man ever sank under the burden of the day. It is when to-morrow's burden is added to the burden of today, that the weight is more than a man can bear. —*George Macdonald*

2803   In adversity a man is saved by hope.   —*Menander*

2804   No pain, no palm; no thorns, no throne; no gall, no glory; no cross, no crown.   —*William Penn*

2805   Behold a thing worthy of a God, a brave man matched in conflict with adversity.   —*Seneca*

2806   Gold is tried by fire, brave men by adversity.   —*Seneca*

2807   Adversity finds at last the man whom she has often passed by.   —*Seneca*

2808   The worst is not
So long as we can say, "This is the worst."   —*Shakespeare*

2809   He is not worthy of the honeycomb
That shuns the hive because the bees have stings.   —*Shakespeare*

2810   O benefit of ill! now I find true
That better is by evil still made better.   —*Shakespeare*

2811   Every wind is fair
When we are flying from misfortune.   —*Sophocles*

2812   The Lord gets his best soldiers out of the highlands of affliction.   —*C. H. Spurgeon*

2813   Adversity makes a man wise, though not rich.

2814   Who speaks of insignificant incidents as misfortunes, suffers as much as if they were disaster.

2815   A man ever supports great and inevitable misfortunes with more calmness and resignation than trifling accidents.

2816   Sweet are the uses of adversity to the party it doesn't happen to.

2817   A gem cannot be polished without friction, nor a man perfected without trials.

RELATED SUBJECTS
Danger
Disappointment
Grief
Poverty

HASTE

2821 He is invariably in a hurry. Being in a hurry is one of the trib-
utes he pays to life.   —*Elizabeth A. Bibesco*

2822 Sir Amice Pawlett, when he saw too much haste made in any
matter, was wont to say, "Stay a while, that we may make an
end the sooner."   —*Bacon*

2823 Ther nis no werkman, what-so-ever he be,
That may bothe werke wel and hastily.   —*Chaucer*

2824 No man who is in a hurry is quite civilized.   —*Will Durant*

2825 In skating over thin ice our safety is our speed.   —*Emerson*

2826 Who eat their corn while yet 'tis green.
At the true harvest can but glean.   —*Saadi*

2827 He gets through too late who goes too fast.   —*Publilius Syrus*

2828 To go as fast as a friar that is invited to dinner.

SEE ALSO   RELATED SUBJECT
Courtship 1170   Patience
Deception 1441
Marriage 3852

HATE

2831 I do not love thee, Doctor Fell,
The reason why I cannot tell;
But this alone I know full well,
I do not love thee, Doctor Fell.   —*Thomas Brown*

2832 I hate, yet love: you ask how this may be.
Who knows? I feel its truth and agony.   —*Catullus*

2833 Heaven has no rage like love to hatred turned,
Nor hell a fury like a woman scorned.   —*Congreve*

2834 I don't like you, Sabidius. I cannot say why. All I can say is this:
I don't like you.   —*Martial*

2835 Hatred, as well as love, renders its votaries credulous.
                                                      —*Rousseau*

2836 'Tis a human trait to hate one you have wronged.   —*Seneca*

2837 Savageness is always due to a sense of weakness.   —*Seneca*

2838 I do desire we may be better strangers.   —*Shakespeare*

2839 There is no sport in hate when all the rage
Is on one side.   —*Shelley*

2840 Hate and mistrust are the children of blindness.
—William Watson

2841 As the best wine makes the sharpest vinegar, so the deepest love
turns to the deadliest hatred.

SEE ALSO   RELATED SUBJECTS
Contempt 994   Anger
Epitaphs 1883   Contempt
                     Enemies
                     Jealousy
                     Revenge

HEALTH

2851 "'Tis not *her* coldness, father,
That chills my laboring breast;
It's that confounded cucumber
I've ate and can't digest.   *—R. H. Barham*

2852 Indigestion is—that inward fate
Which makes all Styx through one small liver flow.   *—Byron*

2853 Indigestion is charged by God with enforcing morality on the
stomach.   *—Victor Hugo*

2854 You fall sick ten times or more in the course of a year, a practice
which inconveniences, not yourself, Polycharmus, but us. For
every time you leave your bed you exact the customary presents
of congratulations from your friends. Have some consideration:
fall sick at length, Polycharmus, once for all.   *—Martial*

2855 A great step towards independence is a good-humored stomach.
—Seneca

2856 I have no relish for the country; it is a kind of healthy grave.
—Sydney Smith

2857 Rheumatism has kept many people on the right path of life.

SEE ALSO   RELATED SUBJECTS
Character 717   Body
Poverty 4580   Doctors
Wealth 5791   Life
                     Medicine
                     Sickness

HEAVEN

2861 And in that Heaven of all their wish,
There shall be no more land, say fish.   *—Rupert Brooke*

2862 All places are distant from heaven alike.   *—Burton*

2863 All the way to heaven is heaven.   *—Canon Farrar*

2864   A Persian's heaven is easily made:
       'Tis but black eyes and lemonade.   —*Moore*

2865   Taking the first footstep with a good thought, the second with a
       good word, and the third with a good deed, I entered Paradise.
                                                            —*Zoroaster*

2866   A good key is necessary to enter Paradise.

SEE ALSO	RELATED SUBJECTS
Beauty 350	God
Death 1323	World
Man 3815	
Money 4050	
Passion 4311	
Wealth 5800	

HELP

2871   He too serves a certain purpose who only stands and cheers.
                                                    —*Henry Adams*

2872   No one is useless in this world who lightens the burden of it to
       any one else.   —*Dickens*

2873   What do we live for, if it is not to make life less difficult to each
       other?   —*George Eliot*

2874   Is not a patron, my lord (Chesterfield), one who looks with un-
       concern on a man struggling for life in the water, and when he
       has reached ground encumbers him with help?   —*Johnson*

2875   *Patron:* Commonly a wretch who supports with insolence, and is
       paid with flattery.   —*Johnson*

2876   Keeping from falling, is better than helping up.

2877   To believe in men is the first step toward helping them.

SEE ALSO	RELATED SUBJECTS
Advice 106	Charity
Prayer 4603	Kindness
	Selfishness

HERO

2881   When ye build yer triumphal arch to yer conquerin' hero, Hin-
       nissey, build it out of bricks so the people will have somethin'
       convanient to throw at him as he passes through.—*F. P. Dunne*

2882   Every hero becomes a bore at last.   —*Emerson*

2883   No man is a hero to his valet. This is not because the hero is no
       hero, but because the valet is a valet.   —*Hegel*

2884   He who aspires to be a hero must drink brandy.   —*Johnson*

2885   Hail, ye indomitable heroes, hail!
       Despite of all your generals ye prevail.   *—W. S. Landor*

2886   No one is a hero to his valet.   *—Mme. de Sevigné*

SEE ALSO   RELATED SUBJECTS
Wealth 5776   Courage
                    Fame
                    Martyr
                    Sacrifice

HISTORY

2891   Happy the people whose annals are blank in history-books.
                                                              —Carlyle

2892   All the historical books which contain no lies are extremely
       tedious.   *—Anatole France*

2893   Before us men have flourished just as we
       Now flourish: others yet again shall be
       Whose generations we shall never see.   *—Greek epigram*

2894   It is not deeds or acts that last: it is the written record of those
       deeds and acts.   *—Elbert Hubbard*

2895   The only good histories are those that have been written by the
       persons themselves who commanded in the affairs whereof
       they write.   *—Montaigne*

2896   History is merely gossip.   *—Oscar Wilde*

2897   History is what enables each nation to use the other fellow's past
       record as an alibi.

SEE ALSO   RELATED SUBJECTS
Age 136   America
Beauty 371   Ancestors
Christianity 802   Books
Difficulty 1594   Memory
Man 3814
Prophecy 4704
Women 5975

HOME

2901   A house is no home unless it contain food and fire for the mind
       as well as for the body.   *—Margaret Fuller*

2902   The man who has a house everywhere has a home nowhere.
                                                              —Martial

2903   Eretrians, of Euboa; and at Susa; buried here.
       Exiles learn how far home is—and how dear!   *—Plato*

2904 A man without an address is a vagabond.
      A man with two addresses is a libertine.   —*G. B. Shaw*

2905 A hundred men can make an encampment, but it requires a
      woman to make a home.

2906 Home, to the small boy, is merely a filling station.

See Also	Related Subjects
Charity 736	Family
Inn 3153	Marriage

HONESTY

2911 He who says there is no such thing as an honest man, you may be
      sure is himself a knave.   —*Bishop Berkeley*

2912 Make yourself an honest man, and then you may be sure that
      there is one rascal less in the world.   —*Carlyle*

2913 He hath freedom whoso beareth clean and constant heart within.
                                                          —*Ennius*

2914 A shady business never yields a sunny life.   —*B. C. Forbes*

2915 As innocent as a new-laid egg.   —*W. S. Gilbert*

2916 In this Age, when it is said of a man, "He knows *how to live*," it
      may be implied he is not very honest.   —*Lord Halifax*

2917 If he does really think that there is no distinction between vice
      and virtue, when he leaves our houses let us count our spoons.
                                                          —*Johnson*

2918 To strictest justice many ills belong,
      And honesty is often in the wrong.   —*Lucan*

2919 Never esteem anything as of advantage to thee that shall make
      thee break thy word or lose thy self-respect.—*Marcus Aurelius*

2920 I'd rather know a square guy than own a square mile.
                                                      —*Wilson Mizner*

2921 God defend me from being an honest man according to the de-
      scription which every day I see made by each man to his own
      glorification.   —*Montaigne*

2922 A wit's a feather, and a chief a rod;
      An honest man's the noblest work of God.   —*Pope*

2923 I thank God, I am as honest as any man living, that is an old
      man and no honester than I.   —*Shakespeare*

2924 The only disadvantage of an honest heart is credulity.
                                                      —*Philip Sidney*

2925 He never sold the truth to serve the hour.   *—Tennyson*

2926 He that steals an egg will steal an ox.

2927 It is not a sin to sell dear, but it is to make ill measure.

2928 An honest man is one who is always one step behind opportunity.

2929 Honesty is not the best policy—merely the safest.

2930 Every honest man secretly welcomes a press agent.

2931 Man's honesty is a cowardly attempt to establish a safe precedent.

2932 When a man repeats a promise again and again, he means to fail you.

SEE ALSO
Politics 4485

RELATED SUBJECTS
Character
Cheating
Honor
Sincerity
Temptation
Trust

HONOR

2941 One of the greatest sources of suffering is to have an inborn sense of honor.   *—De Casseres*

2942 Woman's honor is nice as ermine; it will not bear a soil.*—Dryden*

2943 Honor is not a matter of any man's calling merely, but rather of his own actions in it.   *—Dwight*

2944 Honor is but an itch in youthful blood
Of doing acts extravagantly good.   *—Samuel Howard*

2945 The difference between a moral man and a man of honor is that the latter regrets a discreditable act even when it has worked.   *—Mencken*

2946 Honor, the spur that pricks the princely mind.   *—Peele*

2947 Honor and shame from no condition rise;
Act well your part, there all the honor lies.   *—Pope*

SEE ALSO
Money 4040
Prophecy 4702

RELATED SUBJECTS
Dignity
Fame
Greatness
Honesty
Oath
Reputation

HOPE

2951 Hope warps judgment in council, but quickens energy in action.
          —*Bulwer-Lytton*

2952 Hope! of all ills that men endure,
        The only cheap and universal cure.   —*Cowley*

2953 Hope is the gay, skylarking pajamas we wear over yesterday's
        bruises.   —*De Casseres*

2954 To the last moment of his breath,
          On hope the wretch relies;
        And even the pang preceding death
          Bids expectation rise.   —*Goldsmith*

2955 Hope is the poor man's bread.   —*George Herbert*

2956 There is nothing so well known as that we should not expect
        something for nothing—but we all do and call it Hope.
          —*E. W. Howe*

2957 The triumph of hope over experience.
          —*Johnson, in comment on a hasty second marriage*

2958 We speak of hope; but is not hope only a more gentle name for
        fear?   —*L. E. Landon*

2959 One does not expect in this world; one hopes and pays carfares.
          —*Josephine P. Peabody*

2960 Hope springs eternal in the human breast:
        Man never is, but always to be, blest.   —*Pope*

2961 Hope is but the dream of those that wake.   —*Prior*

2962 Patience is the art of hoping.   —*Vauvenargues*

2963 There are no hopeless situations; there are only men who have
        grown hopeless about them.

2964 He that lives on hope has but a slender diet.

2965 A good hope is better than a bad possession.

2966 Free hope from fear and you become a dreamer.

2967 Wishes are the echo of a lazy will.

2968 None without hope e'er loved the brightest fair;
        But love can hope where reason would despair.

SEE ALSO   RELATED SUBJECTS
Belief 458   Desire
Hardship 2803   Faith
Travel 5474   Optimism

HUMILITY

2971   Extremes meet, and there is no better example than the haughti-
       ness of humility.   —*Emerson*

2972   Nothing is so strong as gentleness, nothing so gentle as real
       strength.   —*St. Francis de Sales*

2973   You've no idea what a poor opinion I have of myself, and how
       little I deserve it.   —*W. S. Gilbert*

2974   He who admits that he, himself, is a worm ought not to complain
       when he is trodden on.   —*Elbert Hubbard*

2975   It's goin' t' be fun t' watch an' see how long th' meek kin keep
       the earth after they inherit it.   —*Kin Hubbard*

2976   One may be humble out of pride.   —*Montaigne*

2977   Be humble or you'll stumble.   —*Dwight L. Moody*

2978   Humility is pride in God.   —*Austin O'Malley*

2979   It is easy to look down on others; to look down on ourselves is
       the difficulty.   —*Peterborough*

2980   Humility is a virtue all preach, none practice; and yet everybody
       is content to hear.   —*John Selden*

2981   Humility is to make a right estimate of one's self.
                                                    —*C. H. Spurgeon*

2982   The meek may inherit the earth, but they'll cease being meek as
       soon as they come into their inheritance.

RELATED SUBJECTS
Modesty
Self-Denial

HUNGER

2991   There's no sauce in the world like hunger.   —*Cervantes*

2992   An empty stomach is not a good political adviser.   —*Einstein*

2993   Hungry rooster don't cackle w'en he fine a wum.
                                              —*Joel Chandler Harris*

2994   Hunger is insolent, and will be fed.   —*Homer*

2995   The belly is the commanding part of the body.   —*Homer*

2996   He who does not mind his belly will hardly mind anything else.
                                                        —*Johnson*

2997   Any of us would kill a cow rather than not have beef.—*Johnson*

2998   No clock is more regular than the Belly.   —*Rabelais*

2999   The eye is bigger than the belly.

3000   An empty belly hears nobody.

3001   The way to a man's heart is through his stomach.

SEE ALSO   RELATED SUBJECTS
Justice 3248   Begging
                         Eating
                         Poverty

HUSBAND

3011   A woman who has made fun of her husband can love him no
       more.   —Balzac

3012   The mate for beauty should be a man, and not a money-chest.
                                                   —Bulwer-Lytton

3013   But, oh! ye lords of ladies intellectual,
       Inform us truly—have they not henpeck'd you all?   —Byron

3014   A husband is always a sensible man; he never thinks of marrying.
                                                          —Dumas

3015   A master of a house, as I have read,
       Must be the first man up, and the last in bed.   —Robert Herrick

3016   The lover in the husband may be lost.   —Lord Lyttleton

3017   Galla, you ask why I'll not marry thee?
       Galla, you are too learned far for me.
       A consort so correct I cannot take:
       For I, as husband, oft might solecisms make.   —Martial

3018   You set a watch upon your husband, Polla: you refuse to have any
       set upon yourself. This, Polla, is making a wife of your hus-
       band.   —Martial

3019   On the tombs of her seven husbands the notorious Chloe placed
       the inscription: "The Work of Chloe." How frank!—Martial

3020   So great is the modesty of your mind and face, Sophronius, that I
       wonder you should ever have become a father.   —Martial

3021   Milo abroad, one wonder all declare:
       His lands lie fallow, yet his wife can bear.
       The contrast strange some deep diviners scan:
       She has, tho' they have not, a husbandman.   —Martial

3022   The only time that most women give their orating husbands un-
       divided attention is when the old boys mumble in their sleep.
                                                   —Wilson Mizner

3023   A husband is a plaster that cures all the ills of girlhood.—Molière

3024 What could he know of sky and stars, or heaven's all-hidden life,
Who did not see in his own house the knave that kissed his wife.
—*Saadi*

3025 Better have an old man to humor than a young rake to break
your heart.

3026 Most women have a good deal of pity for some other woman's
husband.

3027 There are men designed by nature to be husbands—of men, they
are the tamest.

3028 A reformed rake makes the best husband.

SEE ALSO
Beauty 388
Maid 3788
Sailors 4923

RELATED SUBJECTS
Family
Marriage
Wife

HYPOCRISY

3031 Great hypocrites are the real atheists.   —*Bacon*

3032 But here I say the Turks were much mistaken
Who, hating hogs, yet wished to save their bacon.   —*Byron*

3033 Behavior which appears superficially correct but is intrinsically
corrupt always irritates those who see below the surface.
—*James Bryant Conant*

3034 Better make penitents by gentleness than hypocrites by severity.
—*St. Francis de Sales*

3035 No man, for any considerable period, can wear one face to himself, and another to the multitude, without finally getting be-
wildered as to which may be the true.   —*Hawthorne*

3036 We are not hypocrites in our sleep.   —*Hazlitt*

3037 It is no fault of Christianity if a hypocrite falls into sin.
—*St. Jerome*

3038 Hypocrisy is a homage vice pays to virtue.   —*La Rochefoucauld*

3039 He reminds me of the man who murdered both his parents, and
then, when sentence was about to be pronounced, pleaded for
mercy on the grounds that he was an orphan.   —*Lincoln*

3040 O, what may man within him hide,
Though angel on the outward side!   —*Shakespeare*

3041 May the man be damned and never grow fat, who wears two
faces under one hat.

3042 Hypocrisy: a lie in action—the legacy of indecency.

3043   Crows bewail the dead sheep, and then eat them.

3044   No rogue like the godly rogue.

SEE ALSO   RELATED SUBJECTS
Actors 47   Deception
Judgment 3226   Lies
Pleasure 4458   Sincerity

I

IDEALISM

3051   The attainment of an ideal is often the beginning of a disillusion.
                                                —*Stanley Baldwin*

3052   No folly is more costly than the folly of intolerant idealism.
                                                —*Winston Churchill*

3053   An idealist is a person who helps other people to be prosperous.
                                                —*Henry Ford*

3054   Idealism increases in direct proportion to one's distance from the
        problem.   —*Galsworthy*

3055   If I cannot realize my Ideal, I can at least idealize my Real.
                                                —*W. C. Gannett*

3056   Words without actions are the assassins of idealism.
                                                —*Herbert Hoover*

3057   Ideals are like the stars—we never reach them, but like the mari-
        ners of the sea, we chart our course by them.   —*Carl Schurz*

3058   When they come downstairs from their Ivory Towers, Idealists
        are apt to walk straight into the gutter.—*Logan Pearsall Smith*

3059   An uncompromising ideal gives one a sense of uncomfortable sat-
        isfaction.

3060   We are an idealistic people and we'll make any sacrifice for a
        cause that won't hurt business.

SEE ALSO   RELATED SUBJECTS
Advertising 72   Character
                           Faith
                           Good
                           Honor

IDEAS

3061   One of the greatest pains to human nature is the pain of a new
        idea.   —*Walter Bagehot*

3062 A city (Paris) where great ideas perish, done to death by a witticism. —*Balzac*

3063 Only the wise possess ideas; the greater part of mankind are possessed by them. —*Coleridge*

3064 Grey is the color of all theory. —*Goethe*

3065 An Idea isn't responsible for the people who believe in it. —*Don Marquis*

3066 It is certainly not the least charm of a theory that it is refutable. —*Nietzsche*

3067 For an idea ever to be fashionable is ominous, since it must afterwards be always old-fashioned. —*Santayana*

SEE ALSO   RELATED SUBJECTS
Soul 5167   Knowledge
Teaching 5294, 5295, 5301   Thought

IDLENESS

3071 The terrible burden of having nothing to do. —*Boileau*

3072 Idleness is an appendix to nobility. —*Burton*

3073 It is better to play than do nothing. —*Confucius*

3074 An idler is a watch that wants both hands,
As useless if it goes as if it stands. —*Cowper*

3075 Th' feller that sets on a store box with his mouth full of scrap terbacker while his wife is at home sewin' fer a livin' knows jist exactly how t' regulate th' railroads. —*Kin Hubbard*

3076 It is impossible to enjoy idling thoroughly unless one has plenty of work to do. —*Jerome K. Jerome*

3077 Wherever you run up against me, Postumus, you call out immediately: "How do you do?" These are your first words: you say them if you meet me ten times in the course of an hour. Do, indeed. I suppose you have nothing to do. —*Martial*

3078 You declaim prettily, Attalus; you plead causes prettily; you write pretty histories, pretty epigrams. You are a pretty grammarian, a pretty astrologer. You sing prettily, Attalus, and you dance prettily. You are a pretty hand with the lyre, a pretty hand with the ball. Since you do nothing well, and yet everything prettily, shall I tell you what you are? You are a great busybody. —*Martial*

3079 Idleness is the stupidity of the body, and stupidity is the idleness of the mind. —*Seume*

3080   He is not only idle who does nothing but he is idle who might be
        better employed.   —*Socrates*

3081   Shun idleness, it is the rust that attaches itself to the most brilliant
        metals.   —*Voltaire*

3082   An idle fellow is a good fellow; work saps not only a man's
        energy but his kindness as well.

3083   The only nation capable of licking the world is stagnation.

3084   Stand still and silently watch the world go by—and it will.

                        RELATED SUBJECTS
                        Delay
                        Laziness
                        Work

IGNORANCE

3091   Ignorance is the night of the mind, but a night without moon or
        star.   —*Confucius*

3092   Ignorance never settles a question.   —*Disraeli*

3093   In order to have wisdom we must have ignorance.
                                                    —*Theodore Dreiser*

3094   Ignorance of one's misfortunes is clear gain.   —*Euripides*

3095   By ignorance is pride increased;
        Those most assume who know the least.   —*John Gay*

3096   Where ignorance is bliss,
        'Tis folly to be wise.   —*Thomas Gray*

3097   Ignorance gives a sort of eternity to prejudice, and perpetuity to
        error.   —*Robert Hall*

3098   Where ignorance is bliss it's foolish to borrow your neighbor's
        newspaper.   —*Kin Hubbard*

3099   Ignorance is preferable to error; and he is less remote from truth
        who believes nothing, than he who believes what is wrong.
                                                            —*Jefferson*

3100   From ignorance our comfort flows,
        The only wretched are the wise.   —*Prior*

3101   A jury is a group of twelve people of average ignorance.—*Spencer*

3102   Horace he has by many different hands,
        But not one Horace that he understands.

3103   Innocence plays in the back yard of ignorance.

3104 He that boasts of his own knowledge proclaims his ignorance.

SEE. ALSO
Admiration 69
Chance 639
Mistakes 3999
Silence 5041

RELATED SUBJECTS
Knowledge
Prejudice
Stupidity

ILLUSION

3111 No man is happy without a delusion of some kind. Delusions are as necessary to our happiness as realities. —*C. N. Bovée*

3112 Better a dish of illusion and a hearty appetite for life, than a feast of reality and indigestion therewith. —*H. A. Overstreet*

3113 The unknown always seems sublime. *Tacitus*

3114 Don't part with your illusions. When they are gone you may still exist, but you have ceased to live. —*Mark Twain*

3115 If it weren't for our illusions we'd be free from deceptions, and life free from any interests.

3116 Illusions are the mirages of Hope.

3117 There are mortgages on every castle in the air.

3118 It is a sign of passing youth when man begins to check up on his illusions.

SEE ALSO
Age 173
Beauty 379
Experience 2019
Marriage 3894
Wisdom 5910

RELATED SUBJECTS
Error
Imagination
Mistakes

IMAGINATION

3121 That minister of ministers,
Imagination, gathers up
The undiscovered universe,
Like jewels in a jasper cup. —*John Davidson*

3122 To know is nothing at all; to imagine is everything.
—*Anatole France*

3123 Were it not for imagination, Sir, a man would be as happy in the arms of a chambermaid as of a Duchess. —*Johnson*

3124 Fancy rules over two thirds of the universe, the past and future, while reality is confined to the present. —*J. P. Richter*

3125 The lunatic, the lover, and the poet are of imagination all compact. —*Shakespeare*

3126   Castles in the air are all right until we try to move into them.

> RELATED SUBJECTS
> Facts
> Fear
> Illusion

INHERITANCE

3131   The fool inherits, but the wise must get.   —*William Cartwright*

3132   Say not you know another entirely, till you have divided an inheritance with him.   —*Lavater*

3133   A son could bear complacently the death of his father, while the loss of his inheritance might drive him to despair.
—*Machiavelli*

3134   Maro, you'll give me nothing while you live,
But, after death, you cry, then, then, you'll give;
If thou art not indeed turn'd arrant ass,
Thou know'st what I desire to come to pass.   —*Martial*

3135   Fabius has bequeathed you nothing, Bithynicus, although you used to present him yearly, if I remember right, with six thousand sesterces . . . (By dying) he has at least saved you six thousand sesterces a year.   —*Martial*

3136   If you want him to mourn, you had best leave him nothing.
—*Martial*

3137   Happy always was it for that son
Whose father for his hoarding went to hell.   —*Shakespeare*

3138   The tears of an heir are laughter under a mask.
—*Publilius Syrus*

3139   To inherit property is not to be born—is to be still-born, rather.
—*Thoreau*

3140   He is no great heir that inherits not his ancestor's virtues.

SEE ALSO	RELATED SUBJECTS
Death 1348	Lawyers
Doctors 1673	Money
Humility 2975, 2982	Wealth

INJURY

3141   The injuries we do and those we suffer are seldom weighed in the same scales.   —*Aesop*

3142   He who has suffer'd you to impose on him, knows you.   —*Blake*

3143   Christianity commands us to pass by injuries; policy, to let them pass by us.   —*Franklin*

3144 He who has injured thee was either stronger or weaker. If weaker, spare him; if stronger, spare thyself. —*Seneca*

3145 Whom they have injured they also hate. —*Seneca*

RELATED SUBJECTS
Fight
Insult
Pain

INNS

3151 A tavern is a house kept for those who are not housekeepers. —*Chatfield*

3152 There is nothing which has yet been contrived by man by which so much happiness is produced as by a good tavern or inn. —*Johnson*

3153 The great advantage of a hotel is that it's a refuge from home life. —*G. B. Shaw*

3154 Take the din out of dinner and put the rest in restaurant. —*Henry J. Spoone*

3155 Taverns are places where madness is sold by the bottle. —*Swift*

3156 He goes not out of his way, that goes to a good inn.

SEE ALSO
Guests 2702

RELATED SUBJECTS
Drinking
Eating
Guests

INSULTS

3161 When Mr. Wilbur calls his play *Halfway to Hell,* he underestimates the distance. —*Brooks Atkinson*

3162 His face looks like a slateful of wrong answers. *"Bugs" Baer, of Firpo*

3163 *Perfectly Scandalous* was one of those plays in which all of the actors unfortunately enunciated very clearly.—*Robert Benchley*

3164 You, Silo, rude and surly? Zounds!
Deliver back my fifty pounds,
And then you may, for aught I care,
Be rude and surly—if you dare!
But, pray, while pimping is your trade,
Remember, sir, for what you're paid,
And keep, whate'er may lurk beneath,
A civil tongue within your teeth! —*Catullus*

3165 An injury is much sooner forgiven than an insult.—*Chesterfield*

3166 He who allows himself to be insulted deserves to be.—*Corneille*

3167 A viper stung a Cappadocian's hide,
      And poisoned by his blood that instant died.   —*Demodocus*

3168 A gentleman will not insult me, and no man not a gentleman can
      insult me.   —*Frederick Douglass*

3169 The way to procure insults is to submit to them.   —*Hazlitt*

3170 It is better a man should be abused than forgotten.   —*Johnson*

3171 I could do without your face, Chloe, and without your neck, and
      your hands, and your limbs, and, to save myself the trouble of
      mentioning the points in detail, I could do without you alto-
      gether.   —*Martial*

3172 You are an informer, a calumniator, a forger, a secret agent, a
      slave to the unclean, and a trainer of gladiators. I wonder,
      Vacerra, why you have no money.   —*Martial*

3173 You ask me, Linus, what my field
      Out at Nomentum is to yield?
      Well, this it yields to me: the view,
      My Linus, has no sign of *you*.   —*Martial*

3174 Clearinus wears six rings on each of his fingers, and never takes
      them off even at night, or when he bathes. Do you ask the rea-
      son? He has no ring case.   —*Martial*

3175 *The House Beautiful* is the play lousy.   —*Dorothy Parker*

3176 I am going from bad to Hearst.   —*William L. Shirer*

3177 She is intolerable, but that is her only fault.
                        —*Talleyrand, of a young lady of the Court*

3178 Sarcasm: intellect on the offensive.

3179 Jack, eating rotten cheese, did say,
      "Like Samson, I my thousands slay."
      "I vow," quoth Roger, "so you do,
      And with the self-same weapon too."

SEE ALSO   RELATED SUBJECTS
Wit 5942   Epigrams
                            Injury

ITALY

3181 Italy, a paradise for horses, hell for women, as the proverb goes.
                                                            —*Burton*

3182 Italy is only a geographical expression.   —*Metternich*

3183 A paradise inhabited with devils.   —*Sir Henry Wotton*

J

JEALOUSY

3191   Jealousy, the jaundice of the soul.   —*Dryden*

3192   Lots of people know a good thing the minute the other fellow
      sees it first.   —*Job E. Hedges*

3193   Who persuaded you to cut off the nose of your wife's lover?
      Wretched husband, that was not the part which outraged you!
      Fool, what have you done? Your wife has lost nothing by the
      operation.   —*Martial*

3194   There is more self-love than love in jealousy.
                          —*La Rochefoucauld*

3195   Envy is a pain of mind that successful men cause their neighbors.
                          —*Onasander*

3196   Jealousy is the fear or apprehension of superiority: envy our un-
      easiness under it.   —*William Shenstone*

3197   Moral indignation is jealousy with a halo.   —*H. G. Wells*

3198   Plain women are always jealous of their husbands, beautiful
      women never are!   —*Oscar Wilde*

3199   Hunger, revenge, to sleep are petty foes,
      But only death the jealous eyes can close.   —*Wycherley*

3200   To be jealous of the woman one has ceased to love argues a very
      contemptible character.

3201   A lewd bachelor makes a jealous husband.

3202   Well may Suspicion shake its head—
      Well may Clarinda's spouse be jealous,
      When the dear wanton takes to bed
      Her very *shoes*—because they're *fellows*.

SEE ALSO   RELATED SUBJECTS
Competition 893   Enemies
Guilt 2723   Hate
Weather 5806   Love

JOKES

3211   A good storyteller is a person who has a good memory and hopes
      other people haven't.   —*Irvin S. Cobb*

3212 They cannot be complete in aught
    Who are not humorously prone—
    A man without a merry thought
    Can hardly have a funny bone.   *—F. Locher-Lampson*

3213 A joke without a point, inane and bald,
    Itself a joke on joking may be called.   *—Menander*

3214 He must not laugh at his own wheeze:
    A snuff box has no right to sneeze.   *—Keith Preston*

3215 My way of joking is telling the truth. That is the funniest joke
    in the world.   *—G. B. Shaw*

3216 You could read Kant by yourself, if you wanted; but you must
    share a joke with some one else.   *—Stevenson*

3217 Good jests bite like lambs, not like dogs.

3218 The good die young was never said of a joke.

SEE ALSO   RELATED SUBJECTS
Life 3559   Epigrams
                Laughter
                Wit

JUDGMENT

3221 A shoemaker should not judge above his shoes.   *—Apelles*

3222 Good and bad men are each less so than they seem.*—Coleridge*

3223 Where men of judgment creep and feel their way,
    The positive pronounce without dismay.   *—Cowper*

3224 Common sense is, of all kinds, the most uncommon.
                        —Tryon Edwards

3225 You cannot see the mountain near.   *—Emerson*

3226 Things are seldom what they seem,
    Skim milk masquerades as cream.   *—W. S. Gilbert*

3227 The man who called it "near beer" was a bad judge of distance.
                      —Philander Johnson

3228 God himself, sir, does not propose to judge man until the end of
    his days.   *—Johnson*

3229 Everyone complains of his memory, and no one complains of his
    judgment.   *—La Rochefoucauld*

3230 We judge ourselves by what we feel capable of doing; others
    judge us by what we have done.   *—Longfellow*

3231 'Tis with our judgments as our watches, none
    Go just alike, yet each believes his own.   *—Pope*

3232 My salad days.
    When I was green in judgment.   *—Shakespeare*

3233 How little do they see what really is, who frame their judgments
upon that which seems. —*Southey*

3234 Enthusiasm for a cause sometimes warps judgment.
—*William Howard Taft*

3235 Common sense is not so common. —*Voltaire*

3236 In our judgment of human transactions, the law of optics is re-
versed; we see the most indistinctly the objects which are close
around us. —*Whately*

3237 It is only shallow people who do not judge by appearances.
—*Oscar Wilde*

3238 The best we can expect on the Day of Judgment is a suspended
sentence.

3239 When Death puts out our flame, the snuff will tell
If we were wax or tallow, by the smell.

3240 Statistics are no substitute for judgment.

See Also	Related Subjects
Children 775	Criticism
Criticism 1258	Decision
Enemies 1831	Law
Laughter 3366	Wisdom
Secret 4972	
Taste 5276	

JUSTICE

3241 He's just, your cousin, ay, abhorrently;
He'd wash his hands in blood, to keep them clean.
—*E. B. Browning*

3242 Justice while she winks at crimes,
Stumbles on innocence sometimes. —*Samuel Butler*

3243 When one has been threatened with a great injustice, one accepts
a smaller as a favor. —*Mrs. Thomas Carlyle*

3244 Justice is the bread of the nation; it is always hungry for it.
—*Chateaubriand*

3245 Justice is truth in action. —*Disraeli*

3246 Whatever is, is in its causes just. —*Dryden*

3247 Justice delayed is justice denied. —*Gladstone*

3248 The hungry judges soon the sentence sign,
And wretches hang that jurymen may dine. —*Pope*

3249   The love of justice is, in the majority of men, the fear of suffer-
         ing injustice.   —*La Rochefoucauld*

3250   A just man is not one who does no ill,
         But he, who with the power, has not the will.   —*Philemon*

3251   Use every man after his desserts, and who should 'scape whip-
         ping?   —*Shakespeare*

3252   Justice, like lightning, ever should appear to few men's ruin, but
         to all men's fear.   —*Sweetman*

3253   Every man loves justice at another man's house; nobody cares for
         it at his own.

3254   A fox should not be of the jury at a goose's trial.

3255   It is just as well that justice is blind; she might not like some of
         the things done in her name if she could see them.

3256   He has always received condemnation from both sides for his fair
         and impartial handling of cases.

3257   He that buyeth magistracy must sell justice.

SEE ALSO
Death 1359
Honesty 2918
Mercy 3962
War 5723

RELATED SUBJECTS
Crime
Hanging
Judgment
Law
Lawyers
Punishment

K

KINDNESS

3261   Kindness—a language which the dumb can speak, and the deaf
         can understand.   —*C. N. Bovée*

3262   He that has once done you a kindness will be more ready to do
         you another, than he whom you yourself have obliged.
                                                              —*Franklin*

3263   If you can make people kind, not merely respectable, the problem
         will be solved.   —*Elbert Hubbard*

3264   Kindness goes a long ways lots o' times when it ought t' stay at
         home.   —*Kin Hubbard*

3265   Brutality to an animal is cruelty to mankind—it is only the difference in the victim.   —*Lamartine*

3266   The first thing a kindness deserves is acceptance, the second, trans-
mission.   *George Macdonald*

3267   Not always actions show the man; we find
Who does a kindness is not therefore kind.   —*Pope*

3268   A word of kindness is seldom spoken in vain, while witty sayings
are as easily lost as the pearls slipping from a broken string.
     —*Prentice*

3269   To smile at the jest which plants a thorn in another's breast is to
become a principal in the mischief.   —*Sheridan*

3270   A sufficient commentary on human nature is that a mob never
rushes madly across town to do a needed kindness.

SEE ALSO   RELATED SUBJECTS
Civilization 847   Begging
                          Courtesy
                          Gifts
                          Help
                          Mercy
                          Selfishness

KINGS

3271   If Russians knew how to read, they would write me off.
     —*Catherine the Great*

3272   Every chair should be a throne and hold a king.   —*Emerson*

3273   They say kings are made in the image of God. I feel sorry for
God if that is what he looks like.   —*Frederick the Great*

3274   Don't forget your great guns which are the most respectable arguments of the rights of kings.   —*Frederick the Great*

3275   I will not wear a crown of gold where my Saviour wore one of
thorns.   —*Godfrey of Bouillon*

3276   A tomb now suffices him for whom the whole world was not sufficient.   —*Greek epigram on Alexander*

3277   Kings are in the moral order what monsters are in the natural.
     —*Henri Gregoire*

3278   In things a moderation keep;
Kings ought to shear, not skin, their sheep.   —*Robert Herrick*

3279   I am a royalist by trade.   —*Joseph II of Austria*

3280   *Alexander:* I am Alexander the Great.
        Diogenes: And I am Diogenes, the Cynic.
                                              —Diogenes Laertius

3281   Come, Caesar, even by night—let stars delay;
        If thou but come, thy folk will find it day.   *—Martial*

3282   I can easily imagine Socrates in Alexander's place; Alexander in
        that of Socrates—never.   *—Montaigne*

3283   An aristocracy is the true support of a monarchy.   *—Napoleon*

3284   Aristocracy is always cruel.   *—Wendell Phillips*

3285   The right divine of kings to govern wrong.   *—Pope*

3286   What can they see in the longest kingly line in Europe, save that
        it runs back to a successful soldier?   *—Scott*

3287   A King is a thing men have made for their own sakes, for quiet-
        ness' sake. Just as in a family one man is appointed to buy the
        meat.   *—John Selden*

3288   A multitude of executions discredits a king, as a multitude of
        funerals a doctor.   *—Seneca*

3289   A substitute shines brightly as a king,
        Until a king be by.   *—Shakespeare*

3290   He who slays a king and he who dies for him are alike idolaters.
                                                    —G. B. Shaw

3291   Kings are not born: they are made by universal hallucination.
                                                    —G. B. Shaw

3292   Authority forgets a dying king.   *—Tennyson*

3293   The throne is a glorious sepulchre.   *—Empress Theodora*

3294   No man ruleth safely but he that is willingly ruled.
                                                  —Thomas à Kempis

3295   Good kings never make war, but for the sake of peace.

3296   Here lies our sovereign lord the king,
            Whose word no man relies on;
        Who never said a foolish thing,
            And never did a wise one.   *—Epigram on Charles II*

3297   The modern king has become a vermiform appendix—useless when
        quiet, when obtrusive in danger of removal.

SEE ALSO   RELATED SUBJECTS
Actors 43   Courtier
Discretion 1634   Government
Literature 3625

KISS

3301 Two persons who do not part with kisses should part with haste.
      —*Ralph Bergengren*

3302 The kiss I stole, when thou and I,
          Dear girl, were romping in the glade,
      Did nectar in its sweet outvie,
          But oh! how dear for it I paid!   —*Catullus*

3303 I can't forget, nor thou forgive,
          And so, the wretchedest of men,
      I vow I'll never, while I live,
          No, never steal a kiss again!   —*Catullus*

3304 A kiss is sweet; who dares deny it? But when it is sold, it becomes
      bitterer than hellebore.   —*Cillactor*

3305 All the legislation in the world will not abolish kissing.
      —*Elinor Glyn*

3306 What is a kiss? Why this, as some approve:
      The sure, sweet cement, glue, and lime of love.—*Robert Herrick*

3307 Being used but sisterly salutes to feel,
      Insipid things—like sandwiches of veal.   —*Thomas Hood*

3308 Unto that flowery cup I bent once more,
      Again she showed no seeming to abhor,
      But at the third kiss all she asked me was,
      "Is this all you came to see me for?"   —*Wallace Irwin*

3309 What is a kiss? Alacke! at worst,
      A single Dropp to quenche a Thirst,
      Tho' oft it prooves in happie Hour
      The first sweete Dropp of one long showre.   —*Leland*

3310 Not that I'd have my pleasure incomplete,
      Or lose the kiss for which my lips beset you;
      But that in suffering me to take it, sweet!
      I'd have you say—"No! no! I will not let you!"—*Clement Marot*

3311 Why do I not kiss you, Philaenis? You are bold. Why do I not
      kiss you, Philaenis? You are carrotty. Why do I not kiss you,
      Philaenis? You are one-eyed. He who kisses you, Philaenis, sins
      against Nature.   —*Martial*

3312 To some, Postumus, you give kisses, to some your right hand
      "Which do you prefer?" you say, "choose." I prefer your hand.
      —*Martial*

3313 With only half a lip you kiss,
      And half of that I ne'er should miss,
      A greater boon, of worth untold,
      Wilt grant me? That whole half withhold.   —*Martial*

3314   Lord! I wonder what fool it was that first invented kissing.
                                                            —*Swift*

3315   If you can kiss the mistress, never kiss the maid.

3316   It is a noun both common and proper,
        Not very singular, and agrees with both *you* and *me*.

3317   They say there's microbes in a kiss,
        This rumor is most rife,
        Come, lady dear, and make of me
        An invalid for life.

3318   Yesterday's yesterday while today's here,
        Today is today till tomorrow appear,
        Tomorrow's tomorrow until today's past,
        And kisses are kisses as long as they last.

3319   Moon, Moon, thou art happier than I,
        For thou seest her, and I do not;
        But last night I was happier than thou,
        For I kissed her, and thou didst look on.

3320   A bonny bride is soon buskit.

        SEE ALSO   RELATED SUBJECTS
        Taste 5278   Courtship
        Tobacco 5446   Love
                                 Passion

KNOWLEDGE

3321   What one knows is, in youth, of little moment; they know enough
        who know how to learn.   —*Henry Adams*

3322   I cannot know even whether I know or not.
                                    —*Arcesilaus the Sceptic*

3323   He that increaseth knowledge increaseth sorrow.   —*Bible*

3324   I honestly believe it iz better tew know nothing than tew know
        what ain't so.   —*Josh Billings*

3325   An expert is one who knows more and more about less and less.
                                        —*Nicholas Murray Butler*

3326   He knew what's what, and that's as high
        As metaphysic wit can fly.   —*Samuel Butler*

3327   This devil of a man (Poincairé) is the opposite of Briand: the
        latter knows nothing, and understands everything; the other
        knows everything, and understands nothing.   —*Clemenceau*

3328   The essence of knowledge is, having it, to apply it; not having it,
        to confess your ignorance.   —*Confucius*

3329   Knowledge is proud that he has learn'd so much;
        Wisdom is humble that he knows no more.   —*Cowper*

3330   Men who know the same things are not long the best company
       for each other.   —*Emerson*

3331   If you have knowledge, let others light their candles at it.
                                                      —*Margaret Fuller*

3332   Knowledge is a treasure, but practice is the key to it.
                                                      —*Thomas Fuller*

3333   Excepting for knowledge nothing has any meaning, and to have
       no meaning is to be non-existent.   —*Lord Haldane*

3334   Nothing exists because it is known, but things are known because
       they exist.   —*L. T. Hobhouse*

3335   Knowledge and timber shouldn't be much used till they are sea-
       soned.   —*O. W. Holmes*

3336   If a little knowledge is dangerous, where is the man who has so
       much as to be out of danger?   —*T. H. Huxley*

3337   The seeds of knowledge may be planted in solitude, but must be
       cultivated in public.   —*Johnson*

3338   The world does not require so much to be informed as to be re-
       minded.   —*Hannah More*

3339   All I know is just what I read in the papers.   —*Will Rogers*

3340   It is better, of course, to know useless things than to know
       nothing.   —*Seneca*

3341   I am like a book, with pages that have stuck together for want of
       use: my mind needs unpacking and the truths stored within
       must be turned over from time to time, to be ready when oc-
       casion demands.   —*Seneca*

3342   When the wind is southerly, I know a hawk from a handsaw.
                                                      —*Shakespeare*

3343   To me the charm of an encyclopedia is that it knows—and I
       needn't.   —*Francis Yeats-Brown*

3344   One part of knowledge consists of being ignorant of such things
       as are not worthy to be known.

3345   He that imagines he hath knowledge enough hath none.

3346   First-hand knowledge does not become second-hand when used.

L

LABOR

3351 *Labor:* one of the processes by which A acquires property for B.
—*Ambrose Bierce*

3352 Industry cannot flourish if labor languish.   —*Calvin Coolidge*

3353 Labor disgraces no man; unfortunately you occasionally find men disgrace labor.   —*Ulysses S. Grant*

3354 Republican institutions cannot exist for long where there is enforced labor; or for that matter where there is enforced idleness.

SEE ALSO   RELATED SUBJECTS
Temperance 5329   Business
                    Work

LAUGHTER

3361 The man who cannot laugh is not only fit for treasons, stratagems and spoils; but his whole life is already a treason and a stratagem.   —*Carlyle*

3362 Nothing is more significant of men's character than what they find laughable.   —*Goethe*

3363 Laughter is the mind's intonation. There are ways of laughing which have the sound of counterfeit coins.
—*Edmond de Goncourt*

3364 A laugh is worth a hundred groans in any market.   —*Lamb*

3365 No spell were wanting, from the dead to raise me,
But only that sweet laugh wherewith she slays me.
—*Clement Marot*

3366 I can usually judge a fellow by what he laughs at.
—*Wilson Mizner*

3367 Everything is funny as long as it is happening to somebody else.
—*Will Rogers*

3368 One good, hearty laugh is a bombshell exploding in the right place, while spleen and discontent are a gun that kicks over the man who shoots it off.   —*De Witt Talmage*

3369 Laughter is not at all a bad beginning for a friendship, and it is far the best ending for one.   —*Oscar Wilde*

3370 The most completely lost of all days is the one on which we have not laughed.

3371   The most valuable sense of humor is the kind that enables a person to see instantly what it isn't safe to laugh at.

3372   "I laugh," a would-be-sapient cries,
       "At every one that laughs at me."
       "Good Lord!" a sneering friend replies,
       "How merry you must always be!"

SEE ALSO   RELATED SUBJECTS
Happiness 2785   Jokes
Love 3762   Tears
Troubles 5526   Wit

LAW

3381   Such laws do rightly resemble the spider's cob-webs: because they take hold of little flies and gnats which fall into them, but the rich and mighty will break and run through them at will.
                                                          —*Anacharsis*

3382   Wise men, though all laws were abolished, would lead the same lives.   —*Aristophanes*

3383   It becomes not a law-maker to be a law-breaker.   —*Bias*

3384   I sometimes wish that people would put a little more emphasis upon the observance of the law than they do upon its enforcement.   —*Calvin Coolidge*

3385   Men do not make laws. They do but discover them.
                                                      —*Calvin Coolidge*

3386   Probably all laws are useless; for good men do not need laws at all, and bad men are made no better by them.
                                                      —*Demonax the Cynic*

3387   Customs may not be as wise as laws, but they are always more popular.   —*Disraeli*

3388   Man became free when he recognized that he was subject to law.
                                                          —*Will Durant*

3389   The law, in its majestic equality, forbids the rich as well as the poor to sleep under bridges, to beg in the streets, and to steal bread.   —*Anatole France*

3390   The path to which precedents gain admittance may be narrow: they soon find ways of roaming abroad.   —*Gaius Velleius*

3391   Laws grind the poor, and rich men rule the law.   —*Goldsmith*

3392   Laws that do not embody public opinion can never be enforced.
                                                      —*Elbert Hubbard*

3393 It is one of the maxims of the civil law, that definitions are hazardous. —*Johnson*

3394 The law is the last result of human wisdom acting upon human experience for the benefit of the public.   —*Johnson*

3395 The law hath not been dead, though it hath slept.—*Shakespeare*

3396 The law decides questions of *Meum* and *Tuum*.
      By kindly arranging to make the thing *Suum*.

3397 Technicalities are the "safety zones" from justice.

3398 There should be no laws; he who more than unconsciously obeys them is a scoundrel.

3399 Should troubles incline you to law with a friend,
      You'd better remain as you are;
      If you take it to Court both must lose in the end—
      That's the only relief at the Bar.

3400 English law prohibits a man from marrying his mother-in-law.
      This is the limit of useless legislation.

3401 Man is an able creature, but he has made 32,647,389 laws and hasn't yet improved on the Ten Commandments.

3402 The portion of a law usually found unconstitutional is the teeth.

3403 Jack says that of law common sense is the base,
      And, doubtless, in that he is right;
      Though certain am I, that in many a case
      The foundation is quite out of sight.

3404 Men fight for freedom: then they begin to accumulate laws to take it away from themselves.

3405 "Call silence!" the judge to the officer cries;
      "This hubbub and talk, will it never be done?
      Those people this morning have made such a noise,
      We've decided ten cases without hearing one."

See Also	Related Subjects
Crime 1227	Crime
Death 1329	Government
Decency 1422	Guilt
Kiss 3305	Judgment
Patriotism 4346	Justice
	Lawyers
	Punishment

LAWYERS

3411 Go not in and out in the court of justice, that thy name may not stink.
                                                   —*The Wisdom of Anii*

3412 A lawyer is a learned gentleman who rescues your estate from your enemies and keeps it himself.   —*Lord Brougham*

3413 Why, gentlemen, you cannot live without the lawyers, and certainly you cannot die without them.   —*Joseph H. Choate*

3414 This house where once a lawyer dwelt,
Is now a smith's. Alas!
How rapidly the iron age
Succeeds the age of brass!   —*Erskine*

3415 A countryman between two lawyers is like a fish between two cats.   —*Franklin*

3416 Diodorus goes to law, Flaccus. He suffers from gout in his feet. But he pays no fee to his lawyer. This is gout in his hands.
—*Martial*

3417 When there is no will there is a way for the lawyers.
—*Austin O'Malley*

3418 There take, says Justice, take ye each a shell;
We thrive at Westminster on fools like you;
'Twas a fat oyster—live in pleace—adieu.   —*Pope*

3419 Alas! the small discredit of a bribe
Scarce hurts the lawyer, but undoes the scribe.   —*Pope*

3420 A wise lawyer never goes to law himself.

3421 A good lawyer makes an evil neighbor.

3422 Woe be to him whose advocate becomes his accuser.

3423 "Virtue in the middle," said the Devil, as he seated himself between two lawyers.

3424 Fond of doctors, little health,
Fond of lawyers, little wealth.

3425 It is an ill cause that the lawyer thinks shame o'.
RELATED SUBJECTS
Judgment
Law

LAZINESS

3431 To loaf is a science, to loaf is to live.   —*Balzac*

3432 Lazy folk's stummucks don't git tired.   —*Joel Chandler Harris*

3433 Easy street is a blind alley.   —*Wilson Mizner*

3434 You never see no "to let" signs on Easy Street.—*Kin Hubbard*

3435 Whenever I feel the urge to exercise coming on I lie down until it passes over.

3436   People are naturally indolent: it is not necessity, but actual despair that drives them to perfection.

3437   To slothful men the day, night, month and year
Seem long, though posting on with swift career
We trifle out our long-thought time in vain;
Why of life's shortness do we then complain?

3438   The man who waits for things to turn up finds his toes do it first.

3439   The cat is in the parlor, the dog is in the lake;
The cow is in the hammock—what difference does it make?

RELATED SUBJECTS
Delay
Labor

LEARNING

3441   What sculpture is to a block of marble, education is to the soul.
—*Addison*

3442   A beard creates lice, not brains.   —*Ammianus*

3443   Education is an ornament in prosperity and a refuge in adversity.
—*Aristotle*

3444   The nation that has the schools has the future.   —*Bismarck*

3445   Education makes a people easy to lead, but difficult to drive; easy to govern, but impossible to enslave.   —*Lord Brougham*

3446   Education is the cheap defense of nations.   —*Burke*

3447   The school is not the end but only the beginning of an education.
—*Calvin Coolidge*

3448   The secret of education lies in respecting the pupil. —*Emerson*

3449   I am not impressible, but I am impressionable.   —*Emerson*

3450   Drudgery is as necessary to call out the treasures of the mind, as harrowing and planting those of the earth.—*Margaret Fuller*

3451   Take care not to step on the foot of a learned idiot. His bite is incurable.   —*Paul Gauguin*

3452   A college education shows a man how little other people know.
—*T. C. Haliburton*

3453   It is better to be able neither to read nor write than to be able to do nothing else.   —*Hazlitt*

3454   You can lead a boy to college, but you cannot make him think.
—*Elbert Hubbard*

3455   Pedantry is the dotage of knowledge.   —*Holbrook Jackson*

3456   When schools flourish, all flourishes.   —*Luther*

3457   Schoolhouses are the republican line of fortifications.
                                                  —*Horace Mann*

3458   When you educate a man you educate an individual; when you
          educate a woman you educate a whole family.   —*McIver*

3459   Metaphysics is the art of bewildering oneself methodically.
                                                    —*Michelet*

3460   I've known countless people who were reservoirs of learning yet
          never had a thought.   —*Wilson Mizner*

3461   A learned person is not learned in everything; but the capable per-
          son is capable in everything, even in what he is ignorant of.
                                                  —*Montaigne*

3462   A little learning is a dangerous thing:
          Drink deep or taste not the Pierian spring;
          There shallow draughts intoxicate the brain,
          And drinking largely sobers us again.   —*Pope*

3463   'Tis education forms the common mind;
          Just as the twig is bent the tree's inclined.   —*Pope*

3464   The bookful blockhead, ignorantly read,
          With loads of learned lumber in his head.   —*Pope*

3465   No man is the wiser for his learning.   —*John Selden*

3466   No one finds his proficiency in a study just where he dropped it.
                                                    —*Seneca*

3467   A lesson that is never learned can never be too often taught.
                                                    —*Seneca*

3468   It (Oxford) is a sanctuary in which exploded systems and ob-
          solete prejudices find shelter and protection after they have been
          hunted out of every corner of the world.   —*Adam Smith*

3469   Not body enough to cover his mind decently with; his intellect
          is improperly exposed.   —*Sydney Smith*

3470   Training is everything. The peach was once a bitter almond;
          cauliflower is but cabbage with a college education.
                                                  —*Mark Twain*

3471   When he that speaks, and he to whom he speaks, neither of them
          understand what is meant, that is metaphysics.   —*Voltaire*

3472   A wise man gets learning from those who have none themselves.

3473   It is less painful to learn in youth than to be ignorant in age.

3474 Education is only a ladder to gather fruit from the tree of knowledge, not the fruit itself.

3475 Pedantry: stupidity that read a book.

3476 One pound of learning requires ten pounds of common sense to apply it.

3477 "Live and Learn" may be a good motto, but so many people find it necessary to live and unlearn.

3478 An educational system isn't worth a great deal if it teaches boys to get a living and doesn't teach them how to live.

3479 Oxford gave the world marmalade and a manner, Cambridge science and a sausage.

3480 No wonder that Oxford and Cambridge profound,
In learning and science so greatly abound;
Since some carry thither a little each day,
And we meet with so few who bring any away.

See Also	Related Subjects
Books 500	Books
Doubt 1699	Knowledge
Example 1968	Science
Fools 2289, 2292	Wisdom
Mistakes 3999	

LETTERS

3481 "Lives" of great men oft remind us
As we o'er their pages turn,
That we too may leave behind us
Letters that we ought to burn.   —*Thomas Hood*

3482 A short letter to a distant friend is, in my opinion, an insult like that of a slight bow or cursory salutation.   —*Johnson*

3483 Correspondences are like small-clothes before the invention of suspenders; it is impossible to keep them up.   —*Sydney Smith*

See Also	Related Subjects
Love 3681, 3726	Literature
	Writers

LIBERTY

3491 The price of Liberty is eternal vigilance, and the price of wisdom is eternal thought.   —*Frank Birch*

3492 Liberty! eternal spirit of the chainless mind.   —*Byron*

3493 More liberty begets desire of more;
The hunger still increases with the store.   —*Dryden*

3494 There is often as much independence in not being led as in not being driven. —*Tryon Edwards*

3495 If you would liberate me you must be free. —*Emerson*

3496 To open his lips is crime in a plain citizen. —*Ennius*

3497 Freedom is not worth having if it does not connote freedom to err. —*Mahatma Gandhi*

3498 Liberty is not merely a privilge to be conferred; it is a habit to be acquired. —*Lloyd George*

3499 Liberty has restraints but no frontiers. —*Lloyd George*

3500 Doing what we please is not freedom, is not liberty; rather, it is the abuse of true liberty and freedom. —*Cardinal Hayes*

3501 Where the press is free, and every man able to read, all is safe. —*Jefferson*

3502 All theory is against the freedom of the will, all experience for it. —*Johnson*

3503 Liberty may make mistakes but tyranny is the death of a nation. —*Matteotti*

3504 None can love freedom heartily but good men; the rest love not freedom, but licence. —*Milton*

3505 A nation may lose its liberties in a day, and not miss them in a century. —*Montesquieu*

3506 Lean liberty is better than fat slavery. —*Ray*

3507 Liberty will not descend to a people: a people must raise themselves to liberty. It is a blessing to be earned before it can be enjoyed. —*Tilton*

3508 The tree of liberty grows only when watered by the blood of tyrants. —*Bertrand de Vieuzac*

3509 Liberty, guest amiable,
Plants both elbows on the table. —*Voltaire*

3510 Liberty is the one thing you can't have unless you give it to others. —*William A. White*

3511 A free country is one in which there is no particular individual to blame for the existing tyranny.

SEE ALSO
Dictators 1588
Law 3388
Secret 4969
Soldiers 5143

RELATED SUBJECTS
Democracy
Dictators

LIES

3521 A liar will not be believed, even when he speaks the truth.—*Aesop*

3522 Truth is not only violated by falsehood; it may be equally out-
raged by silence. —*Amien*

3523 A truth that's told with bad intent
Beats all the lies you can invent. —*Blake*

3524 Lied is a rough phrase; say he fell from truth. —*Browning*

3525 The best liar is he who makes the smallest amount of lying go the
longest way—who husbands it too carefully to waste it where
it can be dispensed with. —*Samuel Butler*

3526 And, after all, what is a lie? 'Tis but
The truth in masquerade. —*Byron*

3527 There are three kinds of lies: lies, damned lies, and statistics.
—*Disraeli*

3528 I think a lie with a purpose is wan iv th' worst kind an' th' mos'
profitable. —*F. P. Dunne*

3529 When we risk no contradiction,
It prompts the tongue to deal in fiction. —*John Gay*

3530 Dare to be true; nothing can need a lie;
A fault which needs it most, grows two thereby.—*George Herbert*

3531 If you tell a big enough lie and tell it frequently enough, it will
be believed. —*Hitler*

3532 Sin has many tools, but a lie is the handle which fits them all.
—*O. W. Holmes*

3533 Th' first one t' ketch a circus in a lie is a boy. —*Kin Hubbard*

3534 A man had rather have a hundred lies told of him, than one truth
which he does not wish should be told. —*Johnson*

3535 I reckon there's more things told than are true,
And more things true than are told! —*Kipling*

3536 Truth does not do as much good in the world as its counterfeit
does mischief. —*La Rochefoucauld*

3537 No man has a good enough memory to make a successful liar.
—*Lincoln*

3538 No one is such a liar as the indignant man. —*Nietzsche*

3539 Lie on! While my revenge shall be,
To speak the very truth of thee. —*Lord Nugent*

3540 A very honest woman, but something given to lie.—*Shakespeare*

3541 A lie travels round the world while truth is putting on her boots.
—*C. H. Spurgeon*

3542 It is often the case that the man who can't tell a lie thinks he is the best judge of one. —*Mark Twain*

3543 Falsehoods which we spurn today
Were the truths of long ago. —*Whittier*

3544 He may very well be contented that need not lie nor flatter.

3545 Those who think it permissible to tell white lies soon grow color-blind.

3546 If lying were a capital crime,
The hangman would work overtime.

See Also	Related Subjects
Art 307	Cheating
Conceit 955	Deception
Courtship 1168	Error
Debt 1402	Hypocı
Diplomacy 1616	Oath
Marriage 3896	Truth
Politics 4482	
Women 6032	

LIFE

3551 Ah, lives of men! When prosperous they glitter
Like a fair picture; when misfortune comes
A wet sponge at one blow has blurred the painting.
—*Aeschylus*

3552 Nothing seems so tragic to one who is old as the death of one who is young, and this alone proves that life is a good thing.
—*Zoë Akins*

3553 Two parts of Life; and well the theme
May mournful thoughts inspire;
For ah! the past is but a dream,
The future—a desire! —*Arabic epigram*

3554 Do what you will, this life's a fiction,
And is made up of contradiction. —*Blake*

3555 Life is like playing a violin solo in public and learning the instrument as one goes on. —*Bulwer-Lytton*

3556 Life is the art of drawing sufficient conclusions from insufficient premises. —*Samuel Butler*

3557 To live is like to love—all reason is against it, and all healthy instinct for it. —*Samuel Butler*

3558 Life is made of ever so many partings welded together —*Dickens*

3559 Life is a jest, and all things show it,
      I thought so once, and now I know it.—*John Gay's own epitaph*

3560 Life's perhaps the only riddle
      That we shrink from giving up.   —*W. S. Gilbert*

3561 Forbid a man to think for himself or to act for himself and you
      may add the joy of piracy and the zest of smuggling to his life.
                                                    —*Elbert Hubbard*

3562 Be a life long or short, its completeness depends on what it was
      lived for.   —*David Starr Jordan*

3563 The problem of life is not to make life easier, but to make men
      stronger.   —*David Starr Jordan*

3564 No one is really miserable who has not tried to cheapen life.
                                              —*David Starr Jordan*

3565 All ways have their sunny side. Cities are
      Sociable; bide at home would'st thou hide care;
      Country for pleasure; Voyaging for gain;
      For knowledge, learn how foreign races fare.
                                              —*Julianus Aegyptius*

3566 Live thy life! let not Hope's frauds, thefts, fool thee, bidding thee
      wait
      Till a last dawn disposes of works, joys, put off too late.
                                              —*Julius Polyaenus*

3567 Let those who thoughtfully consider the brevity of life remember
      the length of eternity.   —*Bishop Ken*

3568 The significance of life is life itself.   —*Hermann Keyserling*

3569 There is nothing of which men are so fond, and withal so care-
      less, as life.   —*La Bruyère*

3570 Live as if you expected to live a hundred years, but might die
      tomorrow.   —*Ann Lee*

3571 A great part of the happiness of life consists not in fighting bat-
      tles, but in avoiding them. A masterly retreat is in itself a
      victory.   —*Longfellow*

3572 Knowledge the clue to life can give:
      Then wherefore hesitate to live.   —*Martial*

3573 To the wise, life is a problem; to the fool, a solution.

3574   Defer not joys thou mayst not win from fate:
            Judge only what is past to be thine own.
        Cares with a linked chain of sorrow wait.
            Mirth tarries not; but soon on wing is flown.
        With both hands hold it—clasped in full embrace,
            Still from thy breast it oft will glide away!
        To say "I mean to live" is folly's place:
            Tomorrow's life comes late; live, then, today.   *—Martial*

3575   Life's a long headache in a noisy street.   *—Masefield*

3576   Life is just one damned thing after another.*—F. W. O'Malley*

3577   All life is but a game: then gaily play
        Or sadly learn the penalty to pay.   *—Palladas*

3578   A Perilous voyage is Life;
        And often storm-tost, we
        Worse than shipwreck make
        On the rocky shore of the sea.   *—Palladas*

3579   Whoever hath washed his hands of living
        Utters his mind without misgiving.   *—Saadi*

3580   Life is a ticklish business; I have resolved to spend it in reflecting
        upon it.   *—Schopenhauer*

3581   Life is a play! 'Tis not its length, but its performance that counts.
        —Seneca

3582   Life should be like the precious metals, weigh much in little bulk.
        —Seneca

3583   They that mistake life's accessories for life itself are like them
        that go too fast in a maze: their very haste confuses them.
        —Seneca

3584   The time of life is short;
        To spend that shortness basely were too long.   *—Shakespeare*

3585   Those who do not know how to live must make a merit of dying.
        —G. B. Shaw

3586   Life is a flame that is always burning itself out, but it catches fire
        again every time a child is born.   *—G. B. Shaw*

3587   May you live all the days of your life.   *—Swift*

3588   Why is it that we rejoice at a birth and grieve at a funeral? It is
        because we are not the person involved.   *—Mark Twain*

3589   Let us endeavor so to live that when we come to die even the
        undertaker will be sorry.   *—Mark Twain*

3590   All say, "How hard it is that we have to die"—a strange com-
       plaint to come from the mouths of people who have had to live.
                                                                 —*Mark Twain*

3591   I don't want to earn my living; I want to live.   —*Oscar Wilde*

3592   You do not have to live, but you have to live well.

3593   The fear of death is the greatest compliment we pay to life.

3594   Life: a front door to eternity.

3595   Man's life's a vapor,
           And full of woes;
       He cuts a caper,
           And down he goes.

3596   Life is for most of us a continuous process of getting used to
       things we hadn't expected.

3597   The two chief problems are the high cost of living and the
       cheapness of human life.

SEE ALSO	RELATED SUBJECTS
Age 160	Experience
Aim 196	Health
Art 304	Soul
Bed 404	
Time 5407, 5410	
Youth 6204	

LIGHT

3601   If we want light, we must conquer darkness.   —*J. T. Fields*

3602   Lamps make oil-spots, and candles need snuffing; it is only the
       light of heaven that shines pure and leaves no stain.—*Goethe*

3603   The thing to do is to supply light and not heat.
                                                             —*Woodrow Wilson*

3604   A candle lights others and consumes itself.

SEE ALSO	RELATED SUBJECTS
Religion 4806	Day
Science 4947	Eyes

LISTENING

3611   Nature has given to men one tongue, but two ears, that we may
       hear from others twice as much as we speak.   —*Epictetus*

3612   Remember there's always a voice saying the right thing to you
       somewhere if you'll only listen for it.   —*Thomas Hughes*

3613   A good listener is not only popular everywhere, but after a while
       he knows something.   —*Wilson Mizner*

3614 Know how to listen, and you will profit even from those who talk badly. —*Plutarch*

3615 What a story these old walls would tell, if I would only listen.
—*Comment before the Parthenon*

3616 A good listener is a silent flatterer.

SEE ALSO　　　　　　　RELATED SUBJECT
Bores 521　　　　　　　　Conversation
Conversation 1013
Husband 3022

LITERATURE

3621 Literature is an investment of genius which pays dividends to all subsequent times. —*John Burroughs*

3622 There is a great discovery still to be made in Literature, that of paying literary men by the quantity they do not write.
—*Carlyle*

3623 Grammar is the grave of letters. —*Elbert Hubbard*

3624 As for literature, thefts cannot harm it, while the lapse of ages augments its value. —*Martial*

3625 I am king of the Romans, and above grammar.
—*Emperor Sigismund*

3626 A classic is something that everybody wants to have read and nobody wants to read. —*Mark Twain*

3627 Why care for grammar as long as we are good?—*Artemus Ward*

3628 A good description is a magician that can turn an ear into an eye.

SEE ALSO　　　　　　　RELATED SUBJECTS
Man 3816　　　　　　　　Art　　　　　　Poetry
　　　　　　　　　　　　Books　　　　　Writers
　　　　　　　　　　　　Letters

LOGIC

3631 Logic: an instrument used for bolstering a prejudice.
—*Elbert Hubbard*

3632 Logical consequences are the scarecrows of fools and the beacons of wise men. —*T. H. Huxley*

3633 Logic is the anatomy of thought. —*Locke*

3634 Logic is neither an art nor a science but a dodge. —*Stendhal*

RELATED SUBJECTS
Facts　　　　　　Reason
Illusion

LOVE

3641   The wine-cup is glad! Dear Zenophile's lip
It boasts to have touched when she stooped down to sip.
Happy wine-cup! I wish that, with lips joined to mine,
All my soul at a draught she would drink up like wine.

—Acilius

3642   I loved thee beautiful and kind,
    And plighted an eternal vow;
So altered are thy face and mind,
    'Twere perjury to love thee now.   *—Acilius*

3643   Why so coy, my lovely maid?
Why of age so much afraid?
Your cheeks like roses to the sight,
And my hair as lilies white;
In love's garland, we'll suppose
Me the lily, you the rose.   *—Anacreon*

3644   Respect is what we owe; love, what we give.   *—Philip J. Bailey*

3645   Love passes quickly, and passes like a street Arab, anxious to
mark his way with mischief.   *—Balzac*

3646   Make love to every woman you meet; if you get five per cent on
your outlay it's a good investment.   *—Arnold Bennett*

3647   Love iz like the meazles; we kant have it bad but onst, and the
later in life we have it the tuffer it goes with us.
—Josh Billings

3648   The ability to make love frivolously is the chief characteristic
which distinguishes human beings from the beasts.
—Heywood Broun

3649   Let us live, my Lesbia, and love, and value at one farthing all the
talk of crabbed old men.   *—Catullus*

3650   Lesbia always speaks ill of me, and is always talking about me.
May I perish if Lesbia does not love me. By what token? Because it is just the same with me. I am perpetually crying out
upon her, but may I perish if I do not love her.   *—Catullus*

3651   I hate and love—wherefore I cannot tell,
But by my tortures know the fact too well.   *—Catullus*

3652   Absence, that common cure of love.   *—Cervantes*

3653   A mighty pain to love it is,
And 'tis a pain that pain to miss;
But of all pains, the greatest pain
It is to love, but love in vain.   *—Cowley*

3654 Love: A season's pass on the shuttle between heaven and hell.
　　　　　　　　　　　　　　　　　　　—Don Dickerman

3655 Love comes unseen; we only see it go.　　　*—Austin Dobson*

3656 We are shaped and fashioned by what we love.　　*—Goethe*

3657 Love he to-morrow, who loved never;
　　　To-morrow, who hath loved, persever.　　*—Greek epigram*

3658 Love's like a landscape which doth stand
　　　Smooth at a distance, rough at hand;
　　　Or like a fire which from afar
　　　Doth gently warm, consumes when near.　　　*—Hegge*

3659 You say to me-wards your affection's strong;
　　　Pray love me little, so you love me long.　　*—Robert Herrick*

3660 O! love! love! laddie.
　　　　Love's like a dizziness!
　　　It winna let a puir body
　　　　Gang about his business.　　　*—James Hogg*

3661 Dante is terrible, but he has disgusted nobody with Hades because
　　　he has placed in it all those who have loved.
　　　　　　　　　　　　　　　　　　—Arsène Houssaye

3662 Tell me whom you love, and I will tell you what you are.
　　　　　　　　　　　　　　　　　　—Arsène Houssaye

3663 Love, we say, is life; but love without hope and faith is agonizing
　　　death.　　　　　　　　　　*—Elbert Hubbard*

3664 The supreme happiness of life is the conviction of being loved for
　　　yourself, or, more correctly, being loved in spite of yourself.
　　　　　　　　　　　　　　　　　　　　—Victor Hugo

3665 Love is the most terrible, and also the most generous, of the pas-
　　　sions; it is the only one which includes in its dreams the happi-
　　　ness of someone else.　　　　　*—Alphonse Karr*

3666 Man, while he loves, is never quite depraved.　　*—Lamb*

3667 He give her a look that you could of poured on a waffle.
　　　　　　　　　　　　　　　　　　—Ring Lardner

3668 In their first passion women love their lovers, in all the others
　　　they love love.　　　　　*—La Rochefoucauld*

3669 There are few people who would not be ashamed of being loved
　　　when they love no longer.　　*—La Rochefoucauld*

3670 True love is like ghosts, which everybody talks about and few
　　　have seen.　　　　　　*—La Rochefoucauld*

3671   The pleasure of love is in loving. We are happier in the passion
       we feel than in that we inspire.   —*La Rochefoucauld*

3672   A woman often thinks she regrets the lover, when she only regrets
       the love.   —*La Rochefoucauld*

3673   The more one loves a mistress, the nearer one comes to hating her.
                                                   —*La Rochefoucauld*

3674   A man of sense may love like a madman, but never like a fool.
                                                   —*La Rochefoucauld*

3675   Love is the selfishness of two persons.   —*La Salle*

3676   Many men kill themselves for love, but many more women die
       of it.   —*Lemontey*

3677   Either take away, O Eros, all wish for love, or let me be loved!
       Take away all desire, or satisfy it.   —*Lucilius*

3678   Be quicker, and learn Love gives not away
       Pearls of price but to them with cash to pay.
                                                   —*Marcus Argentarius*

3679   Thou seest Dosicleia; she is very thin and sparse in beauty, but
       her ways are honest and pure. There would be no great matter
       between us; but when I hold her in my arms, I feel her heart
       near mine.   —*Marcus Argentarius*

3680   Galla will, and will not comply with my wishes; and I cannot
       tell, with her willing and not willing, what she wills.—*Martial*

3681   I do not know, Faustus, what it is that you write to so many
       girls. But this I know, that no girl writes anything to you.
                                                              —*Martial*

3682   Lais, most beauteous of women—whenever I ask you the price of
       your charms. you forthwith demand a great talent. I do not buy
       repentance, Lais, at so high a price.   —*Martial*

3683   Gemellus is seeking the hand of Maronilla, and is earnest, and
       lays siege to her, and makes presents to her. Is she then so
       pretty? No. Nothing can be more ugly. What then is the great
       object and attraction in her?—Her cough.   —*Martial*

3684   Lesbia protests that no one has ever obtained her favors without
       payment. That is true. When she wants a lover she pays.
                                                              —*Martial*

3685   No lover, Thais, you deny. But if you are not ashamed of that, at
       least be ashamed of this, Thais—of denying nothing.—*Martial*

3686   As I was constantly told that my mistress Polla indulged in im-
       proper connection with a young libertine, I surprised them and
       found it was as proper as my own.   —*Martial*

3687   Asper loves a maiden. She is handsome certainly, but he is blind. Evidently Asper loves better than he sees.   —*Martial*

3688   Galla, say "No!"—love is soon sated unless our pleasures are mixed with some pain, but do not continue, Galla, to say "No!" too long.   —*Martial*

3689   While in the dark on thy soft hand I hung,
And heard the tempting siren in thy tongue,
What flames, what darts, what anguish I endured!
But when the candles entered, I was cured.   —*Martial*

3690   Polla, why send me wreaths of blooms new-born?
I'd rather handle roses you had worn.   —*Martial*

3691   The tragedy of love is indifference.   —*Somerset Maugham*

3692   O Love that flew so lightly to my heart,
Why are thy wings so feeble to depart?   —*Meleager*

3693   Let the man who does not wish to be idle, fall in love.   —*Ovid*

3694   Scratch a lover, and find a foe.   —*Dorothy Parker*

3695   There are two sorts of affection—the love of a woman you respect, and the love for the woman you love.   —*Pinero*

3696   When affection only speaks,
Truth is not always there.   —*Thomas Middleton*

3697   Love is composed of so many sensations, that something new of it can always be said.   —*Saint Prosper*

3698   Love is like red-currant wine—at the first taste sweet, but afterwards shuddery.   —*T. W. Robertson*

3699   Love is a beggar who still begs when one has given him everything.   —*Rochepèdre*

3700   There are different kinds of love, but they have all the same aim: possession.   —*Roqueplan*

3701   Nothing is so embarrassing as the first *tête-à-tête,* when there is everything to say, unless it be the last, when everything has been said.   —*Roqueplan*

3702   In love, somehow, a man's heart is always either exceeding the speed limit, or getting parked in the wrong place.   —*Rowland*

3703   For repeating themselves, from the first kiss to the last sigh, the average man's love-affairs have History blushing with envy.   —*Rowland*

3704   I despise the ingenuous and I scorn the prude; the latter is too slow to give, the former gives too quickly.   —*Rufinus*

3705 If thou wingest thine arrows, Eros, at once upon two hearts, thou
      art a god; but not if thou piercest one only.   —*Rufinus*

3706 Suffering is the true cement of love.   —*Paul Sabatier*

3707 A fire in the bosom often results in ashes in the mouth.—*A. Sachs*

3708 Our ancient love! And now? All gone!
      Shreds of remembered fondness? None.
      Hate, abhorrence, scorn. Not one stray
      Sigh to tell a Ghost passed this way.   —*Sappho*

3709 You write: "I've forgotten." Cans't not forget—
      Dids't never know. Love is a plant that set
      In soil fit to receive it, requires Death
      To uproot it; the Spirit that lives yet.   —*Sappho*

3710 Love is like the moon; when it does not increase it decreases.
                                                          —*Segur*

3711 Love with old men is as the sun upon the snow, it dazzles more
      than it warms them.   —*J. P. Senn*

3712 Cupid is a knavish lad,
      Thus to make poor females mad.   —*Shakespeare*

3713 Love sought is good, but given unsought is better.—*Shakespeare*

3714 Men have died from time to time, and worms have eaten them,
      but not for love.   —*Shakespeare*

3715 Love is my sin, and thy dear virtue hate,
      Hate of my sin, grounded on sinful loving.   —*Shakespeare*

3716 Out upon it, I have loved
          Three whole days together;
      And am like to love three more,
          If it prove fair weather.   —*Suckling*

3717 Why so pale and wan, fond lover?
          Prithee, why so pale?
      Will, when looking well can't move her,
          Looking ill prevail?   —*Suckling*

3718 Inform me next what love will do
          Twill strangely make a one of two.   —*Suckling*

3719 And I would have, now love is over,
          An end to all, an end:
      I cannot, having been your lover,
          Stoop to become your friend!   —*Arthur Symons*

3720 To love and win is the best thing; to love and lose the next best.
                                                          —*Thackeray*

3721   There is no remedy for love but to love more.   —*Thoreau*

3722   In love, as in everything else, experience is a physician who never
       comes until after the disorder is cured.   —*De la Tour*

3723   A man loved by a beautiful woman will always get out of trouble.
                                                              —*Voltaire*

3724   Men never are consoled for their first love, nor women for their
       last.   —*Weiss*

3725   When the heart is a-fire, some sparks will fly out of the mouth.

3726   Rusticus wrote a letter to his love,
         And filled it full of warm and keen desire:
       He hoped to raise a flame, and so he did—
         The lady put his nonsense in the fire.

3727   Phyllis, you little, rosy rake!
         That heart of yours I long to rifle;
       Come, give it me—why should you make
         So much ado about a trifle.

3728   How happily extremes do meet in Jane and Ebenezer:
       She no longer sour, but sweet, and he a lemon squeezer.

3729   Love's of itself too sweet: the best of all
       Is, when Love's honey has a dash of gall.

3730   Love makes time pass, and time makes love pass.

3731   In Love's wars, he who flieth is conqueror.

3732   To couple is a custom,
         All things thereto agree:
       Why should not I then love,
         Since love to all is free?

3733   Nothing kills love like an overdose of it.

3734   The cat and the love you give away come back to you.

3735   The economics of emotions will not allow a man to remain in
       love for too long a time.

3736   He who tries to forget a woman has never loved her.

3737   Love, like the measles, attacks only the young.

3738   The man who is unselfish in love is a freak of instincts.

3739   Platonic love: the interval between events.

3740   Absence sharpens love, presence strengthens it.

3741· Love does not ennoble one for it generally rounds up one's actions to selfish purposes.

3742 There are few affairs of the heart upon which time will not cast a tinge of the absurd.

3743 With a savage, love is reduced to the strictly essential.

3744 Love levels all spirits; the expression of the most exalted feeling never rises above platitudes.

3745 To a woman in love, loving too much is not loving enough.

3746 Absence is the enemy of love.

3747 A woman who loves does not fear ridicule; a man in love knows no pride.

3748 In a woman in love, the hope of discovery is an intoxication; caution exists only in the woman who is indifferent emotionally.

3749 A man in love will take his chances; woman, in her anxiety, throws away hers.

3750 Woman never ceases loving a man until she finds another to replace him.

3751 Love is more tiring than friendship for it demands continuous proofs.

3752 There is too much said about the number of women Don Juan loved, and nothing about their quality; so much fuss about his morals, and none about his taste.

3753 When a woman has an affair of the heart, she goes into ecstasies; a man goes into details.

3754 Out of a love affair a man emerges bored to death; a woman completely exhausted.

3755 Love is an orgy of emotions.

3756 In their love, old men do not reflect the weariness of exhaustion, but rather the instinctive tenacity of despair.

3757 Absence makes the heart grow fonder.

3758 Love is the Fire of Life; it either consumes or purifies.

3759 Smiling then he took his dart,
And drew her picture in my heart.

3760   Love, you know, is a funny thing;
        But the funniest thing about it
        Is you never can tell if it is love
        Until you start to doubt it.

3761   Bachelors are the bootleggers of love.

3762   A woman who pretends to laugh at love is like a child who sings
        at night when he is afraid.

3763   My mistress I've lost it is true;
        But one comfort attends the disaster;
        That had she my mistress remain'd,
        I could not have call'd myself master.

SEE ALSO	RELATED SUBJECTS
Actors 50	Beauty
Aim 186	Courtship
Anger 248, 249	Desire
Clothes 880	Jealousy
Discretion 1633	Kiss
Forgetting 2308	Marriage
Pain 4303	Passion
	Romance
	Sex

LUCK

3771   The best you get is an even break.   *—F. P. A.*

3772   Watch out w'en you er gittin' all you want. Fattenin' hogs ain't
        in luck.   *—Joel Chandler Harris*

3773   Misfortune does not always wait on vice; nor is success the con-
        stant guest of virtue.   *—Havard*

3774   Little is the luck I've had,
        And oh, 'tis comfort small
        To think that many another lad
        Has had no luck at all.   *—Housman*

3775   so unlucky that he runs into accidents which started out to hap-
        pen to somebody else.   *—Don Marquis*

3776   The only sure thing about luck is that it will change.
        —Wilson Mizner

SEE ALSO	RELATED SUBJECTS
Marriage 3890	Chance
Perseverance 4394	Fate
	Fortune
	Gambling
	Opportunity

M

MAID

3781 Maidens, like moths, are ever caught by glare,
And Mammon wins his way where seraphs might despair. *–Byron*

3782 A young girl receives most not from art but from nature.
—Cillactor

3783 My Son, if a maiden deny thee and
    Scufflingly bid thee give o'er,
Yet lip meets with lip at the lastward,
    Get out! She has been there before. *—Kipling*

3784 Do you ask what sort of maid I desire or dislike, Flaccus? I dislike one too easy, and one too coy. The just mean, which lies between the two extremes, is what I approve; I like neither that which tortures, nor that which cloys. *—Martial*

3785 All are good maids, but whence come the bad wives?

3786 Glasses and lasses are brittle ware.

3787 Do as the maids do, say no, and take it.

3788 Maids want nothing but husbands, and when they have them, they want everything.

3789 When maidens sue, men live like gods.

3790 The modern girl may have her little weaknesses, but she isn't effeminate.

3791 Let mathematicians and geometricians
Talk of circles' and triangles' charms,
The figure I prize is a girl with bright eyes,
And the circle that's formed by her arms.

3792 What lass is for my money? Such a one
As all would buy, but vendible to none.

SEE ALSO
Eating 1790

RELATED SUBJECTS
Chastity   Virtue
Modesty   Women

MAN

3801 What is meant by a "knowledge of the world" is simply an acquaintance with the infirmities of men. *—Dickens*

3802 Man is not the creature of circumstances. Circumstances are the creatures of men. *—Disraeli*

3803 Man is a pliable animal, a being who gets accustomed to everything! —*Dostoyevsky*

3804 The fall of the first Adam was the end of the beginning; the rise
of the second Adam was the beginning of the end.
—*S. W. Duffield*

3805 Surely, if all the world was made for man, then man was made
for more than the world. —*Duplessis*

3806 A man is a god in ruins. —*Emerson*

3807 An institution is the lengthened shadow of one man.—*Emerson*

3808 All men in the abstract are just and good. —*Emerson*

3809 The cheapness of man is every day's tragedy. —*Emerson*

3810 Men are like wine; not good before the lees of clownishness be
settled. —*Feltham*

3811 Darwinian Man, though well-behaved,
At best is only a monkey shaved! —*W. S. Gilbert*

3812 Man is a reasoning rather than a reasonable animal.—*Hamilton*

3813 The body is the soul's poor house or home,
Whose ribs the laths are, and whose flesh the loam.
—*Robert Herrick*

3814 There are only two classes of men who live in history: those who
crowd a thing to its extreme limit, and those who then arise and
cry, "Hold!" —*Elbert Hubbard*

3815 Heaven loves man more than man doth love himself.—*Juvenal*

3816 There is no fact more observable in literature than how many
beautiful things have been said about man in the abstract, and
how few about men in particular. —*Mme. L'Estrange*

3817 Your legs and breast bristle with shaggy hair, but your mind,
Pannicus, shows no signs of manliness. —*Martial*

3818 All the power is with the sex that wears the beard. —*Molière*

3819 Every man carries within him the entire form of our human
condition. —*Montaigne*

3820 Since that which bears all things,
O man, bears thee,
Do thou bear and be borne
In thy degree.
But if thou chafe, nor art
From anger free,
Still that which bears all things,
O man, bears thee. —*Palladas*

3821   No man is so great as mankind.   *—Theodore Parker*

3822   Man is but a reed, the weakest in nature, but he is a thinking reed.
       —Pascal

3823   Know then thyself, presume not God to scan;
       The proper study of mankind is man.   *—Pope*

3824   God made man a little lower than the angels, and he has been
       getting a little lower ever since.   *—Will Rogers*

3825   Man at his birth is content with a little milk and a piece of
       flannel: so we begin, that presently find kingdoms not enough
       for us.   *—Seneca*

3826   He that hath a beard is more than a youth, and he that hath no
       beard is less than a man.   *—Shakespeare*

3827   God made him, and therefore let him pass for a man.
       —Shakespeare

3828   The more we study human nature, the less we think of men—
       the more of man.   *—Tilton*

3829   All that I care to know is that a man is a human being—that is
       enough for me; he can't be any worse.   *—Mark Twain*

3830   Adam and Eve had many advantages, but the principal one was,
       that they escaped teething.   *—Mark Twain*

3831   The fam'd *Essays on Man* in this agree,
       That so things are, and therefore so should be:
       The proof inverted would be stronger far;
       So they should be, and therefore so they are.
       —On Pope's Essays on Man

3832   Man, woman, and devil, are the three degrees of comparison.

3833   The real difference between men is not sanity and insanity, but
       more or less insanity.

3834   If man sprang from monkeys he ought to spring once more and
       make it a safe distance.

3835   God made Eve out of Adam's rib so that he might be able to
       shift half of the blame on him.

3836   The white man's real burden is a lot of other white men.

MARRIAGE

3841   If it were not for the Presents, an Elopement would be Preferable.   —*George Ade*

3842   Marriage is that relation between man and woman in which the independence is equal, the dependence mutual, and the obligation reciprocal.   —*L. K. Anspacher*

3843   It is always incomprehensible to a man that a woman should refuse an offer of marriage.   —*Austen*

3844   Women, deceived by men, want to marry them! It is a kind of revenge as good as any other.   —*Beaumanoir*

3845   *Marriage:* a community consisting of a master, a mistress, and two slaves, making in all, two.   —*Ambrose Bierce*

3846   A fool and knave, with different views,
　　　　　For Julia's hand apply;
　　　　The knave to mend his fortune sues,
　　　　　The fool to please his eye.
　　　　Ask you how Julia will behave?
　　　　　Depend on't for a rule,
　　　　If she's a fool she'll wed the knave,
　　　　　If she's a knave, the fool.   —*Samuel Bishop*

3847   One was never married, and that's his hell; another is, and that's his plague.   —*Burton*

3848   Marriage and hanging go by destiny; matches are made in heaven.
　　　　　　　　　　　　　　　　　　　　　　　　　　　　—*Burton*

3849   Talk six times with the same single lady
　　　　And you may get the wedding-dress ready.   —*Byron*

3850   No one, saith my lady, would she rather wed than myself, not even if Jupiter himself crave her. Thus she saith! But what a woman tells an ardent lover ought fitly to be graven on the breezes and in running waters.   —*Catullus*

3851   The only solid and lasting peace between a man and his wife is doubtless a separation.   —*Chesterfield*

3852   Thus grief still treads upon the heels of pleasure;
　　　　Married in haste, we may repent at leisure.   —*Congreve*

3853   Misses! the tale that I relate
　　　　This lesson seems to carry—
　　　　Choose not alone a proper mate,
　　　　But proper time to marry.   —*Cowper*

3854   Wedlock, indeed, hath oft compared been
       To public feasts, where meet a public rout—
       Where they that are without would fain go in,
       And they that are within would fain go out.   —*Sir John Davies*

3855   Being asked whether it was better to marry or not, he (Socrates)
       replied, "Whichever you do you will repent it."
                                                     —*Diogenes Laertius*

3856   Every woman should marry—and no man.   —*Disraeli*

3857   The chain of wedlock is so heavy that it takes two to carry it—
       sometimes three.   —*Dumas*

3858   Men marry to make an end; women to make a beginning.
                                                     —*A. Dupuy*

3859   Men do not know their wives well; but wives know their hus-
       bands perfectly.   —*Feuillet*

3860   Company makes cuckolds.   —*Thomas Fuller*

3861   In marriage, the greater cuckold of the two is the lover.
                                                     —*Paul Gauguin*

3862   Happiness untold awaits them
       When the parson consecrates them.   —*W. S. Gilbert*

3863   Fortune, talent, health—he had everything; but he was married.
                                                     —*C. G. Gleyre*

3864   Marriage is a ghastly public confession of a strictly private in-
       tention.   —*Ian Hay*

3865   For next to that interesting job,
       The hanging of Jack, or Bill, or Bob,
       There's nothing so draws a London mob
       As the noosing of very rich people.   —*Thomas Hood*

3866   A chap ort t' save a few o' the' long evenings he spends with his
       girl till after they're married.   —*Kin Hubbard*

3867   Marriage has many pains, but celibacy has few pleasures.
                                                     —*Johnson*

3868   Valour and courage to the young and strong,
       A crown of wisdom to grey hairs belong.
       Be of good cheer then; to thyself be true,
       Get thee a wife and get thee children too.
                                                     —*Julianus Aegyptius*

3869   If marriage is to be a success, one should obviously begin by
       marrying the right person.   —*Hermann Keyserling*

3870   You may write it on his tombstone,
      You may cut it on his card,
      That a young man married
      Is a young man marred.   *—Kipling*

3871   Pleasant the snaffle of Courtship, improving the manners and
      carriage,
      But the colt who is wise will abstain from the terrible thorn-bit
      of marriage.   *—Kipling*

3872   Since you are so well matched, and so much alike—a very bad
      wife, and a very bad husband—I wonder that you do not agree.
         —Martial

3873   Paula wants to marry me, but I don't want to marry Paula: she
      is so old. I might be willing if she were older.   *—Martial*

3874   Paula, you want to marry Priscus,
      I am not surprised: you are wise.
      Priscus does not want to marry you.
      He is wise too.   *—Martial*

3875   Fabius buries all his wives:
      Chrestilla ends her husbands' lives.
      The torch, which from the marriage-bed
      They brandish, soon attends the dead.
      O Venus, link this conquering pair!
      Their match will meet with issue fair,
      Whereby for such dangerous *two*
      A single funeral will do.   *—Martial*

3876   Marriage, if truth be told (of this be sure),
      An evil is—but one we must endure.   *—Menander*

3877   The days just prior to marriage are like a snappy introduction to
      a tedious book.   *—Wilson Mizner*

3878   Marriage may often be a stormy lake, but celibacy is almost
      always a muddy horse-pond.   *—T. L. Peacock*

3879   Let sinful bachelors their woes deplore,
      Full well they merit all they feel, and more.   *—Pope*

3880   There swims no goose so gray, but soon or late,
      She finds some honest gander for her mate.   *—Pope*

3881   At the age of sixty, to marry a beautiful girl of sixteen is to imi-
      tate those ignorant people who buy books to be read by their
      friends.   *—Ricard*

3882   The honeymoon is not actually over until we cease to stifle our
      sighs and begin to stifle our yawns.   *—Rowland*

3883   Marriage is a state of antagonistic cooperation.   —*Schlossberg*

3884   Marriage is popular because it combines the maximum of temptation with the maximum of opportunity.   —*G. B. Shaw*

3885   What God hath joined together no man shall ever put asunder:
God will take care of that.   —*G. B. Shaw*

3886   Some pray to marry the man they love,
My prayer will somewhat vary:
I humbly pray to Heaven above
That I love the man I marry.   —*Rose P. Stokes*

3887   This I set down as a positive truth. A woman with fair opportunities, and without an absolute hump, may marry whom she
likes.   —*Thackeray*

3888   Remember, it's as easy to marry a rich woman as a poor woman.
—*Thackeray*

3889   Nowadays all the married men live like bachelors, and all the
bachelors like married men.   —*Oscar Wilde*

3890   When a woman marries again, it is because she detested her first
husband. When a man marries again, it is because he adored
his first wife. Women try their luck; men risk theirs.
—*Oscar Wilde*

3891   When man and wife at odds fall out,
Let Syntax be your tutor;
'Twixt masculine and feminine,
What should one be but neuter?

3892   When Loveless married Lady Jenny,
Whose beauty was the ready-penny,
"I chose her," says he, "like old plate,
Not for the fashion, but the weight."

3893   Marino Falieri of the beautiful wife;
Others enjoy her, he maintains her.

3894   "Marriage, not mirage, Jane, here in your letter:
With your education, you surely know better."
Quickly spoke my young wife, while I sat in confusion,
"'Tis quite correct, Thomas: they're each an illusion."

3895   When Adam, waking, first his lids unfolds
In Eden's groves, beside him he beholds
Bone of his bone, flesh of his flesh, and knows
His earliest sleep has proved his last repose.

3896 "Figures can never lie?" They can.
Do one and one make two?
Not when marriage addeth them up
And getteth answer true.

3897 More belongs to marriage than four bare legs in a bed.

3898 "I wish," he said, "you could make pies
Like Mother used to bake."
"And I," said she, "wish that you made
The dough pa used to make!"

3899 In marriage the eye finds, the heart chooses, the hand binds, and
death looses.

3900 You cannot weld cake-dough to cast iron, nor a girl to an old
man.

3901 Women make marriage enduring; they do not seem to weary of
its commonplace.

3902 When a woman marries her equal she condescends.

3903 Marriage lasts if love does not end before inertia sets in.

3904 The legend that "matrimony" is a lottery has almost ruined the
lottery business.

3905 Women wish to marry their first love; men do not marry even
their last.

3906 Marriage seems a tie that binds until it proves a veritable Gor-
dian knot.

3907 People who marry tease Fate.

3908 Love is a tie that binds; matrimony straps them together.

3909 Love makes marriage possible; habit makes it endurable.

3910 The life of a married man may be full of excitement, never of
surprises.

3911 The bride goes to her marriage-bed, but knows not what shall
happen to her.

3912 Commend a wedded life, but keep thyself a bachelor.

3913 A good many things are easier said than done—including the
marriage ritual.

3914 My heart still hovering round about you,
I thought I could not live without you;
Now we've liv'd three months asunder,
How I liv'd with you is the wonder.

3915 Many a man in love with a dimple makes the mistake of marrying the whole girl.

3916 Marriage has many thorns, but celibacy no roses.

3917 It goes far toward reconciling me to being a woman, when I reflect that I am thus in no danger of marrying one.

SEE ALSO	RELATED SUBJECTS
Age 141	Courtship
Beauty 390	Family
Bed 407	Home
Grief 2685	Husband
Preachers 4615	Love
Theatre 5361	Widow
	Wife

MARTYR

3921 They stood before the altar and supplied
The fire themselves in which their fat was fried.
—*Ambrose Bierce*

3922 Who would die a martyr to sense in a country where the religion is folly? —*Congreve*

3923 I die for your poverty and my wealth. —*Fra Moriale*

3924 It is the cause, and not the death, that makes the martyr.
—*Napoleon*

3925 Some that will hold a creed unto martyrdom will not hold the truth against a sneering laugh. —*Austin O'Malley*

3926 It is interesting to realize that not all the people who have died for an absurd idea lived an absurd life.

3927 In nature there are no martyrs: there are simply the dead and the dying.

3928 It is pitiful that martyrdom fits women so well.

SEE ALSO	RELATED SUBJECTS	
Conviction 1034	Belief	Hero
Opinion 4238	Christianity	Sacrifice
	Courage	
	Faith	

MEDICINE

3931 Medicine, the only profession that labors incessantly to destroy the reason for its own existence. —*Lord Bryce*

3932 Nearly all men die of their remedies, and not of their illnesses.
—*Molière*

3933 The desire to take medicine is perhaps the greatest feature which distinguishes man from animals. —*Sir William Osler*

3934 If physic do not work, prepare for the kirk.

3935 I was well, would be better, took physic, and died.

SEE ALSO
Bed 409
Habit 2742

RELATED SUBJECTS
Doctors
Health
Sickness

MEMORY

3941 I sit besides my lonely fire
And pray for wisdom yet:
For calmness to remember
Or courage to forget. —*Aide*

3942 God gave us our memories so that we might have roses in December. —*J. M. Barrie*

3943 My memory is the thing I forget with —*A child's definition*

3944 How cruelly sweet are the echoes that start
When memory plays an old tune on the heart. —*Cook*

3945 A long memory an' a long tongue er reg'lar ole cronies. —*Kin Hubbard*

3946 Cold natures have only recollections; tender natures have remembrances. —*Mme. de Krüdener*

3947 The proper memory for a politician is one that knows what to remember and what to forget. —*John Morley*

3948 A great memory does not make a philosopher, any more than a dictionary can be called a grammar. —*Cardinal Newman*

3949 Those who cannot remember the past are condemned to repeat it. —*Santayana*

3950 The Right Honorable gentleman is indebted to his memory for his jests, and to his imagination for his facts. —*Sheridan*

3951 Memory is the diary that we all carry about with us. —*Oscar Wilde*

3952 Memory is the treasurer of the mind.

SEE ALSO
Credit 1204
Gratitude 2612
Grief 2683, 2699
Jokes 3211
Judgment 3229
Lies 3537

RELATED SUBJECTS
History
Monument

MERCY

3961 We hand folks over to God's mercy, and show none ourselves.
—*George Eliot*

3962 Being all fashioned of the self-same dust,
Let us be merciful as well as just.   —*Longfellow*

3963 Tigers have courage and the rugged bear,
But man alone can, whom he conquers spare.   —*Waller*

RELATED SUBJECTS
Forgiveness
Justice
Kindness
Pity

MIRROR

3971 The mirror reflects all objects without being sullied.—*Confucius*

3972 What I admire most in men—
To sit opposite a mirror at dinner and not look in it.
—*Richard Harding Davis*

3973 There was never yet fair woman but she made mouths in a glass.
—*Shakespeare*

3974 Your looking-glass will tell you what none of your friends will.

3975 I change, and so do women too;
But I reflect, which women never do.

3976 There are gods in the mirror.

3977 A blind man will not thank you for a looking-glass.

SEE ALSO   RELATED SUBJECTS
Beauty 354   Conceit
Credit 1209   Vanity
Hardship 2796
Theatre 5364
Truth 5553

MISANTHROPE

3981 When the devil grows old he turns hermit.   —*Ariosto*

3982 To fly from, need not be to hate mankind.   —*Byron*

3983 The peculiarity of the New England hermit has not been his
desire to get near to God, but his anxiety to get away from
man.   —*H. W. Mabie*

3984 A hermit is a deserter from the army of humanity. —*Southgate*

3985 A misanthrope I can understand—a womanthrope never.
—Oscar Wilde

RELATED SUBJECTS
Cynicism
Selfishness

MISTAKES

3991 And one by one in turn, some grand mistake,
Casts off its bright skin yearly like the snake. *—Byron*

3992 There is a glory
In a great mistake. *—Nathalia Crane*

3993 The individual is always mistaken. *—Emerson*

3994 The greatest mistake you can make in this life is to be continually
fearing you will make one. *—Elbert Hubbard*

3995 Woman was God's *second* mistake. *—Nietzsche*

3996 The only man who never makes a mistake is the man who never
does anything. *—Theodore Roosevelt*

3997 The only things one never regrets are one's mistakes.
—Oscar Wilde

3998 Wise men learn by other men's mistakes, fools by their own.

3999 By ignorance we mistake, and by mistakes we learn.

SEE ALSO   RELATED SUBJECTS
Crime 1225   Error
Experience 2018   Illusion
Opinion 4221   Understanding
Optimism 4287

MODESTY

4001 Modesty is the conscience of the body. *—Balzac*

4002 It is only the first obstacle which counts to conquer modesty.
—Bossuet

4003 A lady is one who never shows her underwear unintentionally.
—Lillian Day

4004 I have done one braver thing
Than all the Worthies did;
And yet a braver thence doth spring,
Which is, to keep that hid. *—John Donne*

4005 The peculiarity of prudery is to multiply sentinels, in proportion
as the fortress is less threatened. *—Victor Hugo*

4006 Modesty in woman is a virtue most deserving, since we do all we
can to cure her of it. *—Lingrée*

4007   To read my book, the virgin shy
        May blush, while Brutus standeth by:
        But when he's gone, read through what's writ,
        And never stain a cheek for it.   —*Martial*

4008   If any one remains modest under blame, be assured he is so.
                                                           —*J. P. Richter*

4009   Prudery is a kind of avarice, the worst of all.   —*Stendhal*

4010   The statue that advertises its modesty with a fig leaf really brings
        its modesty under suspicion.   —*Mark Twain*

4011   As demure as an old whore at a christening.

4012   He that has no modesty has all the town for his own.

4013   He that refuseth praise the first time does it because he would
        have it the second.

4014   A blush is modesty's first impulse and sophistication's afterthought.

SEE ALSO   RELATED SUBJECTS
Vanity 5631   Blushing
                       Chastity
                       Conceit
                       Humility
                       Virtue

MONEY

4021   What this country needs is a good five cent nickel.   —*F. P. A.*

4022   A money-lender. He serves you in the present tense; he lends you
        in the conditional mood; keeps you in the subjunctive; and
        ruins you in the future.   —*Addison*

4023   Money is like manure, of very little use except it be spread.
                                                           —*Bacon*

4024   To a shower of gold most things are penetrable.   —*Carlyle*

4025   The use of money is all the advantage there is in having it.
                                                           —*Franklin*

4026   He that makes money before he gets wit,
        Will be but a short while the master of it.   —*Thomas Fuller*

4027   A penny will hide the biggest star in the universe if you hold it
        close enough to your eye.   —*Samuel Grafton*

4028   The darkest hour in any man's life is when he sits down to plan
        how to get money without earning it.   —*Horace Greeley*

4029   In order to make money the first thing is to have no need of it.
                                                           —*Ludovic Halévy*

4030 There'll be no pockets in your shroud. —*James J. Hill*

4031 Put not your trust in money, but put your money in trust.
—*O. W. Holmes*

4032 Money is a handmaiden if thou knowest how to use it; a mistress if thou knowest not. —*Horace*

4033· Money and time are the heaviest burdens of life, and the unhappiest of all mortals are those who have more of either than they know how to use. —*Johnson*

4034 That for which all virtue now is sold,
And almost every vice—almighty gold. —*Jonson*

4035 The plainest print cannot be read through a gold eagle.—*Lincoln*

4036 A man left gold; another took it; left a noose,
So the first hanged himself; having but life to lose. —*Plato*

4037 Oh, what a world of vile ill-favored faults looks handsome in three hundred pounds a year! —*Shakespeare*

4038 Let all the learned say what they can,
'Tis ready money makes the man. —*William Somerville*

4039 No man will take counsel, but every man will take money. Therefore, money is better than counsel. —*Swift*

4040 But the jingling of the guinea helps the hurt that Honor feels.
—*Tennyson*

4041 Broadway is a place where people spend money they haven't earned to buy things they don't need to impress people they don't like. —*Walter Winchell*

4042 If breath were made for every man to buy,
The poor man could not live, rich would not die.
—*Sir Henry Wotton*

4043 You can't take it with you.

4044 Though confidence is very fine,
And makes the future sunny;
I want no confidence for mine,
I'd rather have the money.

4045 Mud with a little gold in it is often more highly prized than gold with a little mud on it.

4046 Money talks; little of it palavers.

4047 Money polishes the poor, but with a very dull finish.

4048   If money is at the root of all evil, it is also at the root of all morality.

4049   When money talks it registers a lively conversation.

4050   Gold goes in at any gate except heaven's.

4051   Why "golden," when that age alone, we're told,
Was blessed with happy ignorance of gold?
More justly we our venal times might call
"The golden age," for gold is all in all.

4052   Some people think they are worth a lot of money because they have it.

4053   There has been much argument in recent years about a fitting motto for the coin of the realm. We suggest "Abide With Me."

4054   Money may talk, but have you ever noticed how hard of hearing it is when you call it?

4055   Money, in the opinion of the world, makes a man wise and virtuous; the want of it, foolish and wicked.

4056   Money and man a mutual friendship show;
Man makes false money, money makes man so.

4057   Your Bible, madam, teems with wealth;
    Within the leaves it floats.
Delightful is the sacred text,
    But heavenly the notes.
                    —*On a lady who kept her bank-notes in a Bible*

See Also	Related Subjects
Patriotism 4336	Business
Politics 4508	Credit
Virtue 5697	Wealth
Youth 6213	

MONUMENT

4061   Th' dead ar-re always pop'lar. I knowed a society wanst to vote a monyment to a man an' refuse to help his fam'ly, all in wan night.   —*F. P. Dunne*

4062   In lapidary inscriptions a man is not upon oath.   —*Johnson*

4063   See nations slowly wise, and meanly just,
To buried merit raise the tardy bust.   —*Johnson*

4064 Cato said, "I had rather men should ask why my statue is not set
      up, than why it is."   —*Plutarch*

SEE ALSO   RELATED SUBJECTS
Criticism 1257   Epitaphs
Peace 4354   Fame
                         Memory

MORALITY

4071 "Tut, tut, child!" said the Duchess.
      "Everything's got a moral, if you only can find it.   —*Carroll*

4072 If good men were only better,
      Would the wicked be so bad?   —*J. W. Chadwick*

4073 Every man is to be had one way or another, and every woman
      almost any way.   —*Chesterfield*

4074 From the point of view of morals, life seems to be divided into
      two periods; in the first we indulge, in the second we preach.
                                                   —*Will Durant*

4075 Moral qualities rule the world, but at short distances the senses
      are despotic.   —*Emerson*

4076 A man's acts are usually right, but his reasons seldom are.
                                                   —*Elbert Hubbard*

4077 This story is slightly immoral, but so, I guess, are all stories based
      on truth.   —*Ring Lardner*

4078 Understanding the rainbow is physics, but delight at the rainbow
      is morality!   —*Lin Yutang*

4079 The Puritan hated bear-baiting, not because it gave pain to the
      bear, but because it gave pleasure to the spectators.
                                                   —*Macaulay*

4080 To him in whose eyes no one is bad, who can appear good?
                                                   —*Martial*

4081 All the dissolute rascals invite you to dinner, Phoebus. He whom
      impurity feeds is not, I opine, a spotless person.   —*Martial*

4082 A straight line is shortest in morals as well as in geometry.
                                                   —*Rachel*

4083 An Englishman thinks he is moral when he is only comfortable.
                                                   —*G. B. Shaw*

4084 The more things a man is ashamed of, the more respectable he is.
                                                   —*G. B. Shaw*

4085 Better keep yourself clean and bright: you are the window
through which you must see the world.   —*G. B. Shaw*

4086 Every generation needs regeneration.   —*C. H. Spurgeon*

4087 The Puritan through Life's sweet garden goes
To pluck the thorn and cast away the rose.

4088 Morality curtails the chance to entertain.

4089 Morality is based on a consideration of circumstances—not principles.

4090 There is no woman who couldn't be cajoled into the belief that
she has a perfect right to be immoral if she wants to be.

4091 No man is better than his morals nor worse than his principles.

4092 Morals make characters, not personalities.

4093 Morality is nothing but a struggle for safety.

4094 Morals are set up by men who hate or women who envy.

4095 Conventions are the *valet de chambre* of morality.

SEE ALSO	RELATED SUBJECTS
Beauty 378	Censorship
Example 1962	Crime
Honor 2945	Decency
Pity 4444	Good
Rank 4769	Sin
Taste 5272	Vice
	Virtue
	Wickedness

MOTHER

4101 Where yet was ever found a mother
Who'd give her booby for another?   —*John Gay*

4102 Simply having children does not make mothers.   —*A. Shedd*

4103 The mother knows best whether the child be like the father.

SEE ALSO	RELATED SUBJECTS
Courtship 1175	Children
France 2347	Family
Tongue 5463	Father

MUSIC

4111 Life has its music; let us seek a way
Not to jangle the chords whereon we play.
—*Archilochus of Paros*

4112   Music washes away from the soul the dust of every-day life.
                                                             —*Auerbach*

4113   In my opinion, the great object of music is to touch the heart, and
         this end can never be obtained by mere noise, drumming and
         arpeggios. At all events not by me.
                                         —*Karl Philipp Emanuel Bach*

4114   Swans sing before they die; 'twere no bad thing
         Should certain persons die before they sing.   —*Coleridge*

4115   And music pours on mortals
         Her magnificent disdain.   —*Emerson*

4116   Music is the only language in which you cannot say a mean or
         sarcastic thing.   —*John Erskine*

4117   Music expresses that which cannot be said and on which it is
         impossible to be silent.   —*Victor Hugo*

4118   A squeak's heard in the orchestra,
         The leader draws across
         The intestines of the agile cat
         The tail of the noble hoss.   —*Lanigan*

4119   Music is the universal language of mankind.   —*Longfellow*

4120   The fantasies of music are governed by art, mine by chance.
                                                             —*Montaigne*

4121   Piano playing is more difficult than statesmanship. It is harder to
         awake emotions in ivory keys than it is in human beings.
                                                             —*Paderewski*

4122   Music that gentler on the spirit lies
         Than tired eyelids upon tired eyes.   —*Tennyson*

4123   Opera: the graveyard of melody.

4124   Millions of dollars are spent on the opera which could be used in
         abolishing it.

SEE ALSO   RELATED SUBJECTS
Architecture 263   Art
Trifles 5507   Beauty

N

NATURE

4131   In nature things move violently to their place, and calmly in their
         place.   —*Bacon*

4132   Nature is the art of God.   —*Sir Thomas Browne*

4133   I shall not ask Jean Jacques Rousseau
       If birds confabulate or no.   —*Cowper*

4134   We talk of our mastery of nature, which sounds very grand; but
       the fact is we respectfully adapt ourselves, first, to her ways.
                                                             —*Clarence Day*

4135   Frost is the greatest artist in our clime—
       He paints in nature and describes in rime.   —*Thomas Hood*

4136   The birds, God's poor who cannot wait.   —*Longfellow*

4137   All are but parts of one stupendous whole,
       Whose body Nature is, and God the soul.   —*Pope*

4138   All Nature is but Art, unknown to thee;
       All Chance, Direction, which thou canst not see.   —*Pope*

4139   A stern discipline pervades all nature, which is a little cruel that
       it may be very kind.   —*Herbert Spencer*

4140   There's no time for a man to recover his hair that grows bald by
       nature.   —*Shakespeare*

4141   So, naturalists observe, a flea
       Hath smaller fleas that on him prey;
       And these have smaller still to bite 'em;
       And so proceed *ad infinitum*.   —*Swift*

4142   Few folk hae seen oftener than me Natur gettin' up i' the morn-
       ing . . . Never see ye her hair in papers.   —*John Wilson*

4143   The course of Nature is the art of God.   —*Young*

4144   In nature there are no rights; there are only duties.

4145   The poet and ornithologist
       Differ in ways absurd.
       One writes—"The bird is on the wing;"
       The other answers—"No such thing! The wing is on the bird."

4146   Never look for birds of this year in the nests of the last.

SEE ALSO   RELATED SUBJECTS
Art 274, 281, 306, 311   Beauty
Death 1341, 1364   God
Fools 2286   Tree
Maid 3782
Virtue 5692
Women 5970

NECESSITY

4151   Necessity makes an honest man a knave.   —*Defoe*

4152 Make yourself necessary to somebody. —*Emerson*

4153 Necessity never made a good bargain. —*Franklin*

4154 Necessity may render a doubtful act innocent, but it cannot make it praiseworthy. —*Joubert*

4155 Necessity is the argument of tyrants; it is the creed of slaves. —*Pitt*

4156 A wise man never refuses anything to necessity.—*Publilius Syrus*

4157 Where necessity pinches, boldness is prudence.

SEE ALSO	RELATED SUBJECTS
Excess 1980	Fate
Friend 2426	Poverty
Virtue 5665	Wealth

NEIGHBOR

4161 For many reasons 'tis unwisely said
To know thyself; more profitable it is
To know thy neighbors! —*Menander*

4162 A happy creature is your snail indeed!
Just where he pleases he can live and feed.
And if a neighbor gives him any bother,
With house on back he moves off to another. —*Philemon*

4163 Good neighbours and true friends are two things.

4164 Love your neighbor, yet pull not down your hedge.

4165 We can live without our friends, but not without our neighbours.

SEE ALSO	RELATED SUBJECT
France 2348	Friend
Lawyers 3421	
Peace 4353, 4357	
Selfishness 4996	

NEWS

4171 Journalism is organized gossip. —*Edward Eggleston*

4172 Do not read newspapers column by column; remember they·are made for everybody, and don't try to get what isn't meant for you. —*Emerson*

4173 Tilford Moots wuz over t' th' Henryville poor farm th' other day t' see an ole friend o' his thet used t' publish a newspaper thet pleased ever'buddy. —*Kin Hubbard*

4174 The most truthful part of a newspaper is the advertisements. —*Jefferson*

4175 Newspapers always excite curiosity. No one ever lays one down
      without a feeling of disappointment.   —*Lamb*

4176 In the case of news, we should always wait for the sacrament
      of confirmation.   —*Voltaire*

4177 The word explains itself, without the muse,
      And the four letters speak from whence comes *news*.
      From North, East, West, South, the solution's made,
      Each quarter gives accounts of war and trade.

SEE ALSO   RELATED SUBJECTS
Wife 5868   Curiosity
                            Gossip

NOISE

4181 He who sleeps in continual noise is wakened by silence.
                                                  —*W. D. Howells*

4182 People who make no noise are dangerous.   —*La Fontaine*

4183 If you love not the noise of the bells, why pull the ropes?

SEE ALSO   RELATED SUBJECT
Virtue 5666   Listening

NONSENSE

4191 For daring nonsense seldom fails to hit,
      Like scattered shot, and pass with some for wit.—*Samuel Butler*

4192 No one is exempt from talking nonsense; the misfortune is to do
      it solemnly.   —*Montaigne*

4193 A little nonsense now and then
      Is relished by the wisest men.

                            RELATED SUBJECTS
                            Fools
                            Laughter

O

OATH

4201 It is not the oath that makes us believe the man, but the man the
      oath.   —*Aeschylus*

4202 Oaths are the fossils of piety.   —*Santayana*

4203 The vow that binds too strictly snaps itself.   —*Tennyson*

4204 Better break your word than do worse in keeping it.

See Also   Related Subjects
Character 705   Honor
Dictators 1589   Lies
Monument 4062

OBSTINACY

4211 Obstinacy in a bad cause is but constancy in a good.
—*Thomas Browne*

4212 An obstinate man does not hold opinions, but they hold him.
—*Samuel Butler*

4213 A narrow mind begets obstinacy; we do not easily believe what
we cannot see.   —*Dryden*

4214 There is no bigotry like that of "free thought" run to seed.
—*Horace Greeley*

4215 None so blind as those that will not see.   —*Matthew Henry*

4216 The mind of the bigot is like the pupil of the eye; the more light
you pour upon it, the more it will contract. —*O. W. Holmes*

4217 Arrogance is the obstruction of wisdom.

Related Subjects
Opinion
Prejudice
Perseverance

OPINION

4221 *To be positive:* to be mistaken at the top of one's voice.
—*Ambrose Bierce*

4222 Opinion governs all mankind,
Like the blind's leading of the blind.   —*Samuel Butler*

4223 He that complies against his will
Is of his own opinion still.   —*Samuel Butler*

4224 Whoso would be a man must be a non-conformist. —*Emerson*

4225 As our inclinations, so our opinions.   —*Goethe*

4226 Any stigma will do to beat a dogma.   —*Philip Guedalla*

4227 None so deaf as those that will not hear.   —*Matthew Henry*

4228 Dogmatism is puppyism come to its full growth.—*Douglas Jerrold*

4229 A bigot is a person who, under an atheist king, would be an
atheist.   —*La Bruyère*

4230   Opinions is a species of property
      I am always desirous of sharing.   —*Lamb*

4231   We hardly find any persons of good sense save those who agree
      with us.   —*La Rochefoucauld*

4232   Opinion! which on crutches walks,
      And sounds the words another talks.   —*Lloyd*

4233   The foolish and the dead alone never change their opinion.
                                                      —*Lowell*

4234   I value little my own opinions, but I value just as little those of
      others.   —*Montaigne*

4235   Some praise at morning what they blame at night,
      But always think the last opinion right.   —*Pope*

4236   The difference is as great between
      The optics seeing as the objects seen.   —*Pope*

4237   No errors of opinion can possibly be dangerous in a country where
      opinion is left free to grapple with them.   —*Simms*

4238   A bigot delights in public ridicule, for he begins to think he is a
      martyr.   —*Sydney Smith*

4239   It is difference of opinion that makes horse races.—*Mark Twain*

4240   Contradiction: stubbornness versus stupidity.

4241   Public opinion is the greatest force for good, when it happens to
      be on that side.

4242   After all, public opinion is just what people think other people
      are thinking.

4243   We ask for information, but are interested mostly in what con-
      firms our opinions.

4244   The weakness of public opinion is that so many people express
      it only privately.

4245   A man is oftener raised in the estimation of his fellow-men by
      opposition, than lowered in their esteem.

4246   People's minds are changed through their pockets.

SEE ALSO	RELATED SUBJECTS
Conscience 965	Belief
Error 1935, 1942	Criticism
Genius 2480	Prejudice
Law 3392	Judgment
	Obstinacy

OPPORTUNITY

4251 If you trap the moment before it's ripe,
The tears of repentance you'll certainly wipe;
But if once you let the ripe moment go,
You can never wipe off the tears of woe.   *—Blake*

4252 Not only strike while the iron is hot, but make it hot by striking.
—Cromwell

4253 The secret of success in life is for a man to be ready for his opportunity when it comes.   *—Disraeli*

4254 Seek not for fresher founts afar,
Just drop your bucket where you are.   *—S. W. Foss*

4255 Even a wolf will not stay
Where sounds no bleat to offer hope of prey.   *—Greek epigram*

4256 He knocked at each one
Of the doorways of life, and abode in none.   *—Lucile*

4257 The man who waits for things to turn up has his eyes fixed on his toes.   *—Creswell MacLaughlin*

4258 A pessimist is one who makes difficulties of his opportunities; an optimist is one who makes opportunities of his difficulties.
—Vice-Admiral Mansell, R. N.

4259 On the fall of an oak, every man gathers wood.   *—Menander*

4260 I have known many who could not when they would, for they had not done it when they could.   *—Rabeiais*

4261 God's best gift to us is not things, but opportunities.
—Alice W. Rollins

4262 Never refuse a good offer.

4263 Opportunities always look bigger going than coming.

SEE ALSO	RELATED SUBJECTS
Honesty 2928	Chance
Marriage 3884	Fortune
Remorse 4838	Luck
Tree 5493	
Virtue 5707	

OPTIMISM

4271 The best is yet to be,
The last of life, for which the first was made.   *—Browning*

4272   I hold not with the pessimist that all things are ill, nor with the optimist that all things are well. All things are not well, but all things shall be well, because this is God's ,vorld.
                                                                —*Browning*

4273   This the best day the world has ever seen. Tomorrow will be better.   —*R. A. Campbell*

4274   Be sure to live on the sunny side, and even then do not expect the world to look bright, if you habitually wear gray-brown glasses.   —*Charles H. Eliot*

4275   The place where optimism most flourishes is the lunatic asylum.
                                                            —*Havelock Ellis*

4276   So of cheerfulness, or a good temper, the more it is spent, the more of it remains.   —*Emerson*

4277   An ounce of cheerfulness is worth a pound of sadness to serve God with.   —*Thomas Fuller*

4278   A widespreading, hopeful disposition is the best umbrella for this vale of tears.   —*W. D. Howells*

4279   Optimism is a kind of heart stimulant—the digitalis of failure.
                                                            —*Elbert Hubbard*

4280   It is worth a thousand pounds a year to have the habit of looking on the bright side of things.   —*Johnson*

4281   Keep your face to the sunshine and you cannot see the shadow.
                                                            —*Helen Keller*

4282   Optimism is the madness of maintaining that everything is right when it is wrong.   —*Voltaire*

4283   'Twixt optimist and pessimist
       The difference is droll:
       The optimist sees the doughnut,
       The pessimist, the hole.   —*McLandburgh Wilson*

4284   If it wasn't for the optimist the pessimist would never know how happy he isn't.

4285   To become an optimist close one eye and believe with the other.

4286   Optimist: one who is satisfied with little here below and generally gets below that little.

4287   An optimist may be wrong, but he bears mistakes with fortitude.

SEE ALSO   RELATED SUBJECTS
Opportunity 4258   Courage   Hope
                           Faith   Pessimism

ORIGINALITY

4291 An original something, dear maid, you would wish me
To write; but how shall I begin?
For I'm sure I have nothing original in me,
Excepting Original Sin. —*Thomas Campbell*

4292 Originality is simply a pair of fresh eyes. —*T. W. Higginson*

4293 Originality is undetected plagiarism. —*Dean Inge*

4294 Though old the thought and oft exprest,
'Tis his at last who says it best. —*Lowell*

4295 Originality is the one thing which unoriginal minds cannot feel
the use of. —*J. S. Mill*

RELATED SUBJECTS
Imagination
Wit

P

PAIN

4301 Those who do not feel pain seldom think that it is felt.—*Johnson*

4302 Nothing begins, and nothing ends,
That is not paid with moan;
For we are born in other's pain,
And perish in our own. —*Thompson*

4303 But, soon or late, the fact grows plain
To all through sorrow's test:
The only folks who give us pain
Are those we love the best. —*E. W. Wilcox*

4304 There are wounds from which it is a pity to recover.

4305 If madness were pain, you'd hear outcries in every house.

SEE ALSO
Experience 2014
Ideas 3061
Love 3653
Patience 4321
Philosophy 4437
Pleasure 4451, 4471, 4473

RELATED SUBJECTS
Bed
Doctors
Grief
Sickness

PASSION

4311 To lepers and to outcasts thou dost show
That passion is the paradise below. —*Baudelaire*

4312   Absence diminishes little passions and increases great ones, just as
        the wind blows out a candle and fans a fire.

        —*La Rochefoucauld*

4313   The passionate are like men standing on their heads; they see all
        things the wrong way.   —*Plato*

4314   The mind by passion driven from its firm hold, becomes a feather
        to each wind that blows.   —*Shakespeare*

4315   Our passions are like convulsion fits, which, though they make us
        stronger for the time, leave us the weaker ever after.   —*Swift*

4316   She parried time's malicious dart,
              And kept the years at bay,
        Till passion entered in her heart
              And aged her in a day!   —*E. W. Wilcox*

4317   There is no virtue in the purity that waits until the fires of
        passion are burned out.

4318   It is the weak who can control their passions—they have such
        weak passions.

SEE ALSO   RELATED SUBJECTS
Coquetry 1065   Anger
Fidelity 2201   Desire
                            Hate
                            Kiss
                            Love
                            Revenge

PATIENCE

4321   He preacheth patience that never knew pain.   —*Bohn*

4322   It is easy finding reasons why other folks should be patient.

        —*George Eliot*

4323   The two powers which in my opinion constitute a wise man are
        those of bearing and forbearing.   —*Epictetus*

4324   Patience is bitter, but its fruit is sweet.   —*Rousseau*

4325   How poor are they who have not patience! What wound did ever
        heal but by degrees.   —*Shakespeare*

4326   A man is as big as the things that annoy him.

SEE ALSO   RELATED SUBJECTS
Genius 2473   Haste
Hope 2962   Philosophy
Philosophy 4437   Resignation
                            Worry

PATRIOTISM

4331 Love of country is like love of woman—he loves her best who seeks to bestow on her the highest good. —*Felix Adler*

4332 Patriotism is a lively sense of collective responsibility. Nationalism is a silly cock crowing on its own dunghill. —*Aldington*

4333 It is not I who have lost the Athenians, but the Athenians who have lost me. —*Anaxagoras*

4334 A wise man's country is the world. —*Aristippus*

4335 He who loves not his country can love nothing. —*Byron*

4336 "The American nation in the Sixth Ward is a fine people," he says, "They love th' eagle," he says, "on the back iv a dollar." —*F. P. Dunne*

4337 I once heard an Irishman say, "Every man loves his native land whether he was born there or not." —*Thomas Fitch*

4338 My country is the world; my countrymen are mankind. —*William Lloyd Garrison*

4339 I don't set up for being a cosmopolite, which to my mind signifies being polite to every country except your own. —*Thomas Hood*

4340 Patriotism is the last refuge of a scoundrel. —*Johnson*

4341 Saving their land that fettered lay and sad,
Themselves in dust of darkness these men clad:
Seeing the praise they won for valour high,
For his dear land a man may dare to die. —*Masalcas*

4342 Patriotism is a kind of religion; it is the egg from which wars are hatched. —*Guy de Maupassant*

4343 Patriotism is the willingness to kill and be killed for trivial reasons. —*Bertrand Russell*

4344 Men love their country, not because it is great, but because it is their own. —*Seneca*

4345 The proper means of increasing the love we bear to our native country is to reside some time in a foreign one. —*William Shenstone*

4346 Stranger, bear this message to the Spartans, that we lie here obedient to their laws. —*Simonides, on the dead at Thermopylae*

4347   If noble death be virtue's chiefest part,
       We above all men are by Fortune blest.
       Striving with freedom's crown to honor Greece,
       We died, and here in endless glory rest.   —*Simonides*

SEE ALSO   RELATED SUBJECTS
Ancestors 222   America
Business 577   Duty
                             Oath

PEACE

4351   Nothing can bring you peace but the triumph of principles.
                                                              —*Emerson*

4352   When your foes die, let all resentment cease;
       Make peace with death, and death shall give you peace!
                                                              —*Greek epigram*

4353   Man's greatest blunder has been in trying to make peace with the
       skies instead of making peace with his neighbors.
                                                              —*Elbert Hubbard*

4354   "Peace has its victories no less than war," but it doesn't have as
       many monuments t' unveil.   —*Kin Hubbard*

4355   They make a desolation and they call it peace.   —*Tacitus*

4356   It is madness for a sheep to treat of peace with a wolf.

4357   Nobody can live longer in peace than his neighbour pleases.

4358   He that makes a good war makes a good peace.

4359   A deceitful peace is more hurtful than open war.

4360   No doubt peace hath its victories, but what the world needs is a
       victory that hath its peace.

4361   The trouble with peace propaganda is that when it's permitted it
       isn't necessary, and when it's necessary it isn't permitted.

4362   Hard to dislike a chap who likes you, isn't it? Well, there's your
       peace plan.

4363   Peace is in danger of becoming a mere skeleton in armor.

4364   The world craves peace that passeth all misunderstanding.

4365   To be enduring, a peace must be endurable.

SEE ALSO   RELATED SUBJECTS
Compromise 927   Content
Kings 3295   Dictators
Marriage 3851   Power
                             War

PEN

4371 Beneath the rule of men entirely great,
The pen is sometimes mightier than the sword.—*Bulwer-Lytton*

4372 Pen and ink is wit's plough. —*John Clarke*

4373 Many wearing rapiers are afraid of goose-quills. —*Shakespeare*

4374 Pens are most dangerous tools, more sharp by odds
Than swords, and cut more keen than whips or rods.
—*John Taylor*

4375 There's no wound deeper than a pen can give,
It makes men living dead, and dead men live. —*John Taylor*

RELATED SUBJECTS
Books
Literature
Writers

PEOPLE

4381 The multitude is always in the wrong. —*Wentworth Dillon*

4382 Whatever you may be sure of, be sure of this, that you are dreadfully like other people. —*Lowell*

4383 People are more fun than anybody. —*Dorothy Parker*

4384 I am a member of the rabble in good standing.
—*Westbrook Pegler*

4385 I've been mixing with humanity today and feel the less humane in consequence. —*Seneca*

4386 Once in a golden hour
I cast to earth a seed.
Up there came a flower,
The people said, a weed. —*Tennyson*

4387 The only real people are the people who never existed.
—*Oscar Wilde*

4388 "The voice of the people" is very much in need of a megaphone.

4389 A psychologist objects to what he calls "herd thinking," but what a majority of people think is always what they've heard.

4390 The public mind is educated quickly by *events*—slowly by *arguments*.

SEE ALSO
Deception 1436, 1443
Fame 2111

RELATED SUBJECTS
Democracy
Government
Man

PERSEVERANCE

4391 Consider the postage stamp, my son. It secures success through its abilit῁ to stick to one thing till it gets there.
—*Josh Billings*

4392 We make way for the man who boldly pushes past us.
—*C. N. Bovée*

4393 A man in earnest finds means, or if he cannot find, creates them.
—*Channing*

4394 Diligence is the mother of good luck.   —*Franklin*

4395 The best way out is always through.   —*Robert Frost*

4396 Not to go back is somewhat to advance.   —*Horace*

4397 The rung of a ladder was never meant to rest upon, but only to hold a man's foot long enough to enable him to put the other somewhat higher.   —*T. H. Huxley*

4398 When firmness is sufficient, rashness is unnecessary.   —*Napoleon*

4399 Stay awhile to make an end the sooner.   —*Paulet*

4400 'Tis known by the name of perseverance in a good cause—and of obstinacy in a bad one.
—*Sterne*

4401 Persistency is a fool's best asset.

4402 The difference between perseverance and obstinacy is that one comes from a strong will and the other from a strong won't.

4403 I will find a way or make one.

SEE ALSO   RELATED SUBJECTS
Fish 2232   Obstinacy
Genius 2471   Work
Love 3657

PERSUASION

4411 Man is a creature of a wilful head,
and hardly driven is, but eas'ly led.   —*Samuel Daniel*

4412 Few are open to conviction, but the majority of men are open to persuasion.   —*Goethe*

4413 If you would win a man to your cause, first convince him that you are his sincere friend.   —*Lincoln*

4414 You have not converted a man because you have silenced him.
—*John Morley*

4415 Conversion is not implanting eyes, for they exist already; but giving them a right direction, which they have not.   —*Plato*

4416 Consideration is half conversion.

RELATED SUBJECTS
Advice
Quarrels
Teaching

PESSIMISM

4421 Pessimism is only the name that men of weak nerves give to wisdom.   —*Bernard De Voto*

4422 She not only expects the worst, but makes the most of it when it happens.   —*Hugh Mearns*

4423 He who foresees calamities, suffers them twice over.—*B. Porteus*

4424 Pessimist: one who sizes himself up and gets sore about it.

SEE ALSO   RELATED SUBJECTS
Opportunity 4258   Cynicism
                           Doubt
                           Despair
                           Optimism

PHILOSOPHY

4431 In Philosophy, on thought's peak, my friend,
Thou countedst years as so much coin to spend
On it, and would'st have thanked death that it used
Bland age, not dull disease to make an end.
                                          —*Dionysius of Cyzicus*

4432 Those who never philosophized until they met with disappointments, have mostly become disappointed philosophers.
                                          —*Arthur Helps*

4433 'Tis well to have a theory, and sit in the center of it.
                                          —*Katharina of Holland*

4434 It is a great advantage for a system of philosophy to be substantially true.   —*Santayana*

4435 Philosophy did not find Plato already a nobleman, it made him one.   —*Seneca*

4436 To be philosophy's slave is to be free.   —*Seneca*

4437 For there was never yet philosopher
That could endure the toothache patiently.   —*Shakespeare*

4438 A man gazing on the stars is proverbially at the mercy of the puddles on the road.   —*Alexander Smith*

4439   Philosophy: despair's shot at happiness.

SEE ALSO   RELATED SUBJECTS
Doubt 1695   Patience
Memory 3948   Thought
                            Wisdom

PITY

4441   Most of our misfortunes are more supportable than the comments of our friends upon them.   —*C. C. Colton*

4442   If every man's internal care
       Were written on his brow,
       How many would our pity share,
       Who raise our envy now!   —*Landor*

4443   I think he needs our pity who likes none.   —*Martial*

4444   Compassion is the basis of all morality.   —*Schopenhauer*

4445   There is no suffering which pity will not insult.

SEE ALSO   RELATED SUBJECTS
Complaint 901   Kindness
Conceit 937   Mercy
Husband 3026

PLEASURE

4451   Pleasure must succeed to pleasure, else past pleasure turns to pain.   —*Browning*

4452   Let us have wine and women, mirth and laughter,
       Sermons and soda-water the day after.   —*Byron*

4453   Thus always teasing others, always teas'd,
       His only pleasure is—to be displeas'd.   —*Cowper*

4454   Whenever you are sincerely pleased your are nourished.
                                                           —*Emerson*

4455   If you would rule the world quietly, you must keep it amused.
                                                           —*Emerson*

4456   Fly the pleasure that bites tomorrow.   —*Herbert*

4457   Follow pleasure, and then will pleasure flee;
       Flee pleasure, and pleasure will follow thee.   —*Heywood*

4458   No man is a hypocrite in his pleasures.   —*Johnson*

4459   Ever let the Fancy roam,
       Pleasure never is at home.   —*Keats*

4460   My theory is to enjoy life, but the practice is against it.—*Lamb*

4461   Since few large pleasures are lent us on a long lease, it is wise to
cultivate a large undergrowth of small pleasures.
—*Mary A. Livermore*

4462   You can't live on amusement. It is the froth on water, an inch
deep, and then the mud!   —*George Macdonald*

4463   A reveler I go, freighted with fire, not wine, beneath the region
of my heart.   —*Meleager*

4464   Find here what each desires: men's pleasure goes
Strange ways: one pulls a thorn and one a rose.   —*Petronius*

4465   Amusement is the happiness of those who cannot think.—*Pope*

4466   The test of an enjoyment is the remembrance which it leaves
behind.   —*J. P. Richter*

4467   To know how to despise pleasure is itself a pleasure.   —*Seneca*

4468   There are two things to aim at in life: first, to get what you want;
and, after that, to enjoy it. Only the wisest of mankind achieve
the second.   —*Logan Pearsall Smith*

4469   Ah that such sweet things should be fleet,
Such fleet things sweet!   —*Swinburne*

4470   And sometimes tell what sweetness is in gall.   —*Wyat*

4471   A man of pleasure is a man of pains.   —*Young*

4472   Most pleasures, like flowers, when gathered, die.   —*Young*

4473   Past pain is pleasure.

4474   There is a sense of immortality in pleasure which is not found in
happiness.

4475   The pleasure is over, but the disgrace remains.

4476   Comfort is the happiness of the indolent, while pleasure is the
comfort of the unhappy.

SEE ALSO   RELATED SUBJECTS
Business 584   Happiness
Conscience 963   Laughter
Good 2543   Sport
Morality 4079
Sickness 5021
Truth 5574

POETRY, *see page 236.*

POLITICS

4481   Practical politics consists in ignoring facts.   —*Henry Adams*

4482   All political parties die at last of swallowing their own lies.
                                                —*John Arbuthnot*

4483   Give the people issues, and you will not have to sell your souls
       for campaign funds.   —*William E. Borah*

4484   In politics, merit is rewarded by the possessor being raised, like a
       target, to a position to be fired at.   —*C. N. Bovée*

4485   An honest politician is one who, when he is bought, will stay
       bought.   —*Simon Cameron*

4486   In politics a capable ruler must be guided by circumstances, con-
       jectures and conjunctions.   —*Catherine II*

4487   A politician thinks of the next election, a statesman, of the next
       generation.   —*J. F. Clarke*

4488   To let politics become a cesspool, and then avoid it because it is
       a cesspool, is a double crime.   —*Howard Crosby*

4489   The world is wearied of statesmen whom democracy has degraded
       into politicians.   —*Disraeli*

4490   Damn your principles! Stick to your party.
                                          —*Disraeli to Bulwer-Lytton*

4491   Policy consists in serving God in such a manner as not to offend
       the devil.   —*Thomas Fuller*

4492   Corruption, the most infallible symptom of constitutional liberty.
                                                —*Gibbon*

4493   A statesman should follow public opinion as a coachman follows
       his horses; having firm hold on the reins, and guiding them.
                                                —*J. C. Hare*

4494   Paramount is making sure I won't be typed. In "Nothing But the
       Truth" I play the part of a fellow who is always truthful and
       in "Louisiana Purchase" I'm a politician.   —*Bob Hope*

4495   Politics is very much like taxes—everybody is against them, or
       everybody is for them as long as they don't apply to him.
                                          —*Fiorello H. LaGuardia*

4496   Ballots are the rightful and peaceful successors of bullets.
                                                —*Lincoln*

4497   Many a live wire would be a dead one except for his connections.
                                                —*Wilson Mizner*

4498   Any party which takes credit for the rain must not be surprised
       if its opponents blame it for the drought.   —*Morrow*

4499 People vote their resentment, not their appreciation. The average man does not vote for anything, but against something.
—*Munro*

4500 There is no more independence in politics than there is in jail.
—*Will Rogers*

4501 I took the Canal Zone and let Congress debate, and while the debate goes on the canal does too.   —*Theodore Roosevelt*

4502 A politician . . . one that would circumvent God.
—*Shakespeare*

4503 Politics . . . are but the cigar smoke of a man.   —*Thoreau*

4504 I am not a politician, and my other habits are good.
—*Artemus Ward*

4505 My pollertics, like my religion, being of an exceedin' accommodatin' character.   —*Artemus Ward*

4506 Politicians are as good as you are, for the way you vote creates politicians.

4507 Bad officials are elected by good citizens who do not vote.

4508 Midas, they say possessed the art, of old,
Of turning whatso'er he touched to gold.
This modern statesmen can reverse with ease;
Touch them with gold, they'll turn to what you please.

4509 The difference is that a statesman thinks he belongs to the State, and a politician thinks the State belongs to him.

4510 One of the most curious things about American politics is that without a single historical exception a partisan is invariably a member of the other party.

4511 Lincoln was right, of course; you can't fool all of the people all of the time; but you only have to fool a majority.

4512 In political matters much may be said on both sides, and it always is.

4513 Another trouble about the growth of the country is that it inevitably means more congressmen.

SEE ALSO
Conscience 964
Conservative 971
Hunger 2992
Memory 3947

RELATED SUBJECTS
Democracy
Diplomacy
Government

POETRY

4521   Poets are all who love, who feel great truths,
And tell them; and the truth of truths is love.—*Philip J. Bailey*

4522   Would you have your songs endure?
Build on the human heart.
                                       —Browning

4523   Troy owes to Homer what whist owes to Hoyle.   *—Byron*

4524   True poets should be chaste, I know,
But wherefore should their lines be so?   *—Catullus*

4525   Most wretched men
Are cradled into poetry by wrong:
They learn in suffering what they teach in song.   *—Catullus*

4526   Free verse is like free love; it is a contradiction in terms.
                                      —Chesterton

4527   Seven wealthy towns contend for Homer dead,
Through which the living Homer begged his bread.
                            —Thomas Seward

4528   I never indulge in poetics
Unless I am down with rheumatics.   *—Ennius*

4529   Vain was the chief's, the sage's pride!
They had no poet, and they died.   *—Horace*

4530   Poetry is the bill and coo of sex.   *—Elbert Hubbard*

4531   Past ruin'd Ilion Helen lives,
Alcestis rises from the shades;
Verse calls them forth; 'tis verse that gives
Immortal youth to moital maids.   *—Landor*

4532   For but two faults our fair poet Eglé the worse is:
She makes her own face, though she don't make her verses!
                                   —Lebrun

4533   There are three kinds of limericks; limericks to be told when
ladies are present; limericks to be told when ladies are absent
but clergymen are present—and limericks.   *—Don Marquis*

4534   Publishing a volume of verse is like dropping a rose-petal down
the Grand Canyon and waiting for the echo. *—Don Marquis*

4535   Poetry is what Milton saw when he went blind.—*Don Marquis*

4536   When a poet presents you with blank leaves you should consider
it no small present.   *—Martial*

4537   When Oppianus lost his color he took to writing verses.—*Martial*

4538   For all their compliments, do verses pay?
         They mayn't, yet these same poems make me gay.   *—Martial*

4539   Lo! I the man for trifles unsurpassed:
         You mayn't admire me, but I hold you fast.
         Great themes are for great bards: enough to see
         You oft re-reading my light poetry.   *—Martial*

4540   Anyone may be an honourable man, and yet write verse badly.
                 —Molière

4541   Sir, I admit your general rule,
         That every poet is a fool;
         But you yourself may serve to show it,
         That every fool is not a poet.   *—Pope*

4542   While pensive poets painful vigils keep,
         Sleepless themselves to give their readers **sleep.**   *—Pope*

4543   Who killed Johnny Keats?
         "I," said the *Quarterly,*
         "So savage and tartarly,
         'Twas one of my feats."   *—Shelley*

4544   Thy verses are eternal, O my friend,
         For he who reads them, reads them to no end.
             —William Shenstone

4545   Poetry is vocal painting, as painting is silent poetry.
               —Simonides

4546   I was promised on a time
         To have reason for my rhyme;
         From that time unto this season,
         I received nor rhyme nor reason.   *— Spenser*

4547   Poets lose half the praise they should have got,
         Could it be known what they discreetly blot.*—Edmund Waller*

4548   Yes, threadbare seem his songs, to lettered ken—
         They were worn threadbare next the hearts of men.
             —William Watson, on Longfellow

4549   To have great poets, there must be great audiences, too.
               —Whitman

4550   A poet can survive everything but a misprint.   *—Oscar Wilde*

4551   In merry old England it once was a rule,
         The King had his poet, and also his fool:
         But now we're so frugal, I'd have you know it,
         That Cibber can serve both for fool and for poet.
             —Epigram on Colley Cibber

4552   Unfortunate lady, how sad is your lot!
        Your ringlets are red, your poems are not.

        SEE ALSO   RELATED SUBJECTS
        Art 297   Art
        Gifts 2508   Books
                            Literature
                            Music
                            Writers

POLITICS, *see page 233.*

POVERTY

4561   The broad highway to poverty and need
        Is, much to build and many mouths to feed.   *—Acilius*

4562   Poverty does not mean the possession of little, but the non-possession of much.   *—Antipater*

4563   Wan iv th' shtrangest things about life is that th' poor, who need th' money th' most, ar-re th' very wans that niver have it.
        —F. P. Dunne

4564   There's many a thing which they
        Whose coats are tattered never dare to say.   *—Juvenal*

4565   Travellers with naught sing in the robber's face.   *—Juvenal*

4566   A poor relation is the most irrelevant thing in nature.   *—Lamb*

4567   O God, how weary am I and how old!
        But Poverty is ever young and fresh,
        And, clinging to me wastes my bones and flesh.   *—Macedonius*

4568   Cinna wishes to seem poor, and is poor.   *—Martial*

4569   You will always be poor if you are poor, Aemilianus. Wealth is given today to none save the rich.   *—Martial*

4570   In your glossy new garments you laugh at my threadbare clothes, Zoilus. Threadbare, indeed, they are, but they are my own.
        —Martial

4571   How the sting of poverty, or small means, is gone when one keeps house for one's own comfort, and not for the comfort of one's neighbors.   *—Dinah Maria Mulock*

4572   It is not the man who has too little but the man who craves more, that is poor.   *—Seneca*

4573   We will do almost anything for the poor man, anything but get off his back.   *—Tolstoi*

4574   He who can bear poverty without shame deserves it.

4575   The most inconvenient feature about poverty is that one is apt to get used to it.

4576   The poor are rightfully the property of the rich, because the rich made them.

4577   It is the weariness of the poor that keeps the rich in power.

4578   Poor people have no obligations: their poverty is their best asset.

4579   Appreciation of beauty in the poor is an infringement upon the exclusive rights of the rich.

4580   To add to the misery of the poor, Providence usually makes them uncomfortably healthy.

SEE ALSO	RELATED SUBJECTS
Architecture 266	Begging
Art 308	Charity
Children 772	Hardship
Civilization 845	Hunger
Family 2131	Necessity
Hope 2955	
Property 4694	

POWER

4581   A friend in power is a friend lost.   *—Henry Adams*

4582   Whoever can do as he pleases, commands when he entreats.
    —Corneille

4583   For what can pow'r give more than food and drink,
To live at ease, and not be bound to think?   *—Dryden*

4584   To have what we want is riches; but to be able to do without is power.   *—George Macdonald*

SEE ALSO	RELATED SUBJECTS
Courtesy 1116	Dictators
Dictators 1585	Government
Man 3818	
Wit 5936	
Women 5982	

PRAISE

4591   A compliment is usually accompanied with a bow, as if to beg pardon for paying it.   *—A. W. & J. C. Hare*

4592   Praise undeserved is satire in disguise.   *—Pope*

4593   It is safer to commend the dead than the living.

4594 Compliments cost nothing, yet many pay dear for them.

PRAYER

4601 People would be surprised to know how much I learned about prayer from playing poker.   —*Mary Austin*

4602 A good deed is the best prayer.   —*Robert Ingersoll*

4603 The hands that help are holier than the lips that pray.
                                                          —*Robert Ingersoll*

4604 Practical prayer is harder on the soles of your shoes than on the knees of your trousers.   —*Austin O'Malley*

4605 The prayers of a lover are more imperious than the menaces of the whole world.   —*George Sand*

4606 Give me good digestion, Lord,
And also something to digest;
But where and how that something comes
I leave to Thee, who knoweth best.   —*Mary Webb*

4607 When the gods wish to punish us they answer our prayers.
                                                              —*Oscar Wilde*

PREACHERS

4611 Actors speak of things imaginary as if they were real, while you preachers too often speak of things real as if they were imaginary.   —*Thomas Betterton*

4612 As the caterpillar chooses the fairest leaves to lay her eggs on, so the priest lays his curse on the fairest joys.   —*Blake*

4613 They said this mystery never shall cease:
The priest promotes war, and the soldier peace.   —*Blake*

4614 "Holy" I may not, "Father" I may call
Thee, since I see thy daughter,
Second Paul.   —*Jean de Cisinge on Pope Paul II*

4615   Cries Sylvia to a reverend dean,
  "What reason can be given,
 Since marriage is a holy thing,
  Why there is none in heaven?"
 "There are no women," he replied.
  She quick returns the jest—
 "Women there are, but I'm afraid
  They cannot find a priest."   *—Dodsley*

4616   A little moralizing's good—a little:
 I like a taste, but not a bath of it.   *—Ennius*

4617   It is no use walking anywhere to preach unless we preach as
 we walk.   *—St. Francis of Assisi*

4618   None preaches better than the ant, and she says nothing.
            —Franklin

4619   The life of a pious minister is visible rhetoric. *—Hooker*

4620   Avoid, as you would the plague, a clergyman who is also a man
 of business.   *—St. Jerome*

4621   Improve your style, monsieur! You have disgusted me with the
 joys of heaven!   *—François de Malherbe*

4622   When an evil deed's to do,
 Friar Lubin is stout and true;
 Glimmers a ray of goodness through it,
 Friar Lubin cannot do it.   *—Clement Marot*

4623   The Christian ministry is the worst of all trades, but the best of
 all professions.   *—J. Newton*

4624   Sermons are like pie-crust, the shorter the better.
         —Austin O'Malley

4625   The half-baked sermon causes spiritual indigestion.
         —Austin O'Malley

4626   To preach more than half an hour, a man should be an angel
 himself or have angels for hearers.   *—Whitefield*

4627   Preaching dogmas is fighting the devil with the scabbard instead
 of the sword.

4628   *Clergyman:* I've lost my brief-case.
 Traveller: I pity your grief.
 Clergyman: My sermons are in it.
 Traveller: I pity the thief.

4629   By our preacher perplexed,
How shall we determine?
"Watch and pray," says the text;
"Go to sleep," says the sermon.

SEE ALSO   RELATED SUBJECTS
Action 12   Christianity
Example 1965   Church
Sex 5015   God
                                  Prayer
                                  Religion

PREJUDICE

4631   Prejudice squints when it looks, and lies when it talks.
—Duchess de Abrantes

4632   He flattered himself on being a man without any prejudices;
and this pretension itself is a very great prejudice.
—Anatole France

4633   People have prejudices against a nation in which they have no
acquaintance.   *—Philip Hamerton*

4634   Fortunately for serious minds, a bias recognized is a bias steri-
lized.   *—Haydon*

4635   Reasoning against a prejudice is like fighting against a shadow;
it exhausts the reasoner, without visibly affecting the prejudice.
—Charles Mildmay

4636   It is never too late to give up our prejudices.   *—Thoreau*

4637   Prejudice, which sees what it pleases, cannot see what is plain.
—Aubrey de Vere

4638   Prejudice is the reason of fools.   *—Voltaire*

4639   They that burn you for a witch lose all their coals.

SEE ALSO   RELATED SUBJECTS
Ignorance 3097   Contempt
Logic 3631   Hate
                                  Ignorance

PRICE

4641   The highest price we can pay for anything, is to ask it.
—W. S. Landor

4642   Everything is worth what its purchaser will pay for it.
—Publilius Syrus

4643   All good things are cheap: all bad are very dear.   *—Thoreau*

4644   Good cheap is dear at long run.

4645   He is never likely to have a good thing cheap that is afraid to ask a price.

4646   He buys honey too dear who licks it from thorns.

4647   If you would have a hen lay, you must bear with her cackling.

SEE ALSO   RELATED SUBJECTS
Love 3682   Business
Praise 4594   Money
Wisdom 5901   Taxes
                     Value

PRIDE

4651   'Tis pride, rank pride, and haughtiness of soul; I think the Romans call it stoicism.   —*Addison*

4652   Snobbery is the pride of those who are not sure of their position.
                                                  —*Berton Braley*

4653   There is this paradox in pride—it makes some men ridiculous, but prevents others from becoming so.   —*C. C. Colton*

4654   Pride had rather go out of the way than go behind.
                                                  —*Thomas Fuller*

4655   There was one who thought himself above me, and he was above me until he had that thought.   —*Elbert Hubbard*

4656   In offering to no one the cup from which you drink, you give a proof, Hormus, not of pride, but of kindness.   —*Martial*

4657   'Tis not the belly's hunger that costs so much, but its pride.
                                                  —*Seneca*

4658   If a proud man makes me keep my distance, the comfort is that he keeps his at the same time.   —*Swift*

4659   There is such a thing as a man being too proud to fight.
                                                  —*Woodrow Wilson*

4660   Pride is the basis of all true courage. There never was a hero without pride, never a coward who could boast of having it.

SEE ALSO   RELATED SUBJECTS
Economy 1814   Conceit
Flattery 2250   Dignity
Ignorance 3095   Vanity

PROHIBITION

4661   Prohibition has made nothing but trouble.   —*Al Capone*

4662 All I kin git out o' the Wickersham position on prohibition is that the distinguished jurist seems to feel that if we'd let 'em have it the problem o' keepin' 'em from gittin' it would be greatly simplified.   —*Kin Hubbard*

4663 Adam was but human—this explains it all. He did not want the apple for the apple's sake, he wanted it only because it was forbidden. The mistake was in not forbidding the serpent; then he would have eaten the serpent.   —*Mark Twain*

RELATED SUBJECTS
Drinking
Temperance
Wine

PROOF

4671 That which needs to be proved cannot be worth much.
—*Nietzsche*

4672 A thing that nobody believes cannot be proved too often.
—*G. B. Shaw*

4673 Some circumstantial evidence is very strong, as when you find a trout in the milk.   —*Thoreau*

SEE ALSO   RELATED SUBJECTS
Belief 462   Crime
Love 3751   Truth

PROPERTY

4681 Men would live exceedingly quiet if those two words, mine and thine were taken away.   —*Anaxagoras*

4682 Them that has china plates themsels is the maist careful not to break the china plates of others.   —*J. M. Barrie*

4683 Who lives content with little possesses everything.   —*Boileau*

4684 Thieves respect property. They merely wish the property to become their property that they may more perfectly respect it.
—*Chesterton*

4685 It sounds like stories from the land of spirits
If any man obtain that which he merits,
Or any merit that which he obtains.   —*Coleridge*

4686 Ultimately property rights and personal rights are the same thing.
—*Calvin Coolidge*

4687 An Achaemenid spoke of me as "mine";
And now Menippus claims me for his line.
Talk of "his" and "their's" is mankind's romance;
Land shifts not; ownership's a word for chance.
—*Greek epigram*

4688   To have a thing is little, if you're not allowed to show it,
And to know a thing is nothing unless others know you know it.
—Lord Neaves

4689   To have may be taken from us, to have had, never.   *—Seneca*

4690   He that is robb'd, not wanting what is stolen,
Let him not know 't and he's not robb'd at all.   *—Shakespeare*

4691   The robb'd that smiles, steals something from the thief.
—Shakespeare

4692   Take care to get what you like or you will be forced to like what
you get.   *—G. B. Shaw*

4693   No man can lose what he never had.   *—Izaak Walton*

4694   If property cannot be abolished, it would be an act of kindness to
abolish the poor.

4695   The world seldom asks, how a man acquired his property. The
only question is, has he got it?

SEE ALSO   RELATED SUBJECTS
Action 4   Money
Change 655   Wealth

PROPHECY

4701   Banish "tomorrows!" Nemesis lays wait
For common speech that claims to be so wise
On the Future, as to anticipate
By light phrases men's unspun destinies.
—Antiphilus of Byzantium

4702   A prophet is not without honor, save in his own country, and
in his own house.   *—Bible*

4703   It has all the contortions of the sibyl without the inspiration.
—Burke

4704   The best of prophets of the future is the past.   *—Byron*

4705   Prophets were twice stoned—first in anger; then, after their
death, with a handsome slab in the graveyard.
—Christopher Morley

SEE ALSO   RELATED SUBJECT
Experience 2009   Future

PUNISHMENT

4711   The public has more interest in the punishment of an injury than
he who receives it.   *—Cato the Censor*

4712   We are not punished for our sins, but by them.*—Elbert Hubbard*

4713   Society does not punish those who sin, but those who sin and con-
        ceal not cleverly.   —*Elbert Hubbard*

4714   Whatever punishment does to a nation, it does not induce a sense
        of guilt.   *—Anne O'Hare McCormick*

4715   Distrust all in whom the impulse to punish is powerful.
                                                                  —*Nietzsche*

4716   That only is a disgrace to a man which he has deserved to suffer.
                                                                  —*Phaedrus*

4717   He hurts the good who spares the bad.   —*Publilius Syrus*

4718   Whilst we have prisons it matters little which of us occupies the
        cells.   —*G. B. Shaw*

4719   The most anxious man in a prison is the governor.—*G. B. Shaw*

4720   This, it seems to me, is the most severe punishment—finding out
        you are wrong!   —*Walter Winchell*

4721   Society produces the rogue so that it may punish him.

4722   Had Cain been Scot, God would have chang'd his doom;
        Not forc'd to wander, but confin'd at home.

4723   Two men looked through prison bars—
        One saw mud; the other, stars.

SEE ALSO   RELATED SUBJECTS
Anger 255   Crime
Prayer 4607   Guilt
Temperance 5331   Hanging
                          Justice
                          Law

PURPOSE

4730   No good fish goes anywhere without a porpoise.   —*Carroll*

4731   The secret of success is constancy of purpose.   —*Disraeli*

4732   Since I have dealt in suds, I could never discover more than two
        reasons for shaving; the one is to get a beard, the other is to
        get rid of one.   —*Fielding*

4733   The world turns aside to let any man pass who knows whither he
        is going.   —*David Starr Jordan*

SEE ALSO   RELATED SUBJECTS
Duty 1757   Aim
Greatness 2637   Decision
Lies 3528   Reason

Q

QUARREL

4740 Arguments out of a pretty mouth are unanswerable. —*Addison*

4741 So I have talked with Betsey, and Betsey has talked with me,
And we have agreed together that we can't never agree.
—Will Carleton

4742 The only way to get the best of an argument is to avoid it.
—Dale Carnegie

4743 A knock-down argument: 'tis but a word and a blow.—*Dryden*

4744 Those who in quarrels interpose
Must often wipe a bloody nose. *—John Gay*

4745 I always get the better when I argue alone. *—Goldsmith*

4746 The evils of controversy are transitory, while its benefits are permanent. *—Robert Hall*

4747 Every quarrel begins in nothing and ends in a struggle for supremacy. *—Elbert Hubbard*

4748 A duellist is only a Cain in high life. *—Douglas Jerrold*

4749 A small country town is not the place in which one would choose to quarrel with a wife; every human being in such places is a spy. *—Johnson*

4750 Quarrels would not last long if the fault was only on one side.
—La Rochefoucauld

4751 It were endless to dispute upon everything that is disputable.
—William Penn

4752 The word that is overbearing is a spur unto strife. *—Pindar*

4753 All discord, harmony not understood. *—Pope*

4754 Opposition always inflames the enthusiast, never converts him.
—Schiller

4755 He that makes a question where there is no doubt, must make an answer where there is no reason.

4756   The difference is wide that the sheets will not decide.

SEE ALSO   RELATED SUBJECTS
Drinking 1734   Opinion
Eating 1777   Tolerance

R

RANK

4761   Conspiracy—a game invented for the amusement of unoccupied
       men of rank.   —*Addison*

4762   A man can dignify his rank; no rank
       Can dignify a man.   —*Attius*

4763   To command, must we not have never met our equal?—*Balzac*

4764   It is a fine thing to command, even if it only be a herd of cattle.
                                                           —*Cervantes*

4765   I have found some of the best reasons I ever had for remaining at
       the bottom simply by looking at the men at the top.
                                                           —*F. M. Colby*

4766   The superiority of some men is merely local. They are great be-
       cause their associates are little.   —*Johnson*

4767   What men prize most is a privilege, even if it be that of chief
       mourner at a funeral.   —*Lowell*

4768   Man's rank is his power to uplift.   —*George Macdonald*

4769   There is no greater immorality than to occupy a place you cannot
       fill.   —*Napoleon*

4770   Man is an imitative creature, and whoever is foremost leads the
       herd.   —*Schiller*

4771   It is a maxim, that those to whom every body allows the second
       place have an undoubted title to the first.   —*Swift*

RELATED SUBJECTS
Ancestors
Dignity
Fame
Greatness

REASON

4781   It is not necessary to believe things in order to reason about them.
                                                           —*Beaumarchais*

4782   The heart has reasons that reason does not understand.—*Bossuet*

4783 I'll not listen to reason. . . . Reason always means what some one
else has got to say. --*Mrs. Gaskell*

4784 To give a reason for anything is to breed a doubt of it.—*Hazlitt*

4785 A man always has two reasons for doing anything—a good reason
and the real reason. —*J. P. Morgan*

4786 Earnestness is enthusiasm tempered by reason. —*Pascal*

4787 When a man has not a good reason for doing a thing, he has one
good reason for letting it alone. —*Thomas Scott*

4788 I have no other but a woman's reason; I think him so, because I
think him so. —*Shakespeare*

4789 Reason only controls individuals after emotion and impulse have
lost their impetus. —*Carlton Simon*

SEE ALSO	RELATED SUBJECTS
Anger 247	Logic
Drinking 1712, 1743	Purpose
Epigram 1867	Thought
Error 1935	Wisdom
Genius 2475	
Man 3812	

REFORM

4791 Those who are fond of setting things to rights, have no great objection to seeing them wrong. —*Hazlitt*

4792 According to the reformers, most of the movies have unsound
effects. —*Olin Miller*

4793 The race could save one-half its wasted labor
Would each reform himself and spare his neighbor. —*Putnam*

4794 Necessity reforms the poor, and satiety the rich. —*Tacitus*

4795 A reformer is a guy who rides through a sewer in a glass-bottomed
boat. —*James J. Walker*

4796 The worst thing about a fanatical reformer is that he makes the
world think all reformers are fanatics.

4797 Among the famous reformers is satiety.

SEE ALSO	RELATED SUBJECTS
Age 169	Censorship
Christianity 792	Morality
Habit 2745	Tolerance
Husband 3028	Virtue

RELIGION

4801 *Impiety:* Your irreverence toward my diety.   —*Ambrose Bierce*

4802 There's naught, no doubt, so much the spirit calms as rum and
      true religion.   —*Byron*

4803 Religion must still be allowed to be a collateral security to Virtue.
                                                      —*Chesterfield*

4804 False doctrine does not necessarily make a man a heretic, but an
      evil heart can make any doctrine heretical.   —*Coleridge*

4805 Bigotry murders religion to frighten fools with her ghost.
                                                      —*C. C. Colton*

4806 I have only a small flickering light to guide me in the darkness
      of a thick forest. Up comes a theologian and blows it out.
                                                         —*Diderot*

4807 The cross is the ladder of heaven.   —*Thomas Draxe*

4808 Theology is Anthropology.   —*Feuerbach*

4809 A religion without its mysteries is a temple without a God.
                                                      —*Robert Hall*

4810 I would give nothing for that man's religion, whose very dog and
      cat are not the better for it.   —*Hill*

4811 Theology is an attempt to explain a subject by men who do not
      understand it. The intent is not to tell the truth but to satisfy
      the questioner.   —*Elbert Hubbard*

4812 Let us put theology out of religion. Theology has always sent the
      worst to heaven, the best to hell.   —*Robert Ingersoll*

4813 Heresy is what the minority believe; it is the name given by the
      powerful to the doctrine of the weak.   —*Robert Ingersoll*

4814 Superstition is the only religion of which base souls are capable.
                                                         —*Joubert*

4815 Where it is a duty to worship the sun it is pretty sure to be a crime
      to examine the laws of heat.   —*John Morley*

4816 Religion is a process of turning your skull into a tabernacle, not of
      going up to Jerusalem once a year.   —*Austin O'Malley*

4817 We are plated with piety, not alloyed with it.—*Austin O'Malley*

4818 I think while zealots fast and frown,
      And fight for two or seven,
      That there are fifty roads to town,
      And rather more to Heaven.   —*Praed*

4819 Creeds grow so thick along the way their boughs hide God.
—*Reese*

4820 Mythology is the religious sentiment growing wild. —*Schelling*

4821 There is only one religion, though there are a hundred versions of it. —*G. B. Shaw*

4822 No man's religion ever survives his morals. —*South*

4823 A religion without mystery must be a religion without God.
—*Jeremy Taylor*

4824 The dispute about religion and the practice of it seldom go together. —*Young*

4825 We use religion like a trolley-car—we ride on it only while it is going our way.

4826 Religion is more than a fire insurance policy.

4827 Writers on the spiritual life are constantly mistaking the liver for the devil.

4828 A son should inherit his father's money—not his religion; he may be too lazy to build up a new fortune but never too slow to catch up with a new creed.

See Also	Related Subjects
Age 169	Belief
Hardship 2801	Christianity
Patriotism 4342	Church
	Faith
	God
	Prayer

REMORSE

4831 R-e-m-o-r-s-e,
Those dry Martinis were too much for me.
Last night I really felt immense,
To-day I feel like thirty cents;
It is no time for mirth and laughter
In the cold gray dawn of the morning after. —*George Ade*

4832 The best part of repentance is little sinning. —*Arabian Proverb*

4833 Our repentance is not so much regret for the ill we have done as fear of the ill that may happen to us in consequence.
—*La Rochefoucauld*

4834 Confession of our faults is the next thing to innocency.
—*Publilius Syrus*

4835   Remorse goes to sleep during a prosperous period and wakes up in adversity.   *—Rousseau*

4836   The world will not believe a man repents;
And this wise world of ours is mainly right.   *—Tennyson*

4837   Late repentance is seldom true, but true repentance is never too late.   *—R. Venning*

4838   It is sweeter to be remorseful over past sins than regretful about lost opportunities.

4839   Adam did not have to repent for he had no alternative.

SEE ALSO   RELATED SUBJECTS
Hanging 2758   Conscience
                    Despair
                    Reform

REPUTATION

4841   Reputation is a bubble which man bursts when he tries to blow it for himself.   *—Carleton*

4842   The reputation of a woman may be compared to a mirror, shining and bright, but liable to be sullied by every breath that comes near it.   *—Cervantes*

4843   The solar system has no anxiety about its reputation.*—Emerson*

4844   It is a sign that your reputation is small and sinking, if your own tongue must praise you.   *—Matthew Hale*

4845   A woman can defend her virtue from men, much more easily than she can protect her reputation from women.*—Elbert Hubbard*

4846   The blaze of reputation cannot be blown out, but it often dies in the socket.   *—Johnson*

4847   No man, however great, is known to everybody and no man, however solitary, is known to nobody.   *—Moore*

4848   There are two very difficult things in the world. One is to make a name for oneself and the other is to keep it.*—Robert Schumann*

4849   I would to God thou and I knew where a commodity of good names were to be bought.   *—Shakespeare*

4850   Get a name to rise early, and you may lie all day.

4851   The harder you throw down a football and a good character, the higher they rebound; but a thrown reputation is like an egg.

4852   Not beauty but respectability is only skin deep.

4853   For Jack's good life to certify,
      Nor friends, nor strangers can be got:
      Those who *don't* know him, know not why;
      Those, who *do* know him, know why not.

> RELATED SUBJECTS
> Character
> Fame
> Greatness
> Honor
> Insults

RESIGNATION

4861   Thus oft a struggle to escape
      But lands us in a still worse scrape.   *—La Fontaine*

4862   For after all, the best thing one can do
      When it is raining, is to let it rain.   *—Longfellow*

4863   There is no good in arguing with the inevitable. The only argument available with an east wind is to put on your overcoat.
      —Lowell

4864   Where there is no choice, we do well to make no difficulty.
      —George Macdonald

4865   Where to elect there is but one,
      'Tis Hobson's choice,—take that or none.   *—Thomas Ward*

4866   O that I were, where I would be,
      Then should I be where I am not,
      But where I am, there must I be,
      And where I would be, I cannot.

4867   For every ill beneath the sun,
      There is some remedy, or none.
      Should there be one, resolve to find it;
      If not, submit, and never mind it.

4868   Resignation is the timid side of courage.

> SEE ALSO   RELATED SUBJECTS
> Trees 5491   Patience
>   Philosophy

REVENGE

4871   Vengeance is the delight of petty minds,
      Paltry and weak. Infer this truth because
      None like a woman dotes upon revenge.   *—Juvenal*

4872   Revenge, at first though sweet,
      Bitter, ere long, back on itself recoils.   *—Milton*

4873   Heat not a furnace for your foe so hot that it do singe thyself.
                                                              —*Shakespeare*

4874   In taking revenge, a man is but even with his enemy; but in pass-
       ing it over, he is superior.

SEE ALSO   RELATED SUBJECTS
Age 133   Anger
Delay 1504   Crime
Forgetting 2310   Enemies
Marriage 3844   Hate
                              Passion

REVOLUTION

4881   Do you think, then, that revolutions are made with rose-water?
                                                              —*De Chamfort*

4882   Political convulsions, like geological upheavings, usher in new
       epochs of the world's progress.   —*Wendell Phillips*

4883   With the exception of capitalism, there is nothing so revolting as
       revolution.   —*G. B. Shaw*

4884   Rebellion to tyrants is obedience to God.

4885   Society punishes rebels; nature kills them.

4886   Revolutions are the toilet of a nation.

4887   Revolutions never turn back, but they sometimes make very acute
       angles.

SEE ALSO   RELATED SUBJECTS
Begging 421, 429   Change
Christianity 799   Government
Science 4942   Politics
                              Poverty

ROMANCE

4891   Romance, like a ghost, eludes touching. It always is where you
       were, not where you are.   —*Curtis*

4892   Romance has been elegantly defined as the offspring of fiction and
       love.   —*Disraeli*

4893   When one is in love one always begins by deceiving oneself, and
       one always ends by deceiving others. That is what the world
       calls a romance.   —*Oscar Wilde*

4894   Romance should never begin with sentiment.
       It should begin with science and end with a settlement.
                                                              —*Oscar Wilde*

4895 To say "mither" instead of "mother" seems to many the acme of
      romance.   —*Oscar Wilde*

4896 Nothing spoils a romance so much as a sense of humor in the
      woman.   —*Oscar Wilde*

4897 A romance that ends in indifference has gone through a full course
      of development.

4898 To most men any romance which runs beyond the limits of an
      episode becomes a nuisance.

4899 Ever so often women spoil a perfectly good romance by falling in
      love with their paramour.

SEE ALSO   RELATED SUBJECTS
Conceit 949   Courtship
                      Love
                      Marriage
                      Passion

S

SACRIFICE
4901 In this world it is not what we take up, but what we give up, that
      makes us rich.   —*H. W. Beecher*

4902 It is good to be helpful and kindly, but don't give yourself to be
      melted into candle grease for the benefit of the tallow trade.
                                                                  —*George Eliot*

4903 A woman can forgive a man for the harm he does her, but she can
      never forgive him for the sacrifices he makes on her account.
                                                                  —*Somerset Maugham*

4904 Not even for the highest principles has anyone the right to sacrifice
      others than himself.

SEE ALSO   RELATED SUBJECTS
Courtesy 1111   Hero
                      Martyr
                      Self-denial

SAFETY
4911 In skating over thin ice our safety is in our speed.   —*Emerson*

4912 Better ride safe in the dark, says the proverb, than in the daylight
      with a cut-throat at your elbow.   —*Scott*

4913 A ship in harbor is safe, but that is not what ships are built for.
                                                                  —*J. A. Shedd*

4914   Security is mortal's chief enemy.   —*Irving Vining*

4915   The drowning man might catch at a straw but never effectively.

SEE ALSO   RELATED SUBJECTS
Honesty 2929   Caution
Morality 4093   Danger

SAILORS

4921   Go where you will, the sea is still the sea.
        Its terrors then we idly strive to flee.   —*Antipater of Sidon*

4922   The winds and waves are always on the side of the ablest navi-
            gators.   —*Gibbon*

4923   Of all the husbands on the earth,
        The sailor has the finest berth,
        For in 'is cabin he can sit
        And sail and sail—and let 'er knit.   —*Wallace Irwin*

4924   Being in a ship is being in a jail, with the chance of being
            drowned.   —*Johnson*

4925   A sailor once I was, a farmer he
        Who now lies slumbering opposite to me,
        For Hades lies beneath both land and sea.   —*Plato*

4926   He goes a great voyage, that goes to the bottom of the sea.

SEE ALSO   RELATED SUBJECTS
Belief 457   Soldiers
Genius 2489   War

SAINT

4931   The way of this world is to praise dead saints and persecute living
            ones.   —*Nathaniel Howe*

4932   A young Saint an old Devil, (mark this, an old saying, and as
            true a one as, a Young Whore an old Saint).   —*Rabelais*

4933   It is easier to make a saint out of a libertine than out of a prig.
                                                            —*Santayana*

4934   The only difference between the saint and the sinner is that every
            saint has a past and every sinner has a future. —*Oscar Wilde*

RELATED SUBJECTS
Martyr
Virtue

SCIENCE

4941   Books must follow sciences, and not sciences books.   —*Bacon*

4942 Don't hesitate to be as revolutionary as science. Don't hesitate to be as reactionary as the multiplication table.—*Calvin Coolidge*

4943 An actually existing fly is more important than• a possibly existing angel. —*Emerson*

4944 There is no royal road to geometry. —*Euclid*

4945 The cradle of every science is surrounded by dead theologians as that of Hercules was with strangled serpents.—*T. H. Huxley*

4946 Mathematics is the science which uses easy words for hard ideas. —*Kasner & Newman*

4947 Nature and Nature's laws lay hid in night
God Said, let Newton be,—and all was light.—*Pope on Newton*

4948 Science is always wrong. It never solves a• problem without creating ten more. —*G. B. Shaw*

4949 Everything has a cause and the cause of anything is everything. —*W. J. Turner*

4950 Science keeps down the weed of superstition not by logic, but by rendering the mental soil unfit for its cultivation. —*Tyndall*

4951 An undevout astronomer is mad. —*Young*

4952 Mathematics is the bell-boy of all sciences.

SEE ALSO	RELATED SUBJECTS
Fools 2269	Knowledge
Genius 2488	Learning
Hardship 2797	
Morality 4078	
Truth 5583	

SECRET

4961 A sekret ceases tew be a sekret if it iz once confided—it iz like a dollar bill, once broken, it iz never a dollar agin. —*Josh Billings*

4962 Women, and young men, are very apt to tell what secrets they know, from the vanity of having been trusted. —*Chesterfield*

4963 Let not your friend your cherished secrets hear;
Then, if you quarrel, you've no cause to fear. —*Menander*

4964 There is something about a closet that makes a skeleton terribly restless. —*Wilson Mizner*

4965 There are no secrets better kept than the secrets that everybody guesses. —*G. B. Shaw*

4966   If you wish to preserve your secret, wrap it up in frankness.
                                              —*Alexander Smith*

4967   The man who has no secrets from his wife either has no secrets or
       no wife.   —*Gilbert Wells*

4968   Thy secret is thy prisoner; if thou let it go, thou art a prisoner to
       it.

4969   To him that you tell your secret you resign your liberty.

4970   Do not speak of secret matters in a field that is full of little hills.

4971   Try your friend with a falsehood, and if he keep it a secret tell
       him the truth.

4972   One should judge by appearance only: what is hidden should re-
       main so.

SEE ALSO	RELATED SUBJECTS
Death 1341	Frankness
Virtue 5703	Honesty
	Lies

SELF-DENIAL

4981   Self-denial is indulgence of a propensity to forego.
                                              —*Ambrose Bierce*

4982   Self-abnegation, that rare virtue, that good men preach and good
       women practice.   —*O. W. Holmes*

4983   Self denial is not a virtue: it is only the effect of prudence on ras-
       cality.   —*G. B. Shaw*

4984   Self-denial is the shining sore on the leprous body of Christianity.
                                              —*Oscar Wilde*

RELATED SUBJECTS
Generosity
Selfishness

SELFISHNESS

4991   Selfishness is that detestable vice which no one will forgive in
       others, and no one is without in himself.   — *H. W. Beecher*

4992   To feel for none is the true social art of the world's stoics—men
       without a heart.   —*Byron*

4993   That man who lives for self alone
       Lives for the meanest mortal known.   —*Joaquin Miller*

4994   We have always known that heedless self-interest was bad morals;
       we know now that it is bad economics.—*Franklin D. Roosevelt*

4995   He who lives only to benefit himself confers on the world a bene-
       fit when he dies.   —*Tertullian*

4996   A man is called selfish, not for pursuing his own good, but for neglecting his neighbor's.   —*Whately*

4997   He is a slave of the greatest slave, who serveth nothing but himself.

SEE ALSO   RELATED SUBJECTS
Love 3675, 3738   Greed
                        Misanthrope

SERVANT

5001   The Spaniard is a bad servant but a worse master.
                                       —*Thomas Adams*

5002   All service ranks the same with God—
There is no last nor first.   —*Browning*

5003   One of the most considerable advantages the great have over their inferiors is to have servants as good as themselves.—*Cervantes*

5004   A service beyond all recompense
Weighs so heavy that it almost gives offense.   —*Corneille*

5005   If you would have a faithful servant, and one that you like, serve yourself.   —*Franklin*

5006   Few men have been admired by their own domestics.—*Montaigne*

                RELATED SUBJECTS
                Help
                Slave

SEX

5011   She hugg'd the offender, and forgave the offence:
Sex to the last.   —*Dryden*

5012   Amoebas at the start
      Were not complex;
They tore themselves apart
      And started Sex.   —*Arthur Guiterman*

5013   Breathes there a man with hide so tough
Who says two sexes aren't enough?
                             —*Samuel Hoffenstein*

5014   A woman never forgets her sex. She would rather talk with a man than an angel, any day.   —*O. W. Holmes*

5015   As the French say, there are three sexes,—men, women, and clergymen.   —*Sydney Smith*

SEE ALSO   RELATED SUBJECTS
Poetry 4530   Man
                        Woman

SICKNESS

5021 I reckon being ill as one of the great pleasures of life, provided one is not too ill and is not obliged to work till one is better.
—*Samuel Butler*

5022 I don't suffer, my friends, but I feel a certain difficulty in existing.
—*Fontenelle*

5023 If I remember right you had, Aelia, four teeth: one fit of coughing shot out two; and another fit, two more. Now you can cough in peace all day.   —*Martial*

5024 You came to see me once only when I was ill. It will go badly with me if I see you often.   —*Martial*

5025 I enjoy convalescence. It is the part that makes the illness worth while.   —*G. B. Shaw*

5026 That sick man is not to be pitied, who hath his cure in his sleeve.

5027 The chamber of sickness is the chapel of devotion.

5028 The purse of the patient protracts his cure.

5029 It is no advantage for a man in a fever to change his bed.

SEE ALSO	RELATED SUBJECTS
Age 143	Doctors
Wealth 5779	Health
	Medicine

SILENCE

5031 Silence is not always tact, and it is tact that is golden—not silence.
—*Samuel Butler*

5032 Silence is deep as eternity; speech is shallow as time.   —*Carlyle*

5033 Let your speech be better than silence, or be silent.—*Dionysius*

5034 "I hardly ever ope my lips," one cries;
"Simonides, what think you of my rule?"
"If you're a fool, I think you're very wise;
"If you are wise, I think you are a fool."   —*Garnett*

5035 A silence, like a poultice, comes
To heal the blows of sound.   —*O. W. Holmes*

5036 You hesitate to stab me with a word,
And know not silence is the sharper sword.   —*Johnson*

5037 Silence in woman is like speech in men; deny it who can.
—*Johnson*

5038 You have not converted a man because you have silenced him.
—*Morley*

5039 She half consents who silently denies. —*Ovid*

5040 Silence in love betrays more woe
Than words, though ne'er so witty;
A beggar that is dumb, you know,
May challenge double pity. —*Sir Walter Raleigh*

5041 Nothing is so good for an ignorant man as silence; if he were
sensible of this he would not be ignorant. —*Saadi*

5042 Be check'd for silence,
But never tax'd for speech. —*Shakespeare*

5043 He (Macaulay) has occasional flashes of silence that make his
conversation perfectly delightful. —*Sydney Smith*

5044 If a word spoken in its time is worth one piece of money, silence
in its time is worth two. —*Talmud*

5045 Silence is a fine jewel for a woman, but it's little worn.

5046 Silence: wisdom in dead storage.

5047 It is better to be silent and be thought a fool than to speak up
and remove all doubt.

5048 More men are sorry for speaking, than keeping silence.

SEE ALSO   RELATED SUBJECTS
Bores 530   Noise
Lies 3522   Speeches
Understanding 5596

SIN

5051 Sin we have explain'd away;
Unluckily, the sinners stay. —*Allingham*

5052 "Thou shalt not get found out" is not one of God's commandments; and no man can be saved by trying to keep it.
—*Leonard Bacon*

5053 Sin is not hurtful because it is forbidden, but it is forbidden because it is hurtful. —*Franklin*

5054 Holy must be the man who treads
The incensed shrine within:
And holy is that man alone
Whose soul is free from sin. —*Greek epigram*

5055 No man's contented just so much to sin
As you may license him. —*Juvenal*

5056 He that plots secret crime his soul within
Is straightway guilty of the actual sin. —*Juvenal*

5057   The sin ye do by two and two ye must pay for one by one!
                                                          —*Kipling*

5058   Man-like it is to fall into sin,
         Fiend-like is it to dwell therein,
         Christ-like is it for sin to grieve,
         God-like is it all sin to leave.   —*Longfellow*

5059   There is often a sin of omission as well as of commission.
                                                  —*Marcus Aurelius*

5060   In all my writings my aim has been to spare sinners and assail sin.
                                                          —*Martial*

5061   In Adam's fall
         We sinned all.   —*New England Primer*

5062   Some rise by sin, and some by virtue fall.   —*Shakespeare*

5063   To say of shame—what is it?
         Of virtue—we can miss it;
         Of sin—we can kiss it,
         And it's no longer sin.   —*Swinburne*

5064   The girl who can her fault deny
         Will always at the end be winner;
         'Tis she who does for pardon cry
         That's held the sinner.   —*F. A. Wright*

5065   Few serve Satan better than sleeping saints.

5066   Actions are not sinful; thoughts actuating them may be.

SEE ALSO	RELATED SUBJECTS
Day 1312	Conscience
Doubt 1696	Crime
God 2531	Devil
Habit 2741	Error
Honesty 2927	Evil
Lies 3532	Guilt
Love 3715	Morality
Originality 4291	Punishment
Stupidity 5226	Remorse
	Temptation
	Vice
	Virtue
	Wickedness

SINCERITY

5071   It is dangerous to be sincere unless you are also stupid.
                                                          —*G. B. Shaw*

5072   To stupid people sincerity is one continuous process of self-
         sacrifice.

5073   Sincerity is a policy and cynicism a pose; in life either is an un-natural attitude.

> RELATED SUBJECTS
> Frankness
> Honesty
> Hypocrisy
> Trust

SLAVE

5081   Zosime's form was once a slave;
Her soul ne'er slavery knew—
And now, the freedom of the grave
Has reached her body too.   *—Damascius*

5082   I bought what you called a fool for twenty thousand sesterces. Return me my money, Gargilianus; he is no fool at all.
        —Martial

5083   You sold a slave yesterday for thirteen hundred sesterces, in order, Calliodorus, that you might dine well once in your life. Nevertheless you did not dine well; a mullet of four pounds' weight which you bought was the chief dish, the very crown of your repast. I feel inclined to exclaim: "It was not a fish, shameless fellow, it was a man, a veritable man, Calliodorus, that you ate."   *—Martial*

5084   A muleteer was lately sold for twenty thousand sesterces, Aulus. Are you astonished at so large a price? He was deaf, (and could not overhear the conversation).   *—Martial*

5085   A slave, branded on the forehead by his master, saved him when proscribed. Thus, while the life of the master was preserved, his infamy was perpetuated.   *—Martial*

5086   Why do you maim your slave, Ponticus, by cutting out his tongue? Don't you know that the public says what he cannot?
        —Martial

> SEE ALSO   RELATED SUBJECTS
> Marriage 3845   Dictators
> Selfishness 4997   Labor
>   Liberty
>   Work

SLEEP

5091   He went to bed and slept the sleep of the good-for-nothing, which, by an anachronism not a single song-writer has yet struck, is proven to be more sound than that of innocence.   *—Balzac*

5092   No small art is it to sleep: it is necessary for that purpose to keep awake all day.   *—Nietzsche*

5093   He sleeps well who knows not that he sleeps ill.—*Publilius Syrus*

5094   O sleep, of death although the image true,
Much I desire to share my bed with you.
O come and tarry, for, how sweet to lie
Thus without life, thus without death to die.

SEE ALSO   RELATED SUBJECTS
Death 1324, 1366   Bed
Fame 2112   Death
Hypocrisy 3036
Marriage 3895
Noise 4181
Poetry 4542

SMELL

5101   I send thee myrrh, not that thou mayest be
By it perfumed, but it perfumed by thee.   —*Greek epigram*

5102   I would rather smell of nothing than of perfume.   —*Martial*

5103   What am I to understand from the circumstances, that your kisses
always smell of myrrh, and that you never have about you an
odor other than unnatural? That you always smell so agree-
ably, Postumus, makes me suspect that you have something to
conceal. He does not smell pleasantly, Postumus, who always
smells pleasantly.   —*Martial*

5104   They that smell least, smell best.

SEE ALSO   RELATED SUBJECT
Guests 2714, 2717   Cleanliness
Virtue 5699

SNOB

5111   Of all the lunacies earth can boast,
The one that must please the devil the most
Is pride reduced to the whimsical terms
Of causing the slugs to despise the worms.   —*Brough*

5112   My thirst I slake from wells that bear my seal;
Forbid retailers of gossip the door;
And half a score of words my soul reveal:
"Whatever is popular I abhor!"   —*Callimachus*

5113   Exclusiveness is a characteristic of recent riches, high society, and
the skunk.

5114   An uppish class sometimes mistakes itself for an upper class.

SEE ALSO   RELATED SUBJECTS
Doctors 1665   Conceit   Vanity
Pride 4652   Society

SOCIETY

5121   A crowd is not company, and faces are but a gallery of pictures.
—*Bacon*

5122   Society is composed of two great classes: those who have more dinners than appetite, and those who have more appetite than dinners.   —*De Chamfort*

5123   No company is preferable to bad, because we are more apt to catch the vices of others than their virtues, as disease is far more contagious than health.   —*C. C. Colton*

5124   Ants are good citizens—they place group interests first.
—*Clarence Day*

5125   Society is a masked ball, where every one hides his real character, and reveals it by hiding.   —*Emerson*

5126   Who does not in some sort live to others, does not live much to himself.   —*Montaigne*

5127   Human society is like an arch, kept from falling by the mutual pressure of its parts.   —*Seneca*

5128   A man's interest in the world is only the overflow of his interest in himself.   —*G. B. Shaw*

5129   A village is a hive of glass,
Where nothing unobserved can pass.   —*C. H. Spurgeon*

5130   I had three chairs in my house: one for solitude, two for friendship, three for society.   —*Thoreau*

5131   The company in which you will improve most will be least expensive to you.   —*Washington*

5132   A man who can dominate a London dinner table can dominate the world. The future belongs to the dandy. It is the exquisites who are going to rule.   —*Oscar Wilde*

5133   Keep not ill men company lest you increase the number.

5134   He keeps his road well enough who gets rid of bad company.

5135   A crowd is not company.

SOLDIERS

5141   I like not your strutters with Captain's air,
Chins smooth as girls' cheeks, crowns of curly hair.
Give me, to fight, bowlegs, squat, on firm feet,
Heart pledging the whole never to be beat.

—Archilochus of Paros

5142   A man in armor is his armor's slave.   *—Browning*

5143   I gave my life for freedom—
This I know:
For those who bade me fight
Had told me so.   *—Ewer*

5144   That city is well fortified which has a wall of men instead of
brick.   *—Lycurgus*

5145   I want to see you shoot the way you shout.*—Theodore Roosevelt*

5146   He who does garrison duty is as much a soldier as he that is in
the fighting line.   *—Seneca*

5147   A soldier's fortune, I tell you plain,
Is a wooden leg or a golden chain.

5148   Advantage is a better soldier than rashness.

5149   Our God and soldier we alike adore
Just at the brink of ruin, not before:
The danger past, both are alike requited;
God is forgotten, and the soldier slighted.

SEE ALSO   RELATED SUBJECTS
Actors 49   Courage
Hardship 2812   Fight
Kings 3286   War

SOLITUDE

5151   I praise the Frenchman, his remark was shrewd—
How sweet, how passing sweet is solitude!
But grant me still a friend in my retreat,
Whom I may whisper, Solitude is sweet.   *—Cowper*

5152   Would you some vexation flee?
Keep from bitter heart-pangs free.
Tie with none too close maintain:
You'll have less gladness—and less pain.   *—Martial*

5153   One can acquire everything in solitude—except character.
—Stendhal

5154   A wise man is never less alone than when he is alone.   *—Swift*

5155   I never found the companion that was so companionable as soli-
       tude.   —*Thoreau*

5156   The man who goes alone can start today; but he who travels with
       another must wait till that other is ready.   —*Thoreau*

5157   The joy of meeting pays the pangs of absence; else who could
       bear it?

SEE ALSO   RELATED SUBJECTS
Cities 839   Philosophy
Thought 5393   Thought

SOUL

5161   Flowers are the sweetest things that God ever made and forgot
       to put a soul into.   —*H. W. Beecher*

5162   "Farewell, O Sun," Cleombrotus cried,
       Then from a lofty wall to Hades hied:
       Him to his death no desperate grief had led,
       But Plato on the Soul this man had read.   —*Callimachus*

5163   Immortality will come to such as are fit for it; and he who
       would be a great soul in the future must be a great soul now.
                                                            —*Emerson*

5164   Eagle! why soarest thou above that tomb?
       To what sublime and starry-paven home
           Floatest thou?
       I am the image of swift Plato's spirit,
       Ascending heaven—Athens doth inherit
           His corpse below.   —*Greek epigram*

5165   Drop anchor anywhere and the anchor will drag—that is, if your
       soul is a limitless, fathomless sea, and not a dogpond.
                                                        —*Elbert Hubbard*

5166   Every spirit makes its house, but as afterwards the house confines
       its spirit, you had better build well.   —*Elbert Hubbard*

5167   The soul occupied with great ideas, best performs small duties.
                                                       —*James Martineau*

5168   God has so arranged the chronometry of our spirits, that there
       shall be thousands of silent moments between the striking hours.
                                                       —*James Martineau*

5169   The finest souls are those that have most variety and suppleness.
                                                           —*Montaigne*

5170   The worth of the soul consists not in going loftily, but orderly.
       Its greatness is not put to the proof in greatness, but in me-
       diocrity.   —*Montaigne*

5171   A kiss, and touch of lips; not strange my Soul should cling,
        Strive to cross, weep to turn, and starve with me, poor thing.
                                                            —*Plato*

5172   We say we exchange words when we meet. What we exchange is
        souls.   —*Minot J. Savage*

5173   Books of science when you print,
        The work should be entire and whole,
        Shou'd you, dear friend, but take the hint,
        And to your *bodies*—add a *soul*.

5174   Enthusiasm is the life of the soul.

        SEE ALSO   RELATED SUBJECTS
        Body 486   Body
        Criticism 1256   Life
        Doubt 1700   Thought
        Friend 2406
        Jealousy 3191
        Thought 5384, 5390
        Time 5423

SPEECHES

5181   Take care of the sense and the sounds will take care of themselves.
                                                        —*Lewis Carroll*

5182   MacDonald has the gift of compressing the largest amount of
        words into the smallest amount of thought.
                                                    —*Winston Churchill*

5183   One orator in a family, nay even in a city, is enough.   —*Cicero*

5184   Do not say all that you know, but always know what you say.
                                                            —*Claudius*

5185   There is no eloquence without a man behind it.   —*Emerson*

5186   The obvious duty of a toastmaster is to be so infernally dull that
        the succeeding speakers will appear brilliant by contrast.
                                                        —*C. B. Kelland*

5187   What a long time you take to say nothing, Cinna!   —*Martial*

5188   When everyone is talking, then and then only, Naevolus, do you
        open your mouth; and you think yourself an advocate and a
        pleader. In such a way everyone may be eloquent. But see,
        everybody is silent; say something now, Naevolus.   —*Martial*

5189   You are always shouting, always interrupting the pleaders, Aelius.
        You don't do this for nothing; you take pay to hold your
        tongue.   —*Martial*

5190 Why do you wrap up your neck in a woolen muffler when you are going to recite? The muffler would be more suitable for our ears. —*Martial*

5191 By way of introduction you complained of a cold in your throat. Since you plead this excuse, Maximus, why recite at all? —*Martial*

5192 I don't know whether Phoebus fled from the dinner-table of Thyestes: at any rate, Ligurinus, we flee from yours. Splendid, indeed, it is, and magnificently supplied with good things, but when you recite you spoil it all. I don't want you to set before me a turbot or a two-pound mullet: I don't want your mushrooms or your oysters. I want you to keep your mouth shut! —*Martial*

5193 You are always wishing, Matho, to speak finely. Speak sometimes merely well, sometimes neither well nor ill, sometimes even ill. —*Martial*

5194 A good talker or writer is only a pitcher. Unless his audience catches him with heart and mind he's defeated. —*Wilson Mizner*

5195 Much talking man, in earth thou soon wilt be:
Be still, and living think what 'tis to die. —*Palladas*

5196 Young man, thy words are like the cypress, tall and large, but they bear no fruit. —*Phocion*

5197 They say
That putting all his words together,
'Tis three blue beans in a blue bladder. —*Prior*

5198 It is but a poor eloquence which only shows that the orator can talk. —*Joshua Reynolds*

5199 Gentlemen, you have just been listening to that Chinese sage, On Too Long. —*Will Rogers*

5200 When words are scarce they are seldom spent in vain. —*Shakespeare*

5201 Let any man speak long enough, he will get believers. —*Stevenson*

5202 It is of eloquence as of a flame; it requires matter to feed it, and motion to excite it; and it brightens as it burns. —*Tacitus*

5203 Nothing produces such an effect as a good platitude. —*Oscar Wilde*

5204 Words are like leaves, and where they most abound
Much fruit of sense beneath is rarely found.

5205   After-dinner speaking is the art of saying nothing briefly.

5206   It is a bad cause, that none dares speak in.

5207   His speeches to an hour-glass
    Do some resemblance show;
Because the longer time they run
    The shallower they grow.

                    RELATED SUBJECTS
                    Conversation
                    Epigrams
                    Wit
                    Words

SPORT

5211   The best thing for the inside of a man is the outside of a horse.
                                      —Lord Palmerston

5212   When a man wants to murder a tiger he calls it sport: when the
    tiger wants to murder him he calls it ferocity.   *—G. B. Shaw*

5213   Mother, may I go out to swim?
Yes, my darling daughter:
Hang your clothes on a hickory limb
But don't go near the water.

5214   We read that a form of baseball was a favorite sport among the
    Greeks. We do remember something about a Homer.

SEE ALSO   RELATED SUBJECTS
Business 579   Gambling
                          Pleasure
                          Laughter

STUPIDITY

5221   Absurdity refutes itself.   *—A. Bartholini*

5222   Every absurdity has a champion to defend it.   *—Goldsmith*

5223   The privilege of absurdity; to which no living creature is subject
    but man only.   *—Thomas Hobbes*

5224   A Zombie has no mind of his own and walks around without
    knowing where he's going or what he's doing . . . In Hollywood
    they call them "pedestrians."   *—Bob Hope*

5225   Against stupidity the very gods
Themselves contend in vain.   *—Schiller*

5226   There is no sin except stupidity.   *—Oscar Wilde*

5227   Genius has limitations; stupidity is boundless.

5228   Stupidity would be very charming if it only had better manners.

5229   Platitudes are the Sundays of stupidity.

5230   What makes stupidity really insufferable is that it is forever in action—idiocy knows no rest.

SEE ALSO   RELATED SUBJECTS
Cleverness 864   Fools
Excess 1982   Ignorance
Gravity 2624
Happiness 2787
Idleness 3079
Sincerity 5071

SUCCESS

5231   Every man who is high up loves to think that he has done it all himself; and the wife smiles, and lets it go at that.
                                                  —J. M. Barrie

5232   It is not the going out of port, but the coming in, that determines the success of a voyage.   *—H. W. Beecher*

5233   The secret of success lies not in doing your own work, but in recognizing the right man to do it.   *—Andrew Carnegie*

5234   In public we say the race is to the strongest; in private we know that a lopsided man runs the fastest along the little side-hills of success.   *—Frank M. Colby*

5235   Be awful nice to 'em goin' up, because you're gonna meet 'em all comin' down.   *—Jimmy Durante*

5236   Success is little more than a chemical compound of man with moment.   *—Philip Guedalla*

5237   The worst use that can be made of success is to boast of it.
                                             —Arthur Helps

5238   Those men who pass most comfortably through the world are those who possess good digestion and hard hearts.
                                  —James Martineau

5239   The gent who wakes up and finds himself a success hasn't been asleep.   *—Wilson Mizner*

5240   The surest way not to fail is to determine to succeed.—*Sheridan*

5241   Nothing recedes like success.   *—Walter Winchell*

5242   The best way to get along is never to forgive an enemy or forget a friend.   *—Walter Winchell*

5243   Success, a sort of suicide, is ruin'd by success.   *—Young*

5244   The reason why men who mind their own business succeed is because they have so little competition.

5245   Next to Death, the most infallible remedy for a guilty conscience is success.

5246   It is an unhealthy attitude to think success a trivial incident in life.

5247   If success comes too late in life it causes more regrets than comforts.

5248   Nothing slackens one like success.

5249   Success is getting what you want; happiness is wanting what you get.

5250   No matter how valuable, advice on how to succeed, coming from an unsuccessful man, will be received with poor grace or even ridicule.

SEE ALSO	RELATED SUBJECTS
Character 670	Aim
Conceit 934	Deeds
Crime 1224	Fame
Greatness 2634	
Purpose 4731	

SUN

5251   I have nothing to ask but that you would remove to the other side, that you may not, by intercepting the sunshine, take from me what you cannot give.   —*Diogenes to Alexander*

5252   Oft did I wonder why the setting sun
Should look upon us with a blushing face:
Is't not for shame at what he hath seen done,
Whilst in our hemisphere he ran his race?   —*Heath*

5253   Thank heavens, the sun has gone in, and I don't have to go out and enjoy it.   —*Logan Pearsall Smith*

5254   The sunrise never failed us yet.   —*Celia Thaxter*

5255   No man sees his shadow who faces the sun.

SEE ALSO	RELATED SUBJECTS
Art 280	Day
Beauty 367	Heaven
Cleanliness 851	Weather

T

TALENT

5261 Doing easily what others find difficult is talent; doing what is impossible for talent is genius.   *—Amiel*

5262 It always seemed to me.a sort of clever stupidity only to have one sort of talent—like a carrier-pigeon. *—George Eliot*

5263 Talent is that which is in a man's power; genius is that in whose power a man is.   *—Lowell*

5264 In the battle of existence, Talent is the punch; Tact is the clever footwork.   *—Wilson Mizner*

5265 How many "coming men" has one known!
Where on earth do they all go to?   *—Pinero*

5266 Young men of talent are seldom popular; they are all vanity and no tact.

SEE ALSO   RELATED SUBJECT
Bores 531   Genius
Business 582

TASTE

5271 Good taste is better than bad taste, but bad taste is better than no taste.   *—Arnold Bennett*

5272 Bad taste is a species of bad morals.   *—C. N. Bovée*

5273 Taste is nothing else than good sense delicately put in force, and genius is reason in its most sublime form. *—Chénier*

5274 I would rather be able to appreciate things I can not have than to have things I am not able to appreciate. *—Elbert Hubbard*

5275 The greatest man is he who forms the taste of a nation; the next greatest is he who corrupts it. *—Joshua Reynolds*

5276 Taste is, so to speak, the microscope of the judgment.*—Rousseau*

5277 Simplicity is the background of good taste.

5278 Everyone to their liking,
    As the old woman said when she kissed the cow.

See Also	Related Subjects
Art 299	Art
France 2344	Eating
Frankness 2355	Judgment
Love 3752	

TAXES

5281 For every benefit you receive a tax is levied.　　*—Emerson*

5282 In this world nothing is certain but death and taxes.*—Franklin*

5283 Here comes Mr. Winter, Collector of Taxes,
    I advise you to give whatever he axes,
    And that, too, without any nonsense or flummery
    For, though his name's Winter, his actions are summary.
        —Theodore Hook on Mr. Winter

5284 "Taxes are equal, is a dogma which
    I'll prove at once," exclaimed a Tory boor;
    "Taxation hardly presses on the rich,
    And likewise presses hardly on the poor."

5285 Protect the birds. The dove brings peace and the stork brings tax
    exemptions.

See Also	Related Subjects
Cities 836	Government
Criticism 1270	Money
Politics 4495	Price
	Wealth

TEACHING

5291 A courage which looks easy and yet is rare; the courage of a
teacher repeating day after day the same lessons—the least
rewarded of all forms of courage.　　*—Balzac*

5292 Knowledge exists to be imparted.　　*—Emerson*

5293 Charming women can true converts make,
    We love the precepts for the teacher's sake.　　*—George Farquhar*

5294 Let our teaching be full of ideas. Hitherto it has been stuffed only
with facts.　　*—Anatole France*

5295 The teacher is one who makes two ideas grow where only one
grew before.　　*—Elbert Hubbard*

5296 The object of teaching a child is to enable him to get along without his teacher.　　*—Elbert Hubbard*

5297 I care not what subject is taught if only it be taught well.
        —T. H. Huxley

5298   For him who fain would teach the world
      The world holds fate in fee—
      For Socrates, the hemlock cup;
      For Christ, Gethsemane.   *—Don Marquis*

5299   I do not teach, I relate.   *—Montaigne*

5300   Men must be taught as if you taught them not,
      And things unknown propos'd as things forgot.   *—Pope*

5301   Delightful task! to rear the tender thought,
      To teach the young idea how to shoot.   *—James Thomson*

SEE ALSO	RELATED SUBJECTS
Doubt 1693	Learning
Time 5408	Knowledge

TEARS

5311   The drying up a single tear has more
      Of honest fame than shedding seas of gore.   *—Byron*

5312   Every woman is wrong until she cries, and then she is right, instantly.   *—Haliburton*

5313   The most efficient water power in the world—women's tears.
      —Wilson Mizner

SEE ALSO	RELATED SUBJECTS
Cowardice 1187	Eyes
Inheritance 3138	Grief
Tobacco 5442	Pain

TEMPERANCE

5321   Abstaining is favorable both to the head and the pocket.
      —Horace Greeley

5322   The more a man denies himself, the more shall he obtain from God.   *—Horace*

5323   Abstinence is as easy to me as temperance would be difficult.
      —Johnson

5324   Indulgence rare to pleasures lendeth zest.   *—Juvenal*

5325   Afer is a sober man; he does not drink. What is that to me? I
      commend a slave for temperance, not a friend.   *—Martial*

5326   Perfect good sense shuns all extremity,
      Content to couple wisdom with sobriety.   *—Molière*

5327   Abstinence is the surety of temperance.   *—Plato*

5328   To abstain that we may enjoy is the epicureanism of reason.
      —Rousseau

5329   Temperance and labor are the two best physicians of man.
                                                       —*Rousseau*

5330   Abstinence is easier than temperance.   —*Seneca*

5331   Choose rather to punish your appetites than to be punished by
       them.   —*Tyrius Maximus*

5332   Moderation is the watchword of people who are capable of only
       a small share of happiness; they wisely refuse tc pay an ex-
       orbitant price for a happiness which, at best, is but petty.

                              RELATED SUBJECTS
                              Drinking
                              Sin
                              Vice

TEMPTATION

5341   All men that are ruined, are ruined on the side of their natural
       propensities.   —*Burke*

5342   Compound for sins they are inclined to,
       By damning those they have no mind to.   —*Samuel Butler*

5343   The Woman tempted me—and tempts me still!
       Lord God, I pray You that she ever will!   —*E. V. Cooke*

5344   When Eve upon the first of men
         The apple pressed, with specious cant,
       Oh! what a thousand pities then
         That Adam was not Adamant!   —*Thomas Hood*

5345   Man's chief merit consists in resisting the impulses of his nature.
                                                       —*Johnson*

5346   How oft the sight of means to do ill deeds
       Makes ill deeds done!   —*Shakespeare*

5347   If he had been as you and you as he,
       You would have slipped like him.   —*Shakespeare*

5348   I can resist everything except temptation.   —*Oscar Wilde*

5349   The only way to get rid of a temptation is to yield to it.
                                                   —*Oscar Wilde*

5350   Anybody can be good in the country. There are no temptations
       there.   —*Oscar Wilde*

5351   The less the temptation, the greater the sin.

5352   Resist no temptation: a guilty conscience is more honorable than
       regret.

5353 Men will always show the wear and tear for having resisted a temptation.

SEE ALSO RELATED SUBJECTS
Chastity 741 Desire
Credit 1201 Devil
Marriage 3884 Honesty
Virtue 5707 Sin
Writers 6144 Vice

THEATER

5361 All tragedies are finished by a death,
All comedies are ended by a marriage. —*Byron*

5362 The first act's doubtful, but we say,
It is the last commends the play. —*Herrick*

5363 The program is nearly over! I can feel the audience is still with me—but if I run faster I can shake them off. —*Bob Hope*

5364 Not to go to the theater is like making one's toilet without a mirror. —*Schopenhauer*

5365 As long as more people will pay admission to a theater to see a naked body than to see a naked brain, the drama will languish.
—*G. B. Shaw*

SEE ALSO RELATED SUBJECTS
Courtesy 1119 Actors
Fools 2266 Art
Music

THOUGHT

5371 To generalize is to be an idiot. —*Blake*

5372 It's all right to have a train of thoughts, if you have a terminal.
—*Bowker*

5373 A New Thinker is only one who does not know what the old thinkers have thought. —*Frank M. Colby*

5374 One thought includes all thought, in the sense that a grain of sand includes the universe. —*Coleridge*

5375 The narrower the mind, the broader the statement.—*Ted Cook*

5376 In order to improve the mind, we ought less to learn, than to contemplate. —*Réné Descartes*

5377 (Cogito, ergo sum.)
I think, therefore I exist. —*Réné Descartes*

5378 All generalizations are dangerous, even this one.
—*Dumas the Younger*

5379   Contemplation is to knowledge what digestion is to food—the
       way to get life out of it.   —*Tryon Edwards*

5380   For just experience tells, in every soil,
       That those who think must govern those who toil.—*Goldsmith*

5381   A man may dwell so long upon a thought that it may take him
       prisoner.   —*Lord Halifax*

5382   The calmer thought is not always the right thought, just as the
       distant view is not always the truest view.   —*Hawthorne*

5383   Thought is the labor of the intellect, reverie is its pleasure.
                                                      —*Victor Hugo*

5384   The soul is dyed with the color of its leisure thoughts.
                                                        —*Dean Inge*

5385   A fat paunch never breeds fine thoughts.   —*St. Jerome*

5386   What is mind? No matter. What is matter? Never mind.
                                                    —*Thomas H. Key*

5387   Where all think alike, no one thinks very much.
                                                   —*Walter Lippmann*

5388   If you make people think they're thinking, they'll love you. If you
       really make them think, they'll hate you.   —*Don Marquis*

5389   The mind ought sometimes to be diverted that it may return to
       better thinking.   —*Phaedrus*

5390   Thinking is the talking of the soul with itself.   —*Plato*

5391   Hundreds can talk to one who can think; thousands can think to
       one who can see.   —*Ruskin*

5392   There is nothing either good or bad,
       But thinking makes it so.   —*Shakespeare*

5393   They are never alone that are accompanied with noble thoughts.
                                                   —*Sir Philip Sidney*

5394   Associate reverently, and as much as you can, with your loftiest
       thoughts.   —*Thoreau*

5395   Monotony mocks at life; thought belittles it.

5396   Paradoxes: Thoughts that do not go to church on Sunday.

5397 Deliberating is not delaying.

SEE ALSO
Action 11, 17
Art 291
Character 709
Drinking 1713
Experience 2002
Man 3822
People 4389
Youth 6204

RELATED SUBJECTS
Ideas
Ignorance
Philosophy
Wisdom

TIME

5401 I consider time as an immense ocean, in which many noble authors are entirely swallowed up. —*Addison*

5402 To choose time is to save time. —*Bacon*

5403 Others mistrust and say: "But time escapes—
Live now or never!"
He said: "What's time? Leave Now for dogs and apes!
Man has For ever. —*Browning*

5404 It was a favorite expression of Theophrastus that time was the most valuable thing that a man could spend.
—*Diogenes Laertius*

5405 Time goes, you say? Ah no!—
Alas, time stays, we go. —*Dobson*

5406 The times are the masquerade of the eternities. —*Emerson*

5407 We ask for long life, but 'tis deep life, or noble moments that signify. Let the measure of time be spiritual, not mechanical.
—*Emerson*

5408 The years teach much which the days never know. —*Emerson*

5409 Time will discover everything to posterity; it is a babbler, and speaks even when no question is put. —*Euripides*

5410 Dost thou love life? Then waste not time; for time is the stuff that life is made of. —*Franklin*

5411 You cannot step twice into the same stream. For as you are stepping in, other and yet other waters flow on. —*Heraclitus*

5412 Made, bitter-sweet, from fruits of life
There is a wine;
It quenches every human thirst—
We call it time. —*Jean Herrick*

5413 Some people can stay longer in an hour than others can in a week. —*W. D. Howells*

5414   Time, whose tooth gnaws away everything else, is powerless
       against truth.   —*T. H. Huxley*

5415   God has commanded Time to console the unhappy.   —*Joubert*

5416   The things of mortals, mortal are as they:
       All pass us by, quickly to fade away,
       If not, we pass by them and they decay.   —*Lucian*

5417   Lost, yesterday, somewhere between sunrise and sunset, two gold-
       en hours, each set with sixty diamond minutes. No reward is
       offered for they are gone forever.   —*Horace Mann*

5418   It is astonishing what a lot of odd minutes one can catch during
       the day, if one really sets about it.   —*Dinah Maria Mulock*

5419   The reason I beat the Austrians is, they did not know the value
       of five minutes.   —*Napoleon*

5420   Those we call the ancients were really new in everything.
                                                          —*Pascal*

5421   Time on its back bears all things far away.
       Full many a change is wrought by many a day.
       Shape, fortune, name, and nature all decay.   —*Plato*

5422   Time carries off all things; would'st thou exchange
       Name, looks, nature, luck? Just give time full range.   —*Plato*

5423   Pythagoras, when he was asked what time was, answered that it
       was the soul of this world.   —*Plutarch*

5424   Time goes, you say? Ah, no!
       Alas, Time stays, *we* go;
           Or else, were this not so,
           What need to chain the hours,
           For Youth were always ours?
       Time goes, you say—Ah, no!   —*Pierre de Ronsard*

5425   Whatever begins, also ends.   —*Seneca*

5426   A man who has taken your time recognizes no debt; yet it is the
       one he can never repay.   —*Seneca*

5427   Time himself is bald, and therefore to the world's end will have
       bald followers.   —*Shakespeare*

5428   We are Ancients of the earth,
       And in the morning of the times.   —*Tennyson*

5429   As if you could kill time without injuring eternity!   —*Thoreau*

5430   There's scarce a point whereon mankind agree
So well as in their boast of killing me;
I boast of nothing, but when I've a mind
I think I can be even with mankind.   *—Voltaire, on Time*

5431   Counting time is not so important as making time count.
—James J. Walker

5432   If you're there before it's over, you're on time.*—James J. Walker*

5433   He was always late on principle, his principle being that punctuality is the thief of time.   *—Oscar Wilde*

5434   It chanceth in an hour, that comes not in seven years.

5435   Old Time kills us all,
Rich, poor, great, and small,
And 'tis therefore we rack our invention,
Throughout all our days,
In finding out ways
To kill by way of prevention.

5436   Time wears out a man and commits outrages upon woman.

5437   No one can pass into Eternity; we are in it.

SEE ALSO	RELATED SUBJECTS
Coquetry 1069	Age
Courtesy 1110	Day
Grief 2695	Delay
Love 3730	Memory

TOBACCO

5441   The man who smokes thinks like a sage and acts like a Samaritan.
—Bulwer-Lytton

5442   A good cigar is as great a comfort to a man as a good cry to a woman.   *—Bulwer-Lytton*

5443   And a woman is only a woman, but a good cigar is a smoke.
—Kipling

5444   For thy sake, tobacco, I
Would do anything but die.   *—Lamb*

5445   What this country needs is a good five-cent cigar.
—Thomas R. Marshall

5446   To smoke a cigar through a mouthpiece is equivalent to kissing a lady through a respirator.

RELATED SUBJECTS
Drinking
Habit
Vice

TOLERANCE

5451 Unfortunately I have an open mind. I let down a window in my brain about six or seven inches from the top even in the bitterest weather.   —*Heywood Broun*

5452 The responsibility of tolerance lies with those who have the wider vision.   —*George Eliot*

5453 By burning Luther's books you may rid your book-shelves of him, but you will not rid men's minds of him.   —*Erasmus*

5454 The only tolerance in the world, the only tolerance that earns the name, is that toward intolerance.   —*Louis Paul*

5455 The eagle suffers little birds to sing,
And is not careful what they mean thereby.   —*Shakespeare*

5456 I do not agree with a word that you say, but I will defend to the death your right to say it.   —*Voltaire*

5457 To some women a broadminded man is one who allows his wife a latitude of actions which he wouldn't dare follow himself.

5458 The objection to an open mind is that convictions get out as often as new ideas get in.

5459 Not to be captious, not unjustly fight,
'Tis to confess what's wrong, and do what's right.

SEE ALSO   RELATED SUBJECTS
Belief 447   Liberty
                           Opinion
                           Reform
                           Religion

TONGUE

5461 No member needs so great a number of muscles as the tongue; this exceeds all the rest in the number of its movements.
                                                          —*Da Vinci*

5462 A sharp tongue is the only edge tool that grows keener with constant use.   —*Washington Irving*

5463 A fluent tongue is the only thing a mother don't like her daughter to resemble her in.   —*Sheridan*

5464 A woman's tongue is her sword and she never lets it rust.

SEE ALSO   RELATED SUBJECTS
Courtship 1171   Conversation
                           Speeches

TRAVEL

5471 How much a dunce that has been sent to roam
Excels a dunce that has been kept at home!   *—Cowper*

5472 A merry companion is as good as a wagon.   *—John Lyly*

5473 The vagabond, when rich, is called a tourist.   *—Paul Richard*

5474 To travel hopefully is a better thing than to arrive.*—Stevenson*

SEE ALSO   RELATED SUBJECTS
Books 508   Automobiles
Poverty 4565   World
Solitude 5156

TREASON

5481 Treason doth never prosper. What's the reason?
For if it prospers, none dare call it treason.
—Sir John Harrington

5482 'Tis not seasonable to call a man a traitor that has an army at his
heels.   *—Selden*

5483 I wondered not when I was told,
The venal Scot his country sold;
But this I very much admire,
Where the deuce he found a buyer!

SEE ALSO   RELATED SUBJECTS
Fear 2176   Crime
Laughter 3361   Patriotism

TREE

5491 I like trees because they seem more resigned to the way they have
to live than other things do.   *—Willa Cather*

5492 Except during the nine months before he draws his first breath,
no man manages his affairs as well as a tree does.*—G. B. Shaw*

5493 The tree is no sooner down, but every one runs for his hatchet.

RELATED SUBJECT
Nature

TRIFLES

5500 He that despiseth little things shall perish by little and little.
—Bible

5501 Exactness in little things is a wonderful source of cheerfulness.
—F. W. Faber

5502 Little minds are too much hurt by little things; great minds are
quite conscious of them, and despise them.*—La Rochefoucauld*

5503   Recollect that trifles make perfection, and perfection is no trifle.
                                                        —*Michelangelo*

5504   A hole is nothing at all, but you can break your neck in it.
                                                        —*Austin O'Malley*

5505   With lovers and sick people there are no trifles.

5506   There is something airy and elusive about the superficial which
          saves it from ridicule.

5507   'Tis the little rift within the lute
          That by and by will make the music mute,
          And, ever widening, slowly silence all.
                                                        —*Tennyson*

5508   Great fleas have little fleas
             Upon their backs to bite 'em,
          And these again have lesser fleas,
             And so—ad infinitum.

SEE ALSO   RELATED SUBJECT
Doctors 1655   Vanity
Love 3727

TROUBLES

5521   He that mischief hatcheth, mischief catcheth. —*William Camden*

5522   Never bear more than one kind of trouble at a time. Some people
          bear three—all they have had, all they have now, and all they
          expect to have.   —*Edward Everett Hale*

5523   Troubles are like babies—they only grow by nursing.
                                                        —*Douglas Jerrold*

5524   there is always
          a comforting thought
          in time of trouble when
          it is not our trouble.   —*Don Marquis*

5525   I am an old man and have known a great many troubles, but
          most of them never happened.   —*Mark Twain*

5526   Laugh a little more at your own troubles and a little less at your
          neighbor's.

5527   He that will have no trouble in this world must not be born in it.

5528   He that seeks trouble it were a pity he should miss it.

SEE ALSO   RELATED SUBJECTS
Drinking 1720   Difficulty
Love 3723   Hardship
Prohibition 4661

TRUST

5531 Let us have a care not to disclose our hearts to those who shut up
theirs against us. —*Francis Beaumont*

5532 Sole friend to worth,
And patroness of all good spirits, Confidence. —*Chapman*

5533 You may be deceived if you trust too much, but you will live in
torment if you do not trust enough. —*Frank Crane*

5534 God has delivered yourself to your care, and says: "I had no
fitter to trust than you." —*Epictetus*

5535 Skill and confidence are an unconquered army.—*George Herbert*

5536 By mutual confidence and mutual aid
Great deeds are done, and great discoveries made. —*Homer*

5537 Confidence is a plant of slow growth; especially in an aged
bosom. —*Johnson*

5538 To be trusted is a greater compliment than to be loved.
—*George Macdonald*

5539 It is an excellent means of gaining the heart of others to submit
and trust in it. —*Montaigne*

5540 Confidence, like the soul, never returns whence it has once de-
parted. —*Publilius Syrus*

5541 If you trust before you try,
You may repent before you die. —*Ray*

5542 He who mistrusts most should be trusted least. —*Theognis*

5543 It is an equal failing to trust everybody, and to trust nobody.

5544 Confidence goeth farther in company than good sense.

5545 Suspicion is the courageous side of weakness.

5546 Alas! when people have confidence again they will again have confidence in the wrong thing.

5547 Man argues woman may not be trusted too far; woman feels man
cannot be trusted too near.

SEE ALSO	RELATED SUBJECTS
Enemies 1836	Belief
Money 4031	Credit
Virtue 5684	Duty
	Faith
	Honesty
	Sincerity

TRUTH

5550 Pure truth cannot be assimilated by the crowd; it must be communicated by contagion.
—*Amiel*

5551 Defeat is a school in which truth always grows strong.
—*H. W. Beecher*

5552 A truth that's told with bad intent
Beats all the lies you can invent.   —*Blake*

5553 Truth is the shattered mirror strown
In myriad bits; while each believes his little bit the whole to own.
—*Burton*

5554 For things said false and never meant,
Do oft prove true by accident.   —*Samuel Butler*

5555 Truths turn into dogmas the moment they are disputed.
—*Chesterton*

5556 Baldwin occasionally stumbles over the truth, but he always hastily picks himself up and hurries on as if nothing had happened.
—*Winston Churchill*

5557 Veracity does not consist in *saying,* but in the intention of *communicating* truth.   —*Coleridge*

5558 Truth is the object of philosophy, but not always of philosophers.
—*Churton Collins*

5559 Every gaudy color
Is a bit of truth.   —*Nathalia Crane*

5560 There is nothing so strong or safe in an emergency of life as the simple truth.   —*Dickens*

5561 The greatest homage we can pay to truth is to use it.—*Emerson*

5562 Truth is the property of no individual but is the treasure of all men.   —*Emerson*

5563 God offers to every mind its choice between truth and repose. Take which you please—you can never have both.—*Emerson*

5564 Craft must have clothes, but truth loves to go naked.
—*Thomas Fuller*

5565 An exaggeration is a truth that has lost its temper.
—*Kahlil Gibran*

5566 Those who honestly mean to be true contradict themselves more rarely than those who try to be consistent.   —*O. W. Holmes*

5567 It is the customary fate of new truths to begin as heresies and to end as superstitions.   —*T. H. Huxley*

5568 Irrationally held truths may be more harmful than reasoned errors.
            —*T. H. Huxley*

5569 It is always the best policy to speak the truth, unless of course, you are an exceptionally good liar. —*Jerome K. Jerome*

5570 When speculation has done its worst, two and two still make four.
            —*Johnson*

5571 What is true by lamplight is not always true by sunlight.
            —*Joubert*

5572 The veracity which increases with old age is not far from folly.
          —*La Rochefoucauld*

5573 Truth uttered before its time is always dangerous. —*Mencius*

5574 The average man does not get pleasure out of an idea because he thinks it is true; he thinks it is true because he gets pleasure out of it.   —*Mencken*

5575 I speak truth, not all I would like to, but as much as I dare to speak.   —*Montaigne*

5576 I may indeed very well happen to contradict myself; but truth, as Demades said, I do not contradict.   —*Montaigne*

5577 Some folks never handle the truth without scratching it.
         —*Austin O'Malley*

5578 The old faiths light their candles all about, but burly truth comes by and blows them out.   —*Lizette W. Reese*

5579 My way of joking is to tell the truth. It's the funniest joke in the world.   —*G. B. Shaw*

5580 It takes two to speak truth—one to speak and another to hear.
          —*Thoreau*

5581 Truth is such a precious article let us all economize in its use.
         —*Mark Twain*

5582 Tell the truth, and so puzzle and confound your adversaries.
        —*Sir Henry Wotton*

5583 Truth belongs to the realm of science; it plays no part in man's happiness.

5584 I don't know if truth is stranger than fiction; it is certainly more disconcerting.

5585 What a mad scramble in search after truth; when truth has invariably proven so inessential.

5586 Seeing's believing, but feeling's the truth.

5587   Absolute truth does not border upon, but actually overlaps, fanaticism.

5588   "Truer words were never spoken—"
Ah, but true words leave hearts broken!
Truth is only for the wise—
Lovers ought to stick to lies.

5589   Some of the things that seem too good to be true—they just aren't true.

5590   Platitudes are among the most useful things in the world for those who know how to use them, for truth is not the worse for being obvious, undeniable, or familiar.

SEE ALSO
Age 171
Beauty 349
Belief 441
France 2341
Hardship 2795
News 4174
Time 5414

RELATED SUBJECTS
Facts
Frankness
Honesty
Lies

U

UNDERSTANDING

5591   It is not the hand, but the understanding of a man, that may be said to write.   —*Cervantes*

5592   There are three things I have always loved, and never understood —painting, music, women.   —*Fontenelle*

5593   It is better to understand little than to misunderstand a lot.
—*Anatole France*

5594   To understand everything is to forgive everything.   —*Gautama*

5595   We shall never understand one another until we reduce the language to seven words.   —*Kahlil Gibran*

5596   He who does not understand your silence will probably not understand your words.   —*Elbert Hubbard*

5597   Men are most apt to believe what they least understand.
—*Montaigne*

5598   Women are wiser than men because they know less and understand more.   —*James Stephens*

SEE ALSO
God 2534

RELATED SUBJECTS
Error   Wisdom
Mistake

V

VALUE

5601 Worth seeing? yes; but not worth going to see.   —*Johnson*

5602 Nothing is so useless as a general maxim.   —*Macaulay*

5603 "So so" is good, very good, very excellent good; and yet it is not;
it is but so so.   —*Shakespeare*

5604 It is no good hen, that cackles in your house and lays in another's.

5605 Half a loaf is better than no bread.

5606 Weeds are as much a part of Life as cultivated plants; they are
misplaced only according to human conceptions.

SEE ALSO   RELATED SUBJECTS
Cynicism 1294   Character
Fools 2261   Price

VANITY

5611 In heaven I yearn for knowledge, account all else inanity;
On earth I confess an itch for the praise of fools—that's vanity.
     —*Browning*

5612 There's no weapon that slays
Its victim so surely (if well aimed) as praise.   —*Bulwer-Lytton*

5613 Men are vain, but they won't mind women's working so long as
they get smaller salaries for the same jobs.   —*Irvin S. Cobb*

5614 If you cannot inspire a woman with love of you, fill her above the
brim with love of herself; all that runs over will be yours.
     —*C. C. Colton*

5615 Vanity, like murder, will out.   —*Cowley*

5616 The solemn fop; significant and budge;
A fool with judges, amongst fools a judge.   —*Cowper*

5617 The black crow thinketh her own birds white.—*Gavin Douglas*

5618 True fops help nature's work, and go to school
To file and finish God Almighty's fool.   —*Dryden*

5619 The time he can spare from the adornment of his person he de-
votes to the neglect of his duties.   —*Jowett*

5620   What makes the vanity of other people insupportable is that it wounds our own.   —*La Rochefoucauld*

5621   Part of your face is clipped, part shaven, part has the hair pulled out. Who would believe that you have but one head?—*Martial*

5622   Zoilus, why do you delight in using a whole pound weight of gold for the setting of a stone, and thus burying your poor sardonyx? Such rings are more suited to your legs; the weight is too great for fingers.   —*Martial*

5623   Since naked on the earth I made my start
       And naked must beneath the earth depart—
       Then, for a naked end why vex my heart?   —*Palladas*

5624   Nature made ev'ry fop to plague his brother,
       Just as one beauty mortifies another.   —*Pope*

5625   She would rather be looked around at than up to.—*Phil Robinson*

5626   Provided a man is not mad, he can be cured of every folly but vanity.   —*Rousseau*

5627   Vanity is the quicksand of reason.   —*George Sand*

5628   He who blushes at riding in a rattle-trap, will boast when he rides in style.   —*Seneca*

5629   Every occasion will catch the senses of the vain man, and with that bridle and saddle you may ride him.—*Sir Philip Sidney*

5630   She is a peacock in everything but beauty.   —*Oscar Wilde*

5631   Vanity as an impulse has without doubt been of far more benefit to civilization than modesty has ever been.—*W. E. Woodward*

5632   Only a vain woman can live by the emotions she inspires.

5633   Tacit admiration flatters only the vain.

SEE ALSO   RELATED SUBJECTS
Coquetry 1070   Conceit
Generosity 2463   Fame
Talent 5266   Flattery
                           Illusion
                           Mirror
                           Snob

VICE

5641   The willing contemplation of vice is vice.   —*Arabian Proverb*

5642   Every vice was once a virtue, and may become respectable again, just as hatred becomes respectable in wartime.—*Will Durant*

5643   There is no man who is not at some time indebted to his vices, as
        no plant that is not fed from manures.   —*Emerson*

5644   What maintains one vice would bring up two children.
                                                            —*Franklin*

5645   One big vice in a man is apt to keep out a great many smaller ones.
                                                            —*Bret Harte*

5646   When our vices quit us, we flatter ourselves with the belief that it
        is we who quit them.   —*La Rochefoucauld*

5647   A vice is a failure of desire.   —*Lee*

5648   It has ever been my experience that folks who have no vices have
        very few virtues.   —*Lincoln*

5649   It is false to say that you are a vicious man, Zoilus; you are not a
        vicious man, you are vice itself.   —*Martial*

5650   Vice leaves, like an ulcer in the flesh, a repentance in the soul,
        which is always scratching itself until it bleeds.—*Montaigne*

5651   The heart resolves this matter in a trice,
        "Men only feel the smart, but not the vice."   —*Pope*

5652   Vice is a monster of so frightful mien,
        As to be hated needs but to be seen;
        Yet seen too oft, familiar with her face,
        We first endure, then pity, then embrace.   —*Pope*

5653   The diff'rence is too nice
        Where ends the virtue or begins the vice.   —*Pope*

5654   Vices that are familiar we pardon, and only new ones do we
        reprehend.   —*Publilius Syrus*

5655   Vices are often habits rather than passions.   —*Rivarol*

5656   Vice repeated is like the wandering wind; blows dust in others
        eyes, to spread itself.   —*Shakespeare*

5657   One usually boasts of a vice that one can get rid of at will.

5658   Assume a vice though you have it not, with the hope that it may
        grow upon you.

VIRTUE

5661   Many wish not so much to be virtuous, as to seem to be —*Cicero*

5662   All bow to virtue, and then walk away.   —*De Finod*

5663   The virtue which requires to be ever guarded is scarcely worth
       the sentinel.   —*Goldsmith*

5664   They who disbelieve in virtue because man has never been found
       perfect, might as reasonably deny the sun because it is not al-
       ways noon.   —*Hare*

5665   Men are virtuous because women are; women are virtuous from
       necessity.   —*E. W. Howe*

5666   Virtue is a beautiful thing in woman when they don't go about
       with it like a child with a drum making all sorts of noise
       with it.   —*Douglas Jerrold*

5667   Let them call it mischief:
       When it is past and prospered 'twill be virtue.   —*Jonson*

5668   Wisdom is knowing what to do next; virtue is doing it.
                                              —*David Starr Jordan*

5669   Virtue by calculation is the virtue of vice.   —*Joubert*

5670   Virtue's admired—and shivers with the cold.   —*Juvenal*

5671   To remain virtuous a man has only to combat his own desires; a
       woman must resist her own inclinations and the continual
       attack of man.   —*De Latena*

5672   The resistance of a woman is not always a proof of her virtue,
       but more frequently of her experience.   —*Ninon de l'Enclos*

5673   Virtue, with some women, is but the precaution of locking doors.
                                                          —*Lemonley*

5674   Abraham Lincoln
       his hand and pen.
       he will be good but
       god knows When.
                                 —*Lincoln in a childhood copy book*

5675   What an antiseptic is a pure life!   —*Lowell*

5676   Nothing is more adroit than irreproachable conduct.
                                              —*Madame de Maintenon*

5677   Affectation hides three times as many virtues as charity does sins.
                                                     —*Horace Mann*

5678   A man should *be* upright, not be *kept* upright.—*Marcus Aurelius*

5679   You say, Senca, that you were violated by robbers, but the rob-
       bers deny it.   *—Martial*

5680   You say, Bassa, that you are beautiful. You say that you are a
       maiden. She who is not so, Bassa, is generally ready to say that
       she is.   *—Martial*

5681   Rumor says, Chione, that you have never had to do with men, and
       that nothing can be purer than yourself. And yet when you
       bathe, you veil not that part which you should veil. If you have
       any modesty, veil your face.   *—Martial*

5682   Good men make life a twofold span to last:
       Twice does he live who can enjoy his past.   *—Martial*

5683   O God, keep me innocent; make others great!
               —Caroline Matilda, Queen of Denmark

5684   Confidence in another man's virtue is no slight evidence of one's
       own.   *—Montaigne*

5685   Disappointment and feebleness imprint upon us a cowardly and
       valetudinarian virtue.   *—Montaigne*

5686   If you would return to virtue, you must shun depravity—
       Fatherland and father follow, more than foreign infamy.
                                    —Naevius

5687   When men grow virtuous in their old age, they only make a sacri-
       fice to God of the devil's leavings.   *—Pope*

5688   The path of a good woman is indeed strewn with flowers; but
       they rise behind her steps, not before them.   *—Ruskin*

5689   No virtue is safe that is not enthusiastic.   *—J. R. Seeley*

5690   Virtue rejects a mean admirer: you must come to her with open
       purse.   *—Seneca*

5691   Hold thou her sinless who has sinned for thee.   *—Seneca*

5692   The good man is Nature's creditor, giving her back better life
       than he had of her.   *—Seneca*

5693   Dost thou think, because thou art virtuous, there shall be no more
       cakes and ale?   *—Shakespeare*

5694   There was never virgin got till virginity was first lost.
                                 —Shakespeare

5695   Virtue consists, not in abstaining from vice, but in not desiring it.
                                  —G. B. Shaw

5696   Blessedness is not the reward of virtue but virtue itself.*—Spinoza*

5697   I think I could be a good woman if I had five thousand a year.
                                                      —*Thackeray*

5698   Be not simply good; be good for something.   —*Thoreau*

5699   There is no odor so bad as that which arises from goodness tainted.
                                                       —*Thoreau*

5700   There are no women to whom virtue comes easier than those who
          possess no attractions.

5701   Only the good want to die young.

5702   Virtue carries its own reward and a mighty sad consolation.

5703   Every whisper in a woman's ear is an attack upon her virtue.

5704   In the generality of men their virtues are nothing else but their
          vices at rest.

5705   Good man: one who is neither clever enough to avoid tempta-
          tions, nor wise enough to yield to them.

5706   Since riches lead to vice,
          And poverty to theft,
          Outside of paradise
          Is any virtue left?

5707   Virtue—in the female, lack of temptation—in the male, lack of
          opportunity.

5708   Virtue which parleys, is near a surrender.

SEE ALSO   RELATED SUBJECTS
Ancestors 232   Blushing
Beauty 391   Character
Blushing 471   Chastity
Crime 1235   Decency
Discretion 1643   Fidelity
Lawyers 3423   Honesty
Passion 4317   Honor
Wealth 5787   Modesty
                                  Morality
                                  Remorse
                                  Saint
                                  Sin

VULGARITY

5711   To the vulgar eye, few things are wonderful that are not distant.
                                                       —*Carlyle*

5712   Vulgarity is simply the conduct of other people.   —*Oscar Wilde*

5713   Details are always vulgar.
                                                    —*Oscar Wilde*

5714   Woman is less vulgar but more commonplace than man.

5715   Vulgarity is the rich man's modest contribution to democracy.

5716   There are fewer vulgar women than men, but they are more re-
        pulsive.

SEE ALSO   RELATED SUBJECTS
Courtesy 1104   Conceit
                          Pride
                          Wealth

W

WAR

5722   On at them! A battle's not lost till 'tis won.
        Both sides owe self-respect. Thus, he who shows
        Triumph in the face of his beaten foes,
        Merits not success.   —*Archilochus of Paros*

5723   Violence does even justice unjustly.   —*Carlyle*

5724   War means fightin', and fightin' means killin'.
                                           —*Gen. N. B. Forrest*

5725   I have always noticed that God is on the side of the heavy bat-
        talions.   —*Marquis de la Ferte Imbault*

5726   A great war leaves the country with three armies—an army of
        cripples, an army of mourners, and an army of thieves.
                                           —*German proverb*

5727   My argument is that War makes rattling good history; but
        Peace is poor reading.   —*Thomas Hardy*

5728   You know what a tank is . . .
        It's a used car with protection from the finance company.
                                           —*Bob Hope*

5729   Waterloo is a battle of the first rank won by a captain of the
        second.   —*Victor Hugo*

5730   The Prussian schoolmaster won the battle of Sadowa.
                                           —*Von Moltke*

5731   When you can use the lightning it is better than cannon.
                                           —*Napoleon*

5732   The battle of Waterloo was won on the playing fields of Eton.
                                           —*Duke of Wellington*

5733   Nothing except a battle lost can be half so melancholy as a battle won.   *—Duke of Wellington*

5734   The real war will never get in the books.   *—Whitman*

5735   Have you heard that it was good to gain the day?
I also say it is good to fall, battles are lost in the same spirit in which they are won.   *—Whitman*

5736   Thought refuses to be stationary, institutions refuse to change, and war is the consequence.   *—E. L. Youmans*

5737   The conquered is never called wise, nor the conqueror rash.

5738   The old Irish when immersing a babe at baptism left out the right arm so that it would remain pagan for good fighting.

5739   The war that will end war will not be fought with guns.

5740   Another thing against war is that it seldom if ever kills off the right people.

5741   War is brought on by countries that want peace at their own price.

5742   The war spark is often fanned by trade winds.

5743   There will be more wars until men grow brave enough to stop them.

5744   War makes fright, fright makes alliances, alliances make war.

5745   And the greatest paradox of them all is still Civilized Warfare.

SEE ALSO	RELATED SUBJECTS
Aim 197	Death
America 202	Enemies
Business 579	Fight
Cowardice 1181	Sailors
Kings 3295	Soldiers
Patriotism 4342	
Time 5419	

WEAKNESS

5751   Better make a weak man your enemy than your friend.
    —Josh Billings

5752   Women are never stronger than when they arm themselves with their weakness.   *—Mme. du Deffand*

5753   Our strength grows out of our weakness.   *—Emerson*

5754   People who have no weaknesses are terrible; there is no way of
        taking advantage of them.   *—Anatole France*

SEE ALSO	RELATED SUBJECTS
Advice 101	Cowardice
Books 493	Failure
Criticism 1262	Fear
Gambling 2446	Sin
Hate 2837	Temptation
Passion 4318	Wickedness

WEALTH

5761   Though thy broad lands beyond the Pillars stretch
        No more thou ownest than the poorest wretch.
        Like Irus, all thy wealth in one dead hand,
        Thy corpse lies mouldering in another's land.   *—Ammianus*

5762   He has not acquired a fortune; the fortune has acquired him.
                                                            —Bion

5763   The worst thing that can happen to a man is to lose his money,
        the next worst his health, the next worst his reputation.
                                                    —Samuel Butler

5764   We call our rich relatives the kin we love to touch.—*Eddie Cantor*

5765   Wealth, after all, is a relative thing, since he that has little, and
        wants less, is richer than he that has much, and wants more.
                                                    —C. C. Colton

5766   Prosperity is only an instrument to be used; not a deity to be
        worshipped.   *—Calvin Coolidge*

5767   He is only rich who owns the day.   *—Emerson*

5768   Riches serve a wise man, but command a fool.—*Thomas Fuller*

5769   Too poor for a bribe, and too proud to importune,
        He had not the method of making a fortune.   *—Thomas Gray*

5770   Poor in my youth, and in life's later scenes
            Rich to no end, I curse my natal hour,
        Who naught enjoyed while young, denied the means;
            And naught when old enjoy'd, denied the power.
                                                    —Greek epigram

5771   Punishment of a miser—to pay the drafts of his heir in his tomb.
                                                    —Hawthorne

5772   Get place and wealth, if possible, with grace;
        If not, by any means get wealth and place.   *—Horace*

5773   If Rockyfeller could eat he wouldn't be so rich.—*Kin Hubbard*

5774   Another bad thing about "prosperity" is that you can't jingle any
       money without bein' under suspicion.   —*Kin Hubbard*

5775   It seems t' me that when a feller hain't got neither time ner
       money t' do a thing our celebrated prosperity has reached th'
       limit.   —*Kin Hubbard*

5776   These heroes of finance are like beads on a string—when one slips
       off, all the rest follow.   —*Ibsen*

5777   'Tis better to live rich than to die rich.   —*Johnson*

5778   How you've got rich, none cares; rich you must be.   —*Juvenal*

5779   When I wish I was rich, then I know I am ill.—*D. H. Lawrence*

5780   They call thee rich; I deem thee poor;
       Since, if thou darest not use thy store,
       But savest only for thine heirs,
       The treasure is not thine, but theirs.   —*Lucillius*

5781   Africanus is a millionaire, yet he is a legacy hunter. Fortune gives
       too much to many, enough to none.   —*Martial*

5782   To be angry is all you know, you rich friends. You do not act
       prettily, but it is more profitable to get angry than to give.
                                                             —*Martial*

5783   You had spent, Apicius, sixty millions of sesterces on your belly,
       but you had still left a loose ten millions. In despair at such a
       reduction, as if you were condemned to endure hunger and
       thirst, you took as a last draught a dose of poison. No greater
       proof of gluttony than this, Apicius, was ever given by you.
                                                             —*Martial*

5784   The only wealth which you will keep forever is the wealth which
       you have given away.   —*Martial*

5785   There's nothing so comfortable as a small bankroll. A big one is
       always in danger.   —*Wilson Mizner*

5786   Money, the only substance which can keep a cold world from
       nicknaming a citizen "Hey, you!"   —*Wilson Mizner*

5787   In the case of our multi-millionaires virtues must necessarily be
       "sterling virtues."   —*Gustavus Myers*

5788   Thou'rt growing rich. What good can riches be?
       Thy coffin has not room for them and thee.
       Thou spendest hours in gathering in thy store,
       Yet cans't not add to life one hour the more.   —*Palladas*

5789   When a man dies he clutches in his hands only that which he has
       given away during his lifetime.   —*Rousseau*

5790   Wealth falls on some men as a copper down a drain.—*Seneca*

5791   Health without wealth is half a sickness.

5792   He that has money is bothered about it;
And he that has none is bothered without it.

5793   Thou canst not serve God, unless thy mammon serve thee.

5794   Riches have made more men covetous, than covetousness hath made men rich.

5795   Riches are like muck, which stink in a heap, but spread abroad, make the earth fruitful.

5796   For one rich man that is content there are a hundred that are not.

5797   God shows His contempt for wealth by the kind of persons He selects to receive it.

5798   This man was wondrous rich, and oft did crave
To bear his riches with him to the grave—
But Death was stern, and stopped them at the door,
So took him only, penniless and poor.

5799   The brother had rather see the sister rich than make her so.

5800   It is about as hard for a rich man to enter heaven as it is for a poor man to remain on earth.

See Also	Related Subjects
Character 717	Greed
Vulgarity 5715	Fortune
	Money
	Property

WEATHER

5801   De win' can blow lak hurricane
     An' s'pose she blow some more
You can't get drown on Lac St. Pierre
So long you stay on shore.   —*W. H. Drummond*

5802   Whichever way the wind doth blow
Some heart is glad to have it so;
Then blow it east or blow it west,
The wind that blows, that wind is best.   —*Caroline A. Mason*

5803   Winter lingered so long in the lap of Spring, that it occasioned a great deal of talk.   —*Bill Nye*

5804   Sunshine is delicious, rain is refreshing, wind braces up, snow is exhilarating; there is really no such thing as bad weather, only different kinds of good weather.   —*Ruskin*

5805   Everybody talks about the weather, but nobody does anything
        about it.   —*Charles Dudley Warner*

5806   There is nothing more universally commended than a fine day; the
        reason is that people can commend it without envy.
                                                         —*William Shenstone*

5807   The melancholy days are come, the saddest of the year;
        Not cold enough for whiskey hot, but too damn cold for beer.

SEE ALSO   RELATED SUBJECTS
Hardship 2811   Day
Resignation 4862   Sun

WICKEDNESS

5811   There never was a bad man that had ability for good service.
                                                         —*Burke*

5812   When Pompey was Rome's consul first,
        'Twas with but two adulterers cursed.
        When next he did the office fill,
        These two remain'd to cuckold still;
        But they had managed so to teach,
        That myriads more had sprung from each:
        So fast it breeds and breeds again,
        The taste for wives of other men.   —*Catullus*

5813   The belief in a supernatural source of evil is not necessary: men
        alone are quite capable of every wickedness.   —*Joseph Conrad*

5814   Corruption never has been compulsory.   —*Anthony Eden*

5815   Sing-Sing has several men who were sent there simply because
        they had Axminster desires and rag-carpet capacities.
                                                         —*Elbert Hubbard*

5816   None in a moment e'er grew wholly vile.   —*Juvenal*

5817   Wickedness sucks in the greater part of its own venom, and poi-
        sons itself therewith.   —*Montaigne*

5818   But when to mischief mortals bend their will, how soon they find
        fit instruments of ill!   —*Pope*

5819   You may be as orthodox as the Devil, and as wicked.
                                                         —*John Wesley*

5820   As good a knave I know as a knave I know not.

5821   Rogues differ little. Each began first as a disobedient son.

5822   Corruption of the best becomes the worst.

5823　Those who admire strength in a rascal do not live in his town.

RELATED SUBJECTS
Character
Conscience
Error
Evil
Guilt
Morality
Sin
Vice

WIDOW

5831　A widow of doubtful age will marry almost any sort of a white man. ―*Horace Greeley*

5832　Easy-crying widows take new husbands soonest; there's nothing like wet weather for transplanting. ―*O. W. Holmes*

5833　A married man can do anything he likes if his wife don't mind. A widower can't be too careful. ―*G. B. Shaw*

5834　He that would woo a maid must feign, lie and flatter,
But he that woos a widow must down with his britches and at her. ―*Nathaniel Smith*

5835　A buxom widow must be either married, buried, or shut up in a convent.

5836　A good occasion of courtship is when the widow returns from the funeral.

5837　Sorrow for a husband is like a pain in the elbow, sharp and short.

5838　Who marries a widow and two daughters marries three thieves.

5839　Be wary how you marry one that hath cast her rider, I mean a widow.

5840　When a man marries a widow his jealousies revert to the past: no man is as good as his wife says her first husband was.

5841　A widow in love tries either to efface her past or re-enact it―she will forever compare.

RELATED SUBJECTS
Husband
Marriage
Wife

WIFE

5851　Wives in their husbands' absences grow subtler,
And daughters sometimes run off with the butler. ―*Byron*

5852 When a man says, "Get out of my house! what would you have
      with my wife?" there's no answer to be made.   —*Cervantes*

5853 My wife has a whim of iron.   —*Oliver Herford*

5854 Lycoris has buried all her female friends, Fabianus. I wish she
      could make friends with my wife.   —*Martial*

5855 You ask why I won't marry a rich wife? Because I don't want to
      pass as my wife's husband. The wife should be inferior to the
      husband, Priscus. That is the only way to insure equality be-
      tween the two.   —*Martial*

5856 There was no one in the whole city, Caecilianus, who desired to
      meddle with your wife, even gratis, while permission was given;
      but now, since you have set a watch upon her, the crowd of gal-
      lants is enormous. You are a clever fellow!   —*Martial*

5857 Amongst Lybian tribes your wife, Gallus, has a bad reputation;
      they charge her foully with insatiate greed. But these stories are
      simply lies; she is not at all in the habit of receiving favors.
      What then is her habit? She gives them.   —*Martial*

5858 This is now the seventh wife that you have buried in your field,
      Phileros. No one gets a better return from his field than you
      do.   —*Martial*

5859 Do you wonder, Caecilianus, why Afer does not retire to rest?
      You see with whom he has to share his couch.   —*Martial*

5860 Alone you possess your farms, Candidus, alone your cash, alone
      your golden and murrhine vessels, alone your Massic wine,
      alone your Caecuban of Opimius' year, alone your heart, alone
      your wit, alone you possess all your property. (Do you think I
      wish to deny it?)—but your wife, Candidus, you share with
      all the world.   —*Martial*

5861 A good wife is a fortune to a man, especially if she is poor.
                                                           —*Michelet*

5862 Pittacus said, "Every one of you hath his particular plague, and
      my wife is mine; and he is very happy who hath this only."
                                                           —*Plutarch*

5863 Try praising your wife, even if it does frighten her at first.
                                                           —*Billy Sunday*

5864 An ideal wife is any woman who has an ideal husband.
                                                           —*Tarkington*

5865 My notion of a wife at forty, is that a man should be able to
      change her, like a bank note, for two twenties.

5866 A fair wife without a fortune, is a fine house without furniture.

5867   He that loseth his wife and a farthing hath a great loss of a far-
       thing.

5868   He that tells his wife news, is but lately married.

5869   It is better to marry a quiet fool than a witty scold.

5870   Ne'er seek a wife till ye ken what to do wi' her.

5871   There is but one good wife in the world, and every man thinks he
       has her.

5872   Wives must be had, be they good or bad.

5873   Many blame the wife for their own thriftless life.

5874   A good wife makes a good husband.

5875   "How like is this picture, you'd think that it breathes!
       What life! What expression! What spirit!
       It wants but a tongue." "Oh, no!" said the spouse,
       "That want is its principal merit."

SEE ALSO
Beauty 385
Dog 1683
Maid 3785
Secret 4967
Success 5231

RELATED SUBJECTS
Family
Husband
Marriage
Widow

WINE

5881   On one occasion some one put a very little wine into a wine-
       cooler, and said that it was sixteen years old. "It is very small
       for its age," said Gnathaena.   —*Athenaeus*

5882   'Tis pity wine should be so deleterious,
       For tea and coffee leave us much more serious.   —*Byron*

5883   When asked what wine he liked to drink, he (Diogenes) replied,
       "That which belongs to another."   —*Diogenes Laertius*

5884   Gracious Bacchus! Accept this empty jar! You will know best,
       What in pious worship of thee became of all the rest.
                                                         —*Eratosthenes*

5885   The Vine to the Goat:
       Though thou gnaw me to the root
       I shall sprout and bear fresh fruit,
       Just enough to make some wine
       To anoint that hide of thine
       When, upon the altar laid,
       A burnt offering thou art made."
                                                         —*Euenus*

5886　Fill me with the old familiar Juice.　　　　*—Omar Khayyam*

5887　I wonder often what the Vintners buy
One half so precious as the stuff they sell.　　*—Omar Khayyam*

5888　Come, come, good wine is a good familiar creature if it be well
used; exclaim no more against it.　　　　*—Shakespeare*

5889　Wine is wont to show the mind of man.　　　*—Theognis*

5890　The corkscrew—a useful key to unlock the storehouse of wit, the
treasury of laughter, the front-door of fellowship, and the gate
of pleasant folly.

See Also	Related Subjects
Age 132	Drinking
Beauty 381	Eating
Death 1345	Pleasure
Epitaphs 1878	Sin
Love 3641, 3698	

WISDOM

5891　Wise men plead causes, but fools decide them.　　*—Anacharsis*

5892　The use of the head abridges the labor of the hands.
　　　　　　　　　　　　　　　　　—H. W. Beecher

5893　Dead flies cause the ointment of the apothecary to send forth a
stinking savor: so doth a little folly him that is in reputation
for wisdom and honor.　　　　　　　*—Bible*

5894　One wise man's verdict outweighs all the fools'.　*—Browning*

5895　A man doesn't begin to attain wisdom until he recognizes that he
is no longer indispensable.　　　　*—Admiral Byrd*

5896　Intelligence is a luxury, sometimes useless, sometimes fatal. It is
a torch or firebrand according to the use one makes of it.
　　　　　　　　　　　　　　　　　—Caballero

5897　If common sense has not the brilliancy of the sun, it has the fixity
of the stars.　　　　　　　　　*—Caballero*

5898　Defer not till to-morrow to be wise,
To-morrow's sun to thee may never rise.　　*—Congreve*

5899　Knowledge is proud that he has learn'd so much;
Wisdom is humble that he knows no more.　　*—Cowper*

5900　If a man empties his purse into his head, no one can take it from
him.　　　　　　　　　　　　　*—Franklin*

5901　Wisdom is never dear, provided the article be genuine.
　　　　　　　　　　　　　　　　—Horace Greeley

5902 He whose wisdom cannot help him, gets no good from being wise.
—*Ennius*

5903 Wisdom is the abstract of the past, but beauty is the promise of the future. —*O. W. Holmes*

5904 Wisdom is knowing what to do next;
Skill is knowing how to do it, and Virtue is doing it.
—*David Starr Jordan*

5905 To perceive things in the germ is intelligence. —*Lao-Tsze*

5906 It is great cleverness to know how to conceal our cleverness.
—*La Rochefoucauld*

5907 The first dawn of smartness is to stop trying things you don't know anything about—especially if they run to anything over a dollar. —*Wilson Mizner*

5908 It is not our follies that make me laugh, it is our sapiences.
—*Montaigne*

5909 He bids fair to grow wise who has discovered that he is not so.
—*Publilius Syrus*

5910 Wisdom comes by disillusionment. —*Santayana*

5911 Intellect is invisible to the man who has none. —*Schopenhauer*

5912 Many persons might have attained to wisdom had they not assumed that they already possessed it. —*Seneca*

5913 God give them wisdom that have it; and those that are fools, let them use their talents. —*Shakespeare*

5914 Wisdom is ever a blessing; education is sometimes a curse.
—*John A. Shedd*

5915 Though a man be wise,
It is no shame for him to live and learn. —*Sophocles*

5916 Common sense is the knack of seeing things as they are, and doing things as they ought to be done. —*C. E. Stowe*

5917 Knowledge comes but wisdom lingers. —*Tennyson*

5918 Be wise with speed;
A fool at forty is a fool indeed. —*Young*

5919 He that is a wise man by day is no fool by night.

5920 Some are wise, and some are otherwise.

5921 A wise man may look ridiculous in the company of fools.

5922 If wise men were hairs, the world would need a wig.

5923   Only the wise can be perplexed.

5924   God and men think him a fool who brags of his own great wisdom.

5925   The Wisdom of the humble—"Lor', chile, when yuh ain't got no
       education, yuh jes' *got* to use yo' brains."

5926   John Wesley Gains!
       John Wesley Gains!
       Thou monumental mass of brains!
       Come in, John Wesley—
       For it rains.   —*On a certain Congressman*

SEE ALSO   RELATED SUBJECTS
Advice 122   Caution
Conversation 1029   Discretion
Cynicism 1292   Example
Fools 2274, 2290, 2295   Experience
Gravity 2621   Learning
Hardship 2813   Knowledge
Law 3394   Wit
Silence 5046

WIT

5931   Wit needs leisure, and certain inequalities of position.   —*Balzac*

5932   The next best thing to being witty one's self, is to be able to quote
       another's wit.   —*C. N. Bovée*

5933   No one can be a wit of the first water who isn't dry behind the
       ears.   —*Fuller*

5934   Wit is the salt of conversation.   —*Hazlitt*

5935   Impropriety is the soul of wit.   —*Somerset Maugham*

5936   A witty woman is a treasure; a witty beauty is a power.
                                                —*George Meredith*

5937   Wit and judgment are often at strife,
       Tho' meant each other's aid, like man and wife.   —*Pope*

5938   True Wit is nature to advantage dress'd,
       What oft was thought, but ne'er so well expressed.   —*Pope*

5939   You beat your pate, and fancy wit will come;
       Knock as you please, there's nobody at home.   —*Pope*

5940   Wit, like tierce claret, when't begins to pall,
       Neglected lies, and's of no use at all,
       But in its full perfection of decay
       Turns vinegar, and comes again in play.   —*Rochester*

5941   What he hath scanted men in hair, he hath given them in wit.
                                                —*Shakespeare*

5942   The malice of a good thing is the barb that make it stick.
                                                —*Sheridan*

5943   Wit consists in knowing the resemblance of things which differ,
        and the difference of things which are alike.—*Mme. De Staël*

5944   You have risen by your *gravity;*
        I have sunk by my *levity.*   —*Horne Tooke*

5945   I prefer cheerful people to witty ones; wit is cheerfulness pain-
        fully intellectualized.

5946   Wit: Intellect on a spree.

5947   A woman of wit acquires the cynicism of man.

5948   Many that are wits in jest, are fools in earnest.

5949   Satire should, like a polished razor keen,
        Wound with a touch that's scarcely felt or seen.

5950   They say his wit's refined. Thus is explained
        The seeming mystery—his wit is strained.

5951   Enough wit places one above his equal; too much of it lowers him
        to the rank of mere entertainer.

See Also	Related Subjects
Anger 242	Cleverness
Brevity 556	Conversation
Fools 2286	Epigrams
Ideas 3062	Jokes
Nonsense 4191	Laughter
	Wisdom

WOMEN

5961   O Bruscus, cease our aching ears to vex
        With thy loud railing at the softer sex;
        No accusation worse than this could be,
        That once a woman did give birth to thee.   —*Acilius*

5962   The woman who is known only through a man is known wrong.
                                                —*Henry Adams*

5963   The woman that deliberates is lost.   —*Addison*

5964   To our shame a woman is never so much attached to us as when
        we suffer.   —*Balzac*

5965   The way to fight a woman is with your hat. Grab it and run.
                                                —*John Barrymore*

5966 Women are happier in the love they inspire than in that which they feel; men are just the contrary. *—De Beauchêne*

5967 Woman would be more charming if one could fall into her arms without falling into her hands. *—Ambrose Bierce*

5968 The cruellest revenge of a woman is often to remain faithful to a man. *—Bossuet*

5969 There will always remain something to be said of woman, as long as there is one on the earth. *—De Bouflers*

5970 Auld Nature swears the lovely dears
Her noblest work she classes, O;
Her prentice han' she tried on man,
And then she made the lasses, O! *—Burns*

5971 I heard a man say that brigands demand your money or your life, whereas women require both. *—Samuel Butler*

5972 We censure the inconstancy of women when we are the victims; we find it charming when we are the objects. *—Desnoyers*

5973 Women swallow at one mouthful the lie that flatters, and drink drop by drop the truth that is bitter. *—Diderot*

5974 It is often woman who inspires us with the great things that she will prevent us from accomplishing. *—Dumas*

5975 The happiest women, like the happiest nations, have no history. *—George Eliot*

5976 I'm not denying the women are foolish: God Almighty made 'em to match the men. *—George Eliot*

5977 Woman, beguiling man, herself beguiles
With hopes that all too quickly turn to fears.
She lights a conflagration with her smiles,
And vainly seeks to quench it with her tears.*—Colin D. B. Ellis*

5978 Women made us lose paradise, but how frequently we find it again in their arms. *—De Finod*

5979 Women are getting dumber as they grow smarter.*—Mary Garden*

5980 Whoever embarks with women embarks with a storm; but they are themselves the safety boats. *—Arsène Houssaye*

5981 Th' woman that tries t' keep up with th' procession don't see near as much as her husband who stands on th' curb.*—Kin Hubbard*

5982 Sir, nature has given woman so much power that the law cannot afford to give her more. *—Johnson*

5983   If men knew all that women think, they would be **twenty times**
       more audacious.   *—Alphonse Karr*

5984   The female of the species is more deadly than the male.*—Kipling*

5985   A woman's guess is much more accurate than a man's certainty.
                                                                        —Kipling

5986   Even if women were immortal, they could never foresee their last
       lover.   *—De Lamennais*

5987   Whatever spiteful fools may say,
       Each jealous ranting yelper,
       No woman ever went astray,
       Without a man to help her.   *—Lincoln*

5988   When a woman once begins to be ashamed of what she ought not
       to be ashamed of, she will not be ashamed of what she ought.
                                                                —Titus Livius

5989   What is your sex's earliest, latest care,
       Your heart's supreme ambition? To be fair.   *—Lord Lyttelton*

5990   The females of all species are most dangerous when they appear to
       retreat.   *—Don Marquis*

5991   Most beautiful of all women that are or have been, but most
       worthless of all that are or have been. Oh, how I wish, Catulla,
       that you could become less beautiful, or more chaste!*—Martial*

5992   A woman is a book, and often found
       To prove far better in the *sheets,* than bound;
       No wonder, then, some students take delight,
       Above all things, to *study in the night.*   *—After Martial*

5993   A woman is necessarily an evil, and he is a lucky man who catches
       her in the mildest form.   *—Menander*

5994   Informal's what women always say they're going to be and never
       are.   *—Christopher Morley*

5995   A woman, like a cross-eyed man, looks one way, but goes another
       —hence her mysteriousness.   *—Austin O'Malley*

5996   Those who always speak well of women do not know them
       enough: those who always speak ill of them do not know them
       at all.   *—Pigault-Lebrun*

5997   Men, some to business, some to pleasure take;
       But every woman is at heart a rake.   *—Pope*

5998   'Tis true, perfection none must hope to find
       In all the world, much less in womankind.   *—Pope*

5999   A man's "ideal woman" is usually the one whom he passes with a worshipful bow—when he is on his way to call on the other kind.   —*Rowland*

6000   The life of a woman can be divided into three epochs; in the first she dreams of love, in the second she experiences it, in the third she regrets it.   —*St. Prosper*

6001   Woman reduces us all to a common denominator.—*G. B. Shaw*

6002   The only way for a woman to provide for herself decently is for her to be good to some man that can afford to be good to her.   —*G. B. Shaw*

6003   Women upset everything. When you let them into your life, you find that the woman is driving at one thing and you're driving at another.   —*G. B. Shaw*

6004   Woman once made equal to man becomes his superior.—*Socrates*

6005   A wise woman never yields by appointment. It should always be an unforeseen happiness.   —*Stendhal*

6006   Women and birds are able to see without turning their heads, and that is indeed a necessary provision, for they are both surrounded by enemies.   —*James Stephens*

6007   Blonde or brunette, this rhyme applies,
Happy is he who knows them not.   —*Villon*

6008   If woman lost us Eden, such
As she alone restore it.   —*Whittier*

6009   Think how poor Mother Eve was brought
To being as God's afterthought.   —*Anna Wickham*

6010   Men always want to be a woman's first love. That is their clumsy vanity. We women have a more subtle instinct about things. What we like is to be a man's last romance.   —*Oscar Wilde*

6011   I am on the side of the Trojans.
They fought for a woman.   —*Oscar Wilde*

6012   A woman is to be from her house three times; when she is christened, married and buried.

6013   A woman that loves to be at the window, is like a bunch of grapes on the highway.

6014   A woman is a well-served table that one sees with different eyes before and after the meal.

6015   The whisper of a beautiful woman can be heard further than the loudest call of duty.

6016   Women are apt to see chiefly the defects of a man of talent and the merits of a fool.

6017   Without woman the two extremes of life would be without succor, and the middle without pleasure.

6018   After man came woman—and she has been after him ever since.

6019   Women are entitled to life, liberty, and the pursuit of man.

6020   When Eve brought woe to all mankind
Old Adam called her woe man,
But when she woo'd with love so kind
He then pronounced her woman.

But now, with folly and with pride,
Their husbands' pockets trimming,
The ladies are so full of whims
That people call them w(h)imen.

6021   Women are seldom reluctant about giving themselves to men who consider their act a folly.

6022   Woman has never created anything as beautiful as she has destroyed.

6023   When you brag of getting the best of a woman, think of the poor woman who brags in the same way about you.

6024   Woman's equality to man is not a claim . . . rather a concession.

6025   Strategy in woman is born of expediency.

6026   If woman's actions are sometimes baffling, her motives are always obvious.

6027   Woman spoils her first lover and practically ruins all the rest.

6028   After a man finds out that the woman is no angel, he tries to ascertain to what extent she isn't.

6029   Woman has no patience with the timid though she bestows it upon the embarrassed.

6030   Women have no principles; they are either above or below them.

6031   No woman is better than two.

6032   The light that lies
In woman's eyes . . .
And lies, and lies, and lies.

6033   Whoever the woman, her final aspirations flatter man's vanity.

6034   Man has shown good logic in encouraging feminine instincts for they have played women stupendous tricks.

6035   Surely God must have been disappointed in Adam: He made Eve so different.

6036   Whilst Adam slept, Eve from his side arose:
Strange his first sleep should be his last repose.

6037   For every woman who makes a fool out of a man there is another woman who makes a man out of a fool.

6038   Women are like socks, you have to change them regularly.

6039   A woman's heart, like the moon, is always changing, but there is always a man in it.

6040   A woman's past is either scandalously indecent or shamefully uninteresting.

See Also	Related Subjects
Civilization 844	Beauty
Courtship 1178	Coquetry
Deception 1434	Maids
Desire 1536	Man
Friend 2392, 2417	Marriage
Mirror 3975	Sex
Misanthrope 3985	Widow
Mistakes 3995	Wife
Temptation 5343	
Tobacco 5443	

WORDS

6041   All words are pegs to hang ideas on.   —*H. W. Beecher*

6042   Words once spoken can never be recalled.   —*Dillon*

6043   Language develops by the felicitous misapplication of words.
—*J. B. Greenough*

6044   Words are wise men's counters, they do but reckon by them; but they are the money of fools.   —*Thomas Hobbes*

6045   Dictionaries are like watches; the worst is better than none, and the best cannot be expected to go quite true.   —*Johnson*

6046   They spell it Vinci and pronounce it Vinchy; foreigners always spell better than they pronounce.   —*Mark Twain*

6047   Many a treasure besides Ali Baba's is unlocked with a verbal key.
—*Henry Van Dyke*

6048 A man of words and not of deeds
Is like a garden full of weeds.

<table>
<tr><td>SEE ALSO</td><td>RELATED SUBJECTS</td></tr>
<tr><td>Action 28</td><td>Books</td></tr>
<tr><td>Brevity 557</td><td>Conceit</td></tr>
<tr><td>Idealism 3056</td><td>Conversation</td></tr>
<tr><td>Silence 5036</td><td>Literature</td></tr>
<tr><td>Understanding 5595, 5596</td><td>Speeches</td></tr>
<tr><td></td><td>Writers</td></tr>
</table>

WORK

6051 The thicker the hay; the easier mowed.   *—Alaric the Goth*

6052 One must work, if not by choice, at least by despair, since it is less annoying to work than to be amused.   *—Baudelaire*

6053 Tools were made, and born were hands,
Every farmer understands.   *—Blake*

6054 Get work:
Be sure it is better than what you work to get.—*E. B. Browning*

6055 Such hath it been—shall be—beneath the sun
The many still must labor for the one.   *—Byron*

6056 Blessed is he who has found his work; let him ask no other blessedness.   *—Carlyle*

6057 When large numbers of men are unable to find work, unemployment results.   *—Calvin Coolidge*

6058 Absence of occupation is not rest
A mind quite vacant is a mind distress'd.   *—Cowper*

6059 It is better to wear out than to rust out.—*Richard Cumberland*

6060 Cecil's saying of Sir Walter Raleigh, "I know that he can toil terribly," is an electric touch.   *—Emerson*

6061 Toil, says the proverb, is the sire of fame.   *—Euripides*

6062 Work is the meat of life, pleasure the dessert.   *—B. C. Forbes*

6063 The fellow who isn't fired with enthusiasm is apt to be fired.   *—B. C. Forbes*

6064 The eye of a master will do more work than both his hands.   *—Franklin*

6065 You do de pullin', Sis Cow, en I'll do de gruntin'.   *—Joel Chandler Harris*

6066 If little labor, little are our gains;
Man's fortunes are according to his pains.   *—Robert Herrick*

6067   The man flaps about with a bunch of feathers: the woman goes
       to work softly with a cloth.   —*O. W. Holmes*

6068   A really busy person never knows how much he weighs.
                                                        —*E. W. Howe*

6069   I would rather have a big burden and a strong back, than a weak
       back and a caddy to carry life's luggage.   —*Elbert Hubbard*

6070   One machine can do the work of fifty ordinary men. No machine
       can do the work of one extraordinary man.—*Elbert Hubbard*

6071   People who take pains never to do any more than they get paid
       for, never get paid for any more than they do.—*Elbert Hubbard*

6072   Better to work and fail than to sleep one's life away.
                                                    —*Jerome K. Jerome*

6073   My father taught me to work; he did not teach me to love it.
                                                        —*Lincoln*

6074   The workman still is greater than his work.   —*Menander*

6075   Executive ability is deciding quickly and getting somebody else to
       do the work.   —*J. G. Pollard*

6076   Can anything be sadder than work left unfinished? Yes; work
       never begun.   —*Christina Rossetti*

6077   There is a great difference between a young man looking for a
       situation and one looking for work.   —*Leslie M. Shaw*

6078   A sword, a spade, and a thought should never be allowed to rust.
                                                     —*James Stephens*

6079   Work consists of whatever a body is *obliged* to do, and Play con-
       sists of whatever a body is not obliged to do. —*Mark Twain*

6080   Work alone will efface the footsteps of work.   —*Whistler*

6081   Not to oversee workmen is to leave them your purse open.

6082   Account not that work slavery that brings in penny savory.

6083   A man of many trades begs his bread on Sundays.

6084   Better have one plough going than two cradles.

6085   An emmet may work its heart out, but can never make honey.

6086   Labor rids us of three great evils; tediousness, vice and poverty.

6087   None knows the weight of another's burden.

6088 It is not the burden, but the over-burden that kills the beast.

6089 One barber shaves not so close but another finds work.

SEE ALSO
Chance 632
Genius 2477
Hanging 2756
Haste 2823
Success 5233

RELATED SUBJECTS
Business
Deeds
Labor

WORLD

6091 Do what you will, this world's a fiction
And is made up of contradiction. —*Blake*

6092 The whole wide ether is the eagle's way:
The whole earth is a brave man's fatherland. —*Euripides*

6093 The world is nothing but a great desire to live and a great dissatisfaction with living. —*Heraclitus*

6094 The great thing in this world is not so much where we are, but in
what direction we are moving. —*O. W. Holmes*

6095 The axis of the earth sticks out visibly through the center of each
and every town or city. —*O. W. Holmes*

6096 The world in all doth but two nations bear,—
The good, the bad; and these mixed everywhere.
—*Andrew Marvell*

6097 The world's a book, writ by the eternal art
Of the great author; printed in man's heart,
'Tis falsely printed, though divinely penned,
And all the *errata* will appear at the end. —*Francis Quarles*

6098 It is a very good world to live in,
To lend or to spend, or to give in;
But to beg or to borrow, or to get a man's own,
It is the very worst world that ever was known.—*John Wilmot*

6099 A man seldom affects to despise the world, unless the world is
regardless of him.

6100 The world is a well-furnished table,
Where guests are promiscuously set;
We all fare as well as we're able,
And scramble for what we can get.

6101 The world ought to be treated like a playful child; whose smiles
should delight, whose gambols should amuse, whose tears should
soften, whose anger should alarm, and whose vices should be
corrected.

6102 Don't call the world dirty because you have forgotten to clean your glasses.

6103 The world's a city of crooked streets;
Death is the market-place where man meets.
If life were merchandise which men could buy,
The rich would always live, the poor alone would die.

SEE ALSO	RELATED SUBJECTS
Art 300	Cities
Change 652	Civilization
Cynicism 1292	Cynicism
Man 3805	Politics
Patriotism 4334, 4338	Wisdom
Remorse 4836	
Society 5132	
Time 5423	

WORRY

6111 There are two days about which nobody should ever worry, and these are yesterday and tomorrow.   —*Robert J. Burdette*

6112 But human bodies are sic fools,
For a' their colleges and schools,
That when nae real ills perplex them,
They mak enow themsels to vex them.   —*Burns*

6113 Keep cool: it will be all one a hundred years hence.   —*Emerson*

6114 I have never yet met a healthy person who worried very much about his health, or a really good person who worried much about his own soul.   —*J. B. S. Haldane*

6115 To carry care to bed is to sleep with a pack on your back.
—*Haliburton*

6116 Worry is interest paid on trouble before it falls due.—*Dean Inge*

6117 I have lost everything, and I am so poor now that I really cannot afford to let anything worry me.   —*Joseph Jefferson*

6118 Worry, the interest paid by those who borrow trouble.
—*George W. Lyon*

6119 Many of our cares are but a morbid way of looking at our privileges.   —*Walter Scott*

6120 The longer we dwell on our misfortunes the greater is their power to harm us.   —*Voltaire*

6121 I'll not willingly offend,
      Nor be easily offended;
      What's amiss I'll strive to mend,
      And endure what can't be mended.   —*Isaac Watts*

6122 A pound of care will not pay an ounce of debt.

6123 Too much care may be as bad as downright negligence.

SEE ALSO   RELATED SUBJECTS
Children 779   Caution
Desire 1548   Debt
                     Hardship
                     Patience

WRITERS

6131 I have very little of Mr. Blake's company; he is always in Para-
      dise.   —*Mrs. William Blake*

6132 Shakespeare was a dramatist of note;
      He lived by writing things to quote.   —*H. C. Bunner*

6133 They lard their lean books with the fat of others' works.
                                                      —*Burton*

6134 One hates an author that's all author.   —*Byron*

6135 On occasion, he (William Randolph Hearst) seems to fancy him-
      self as chosen to be God Almighty's ghost-writer.
                                                    —*Irvin S. Cobb*

6136 The Eighth Commandment was not made for bards.
                                                    —*Coleridge*

6137 I have the conviction that excessive literary production is a social
      offence.   —*George Eliot*

6138 Many contemporary authors drink more than they write.—*Gorky*

6139 Pope came off clean with Homer; but they say
      Broome went before, and kindly swept the way.
                                          —*J. Henley, on Pope's Homer*

6140 I'll write, because I'll give
      You critics means to live;
      For should I not supply
      The cause, th' effect would die.   —*Robert Herrick*

6141 A bad book is as much of a labor to write as a good one; it comes
      as sincerely from the author's soul.   —*Aldous Huxley*

6142 No man but a blockhead ever wrote except for money.—*Johnson*

6143 Who casts to write a living line, must sweat.   —*Jonson*

6144   A good many young writers make the mistake of enclosing a stamped, self-addressed envelope, big enough for the manuscript to come back in. This is too much of a temptation to the editor.   —*Ring Lardner*

6145   The writers who have nothing to say are the ones you can buy; the others have too high a price.   —*Walter Lippmann*

6146   I am that Martial known to all people by my verses of eleven feet, my hendecasyllables, and my jokes, which however are without malice. Why do you envy me? I am not better known than the horse Andraemon.   —*Martial*

6147   He does not write at all whose poems no man reads. —*Martial*

6148   As your desk, Sosibianus, is full of elaborate compositions, why do you publish nothing? "My heirs," you say, "will publish my verses." When? It is time already, Sosibianus, that you should be read.   —*Martial*

6149   You urge me, Pudens, to correct my books for you with my own hand and pen. You are far too partial and too kind thus to wish to possess my trifles in autograph.   —*Martial*

6150   Paulus buys poems. Then Paulus recites the poems as his own, for what you buy you may fairly call your own.   —*Martial*

6151   You pretend to consider' my talent small, Gaurus, because I write poems which please by being brief. I confess that it is so; while you who write the grand wars of Priam in twelve books, are doubtless a great man. I paint the favorite of Brutus to the life. You, great artist, fashion a giant in clay.   —*Martial*

6152   My words are commended, Aulus, by those who read them and by those who hear them read, but a certain poet declares that they are not "correct." This does not trouble me a great deal. I prefer that the dishes on my dinner-table please the guests rather than the cooks.   —*Martial*

6153   You ask me, Avitus, how Philenus became a father, he who never did anything to gain the name? Gaditanus can tell you, he who, without writing anything, claims to be a poet.—*Martial*

6154   Why, simpleton, do you mix your verses with mine? What have you to do, foolish man, with writings that convict you of theft? Why do you attempt to associate oxes with lions, and make owls pass for eagles? Though you had one of Lada's legs you would not be able, blockhead, to run with the other leg of wood.
                                                                —*Martial*

6155   You give no recitations, Mamercus, yet you wish to pass for a poet. Be what you please, provided you give no recitations.
                                                                —*Martial*

6156   Cinna 'gainst me (so 'tis said)
         Verses doth indite.
        He whose lines are never read
         Can't be held to write.   *—Martial*

6157   Give us Maecenases and we shall have no lack of Virgils.
                                                —Martial

6158   I walk you out: I see you home:
        I listen, sir, to all your chatter.
        Your words and deeds I praise through Rome—
        D'you think it really doesn't matter?
        Yet all this time I might instead
        Have fashioned poems in my head.   *—Martial*

6159   Why don't I send you my works, Pontilianus? For fear that you
        might send me yours.   *—Martial*

6160   You press me to present you with my books, Tucca. I shan't. You
        want to sell them, not to read them.   *—Martial*

6161   You write two hundred lines 'twixt each sunrise,
        But never read them, silly!—yet how wise!   *—Martial*

6162   You ask me, Quintus, for a copy of my books. I haven't one but
        Tryphon the bookseller has. "Do you think I am such a fool
        as to part with my money for nonsense and pay for your verses?
        No," you say, "I shan't do anything so absurd." Nor will I.
                                            —Martial

6163   The book, Fidentinus, from which you are giving a reading is
        mine, but when you read it so badly, it gradually becomes your
        own.   *—Martial*

6164   You admire, Vacerra, only the poets of old, and praise only those
        who are dead. Pardon me, I beseech you Vacerra, if I think
        death too high a price to pay for your praise.   *—Martial*

6165   It is rumored, Fidentinus, that you recite my epigrams in public,
        just as if you had written them. I will send you a copy of my
        poems for nothing, if you are willing that they should pass as
        mine. If you wish them to pass as yours, buy them, so that they
        will be mine no longer.   *—Martial*

6166   You publish none of your own verses, Laelius, and you steal mine.
        Stop stealing mine, or else publish your own.   *—Martial*

6167   I suppose the writer of couplets wishes to please by his brevity,
        but what, I ask, is the good of his brevity, if his couplets fill
        a book?   *—Martial*

6168   You affirm, Laberius, that you can write elegant verses: Why
       then are you unwilling? He who can write elegant verses
       should write them down, Laberius. Then I shall think him a
       hero.   —*Martial*

6169   Matho is spreading the report that my work is not of uniform
       quality. The criticism if just, is really a recommendation of my
       verses. Calvinus and Umber write books of uniform quality. A
       bad book, Creticus, is a book of uniform quality.   —*Martial*

6170   Tell me, Labullus, is this right?
       Can any call it honor bright
       That just to swell your client-crew
       The books I write should be too few?
       About a month has gone so fleet
       I've hardly filled a single sheet.
           In this the poet is the sinner
           If he won't stay at home to dinner.   —*Martial*

6171   I wonder, wall, that you have not gone smash—
       You've had to bear so many scribblers' trash.   —*Martial*

6172   He is just a big dreamer, with a good sense of double-entry book-
       keeping.   —*Harpo Marx, of Alexander Woollcott*

6173   We do not write as we want to but as we can.
                                              —*Somerset Maugham*

6174   When a man's talk is commonplace and his writings uncommon,
       it means that his talent lies in the place from which he borrows
       it, and not in himself.   —*Montaigne*

6175   In my district of Gascony, it is thought a joke to see me in print.
       The further from my home the knowledge of me travels, the
       higher am I valued.   —*Montaigne*

6176   An author departs; he does not die.   —*Dinah Maria Mulock*

6177   The graces once made up their mind
       A shrine inviolate to find:
       And thus they found, and that with ease,
       The soul of Aristophanes.   —*Plato*

6178   Next o'er his books his eyes begin to roll,
       In pleasing memory of all he stole.   —*Pope*

6179   True ease in writing comes from art, not chance,
       As those move easiest who have learn'd to dance.   —*Pope*

6180   The pen is a formidable weapon, but a man can kill himself with
       it a great deal more easily than he can other people.
                                         —*George Denison Prentice*

6181   In Hollywood the woods are full of people that learned to write, but evidently can't read. If they could read their stuff, they'd stop writing.   *—Will Rogers*

6182   You write with ease to show your breeding,
But easy writing's curst hard reading.   *—Sheridan*

6183   In composing, as a general rule, run your pen through every other word you have written; you have no idea what vigor it will give your style.   *—Sydney Smith*

6184   I have been an author for 22 years and an ass for 55.
    —Mark Twain

6185   Only presidents, editors and people with tapeworm have the right to use the editorial "we."   *—Mark Twain*

6186   As to the Adjective; when in doubt, strike it out.*—Mark Twain*

6187   He became mellow before he became ripe.
    —Alexander Woollcott, of Christopher Morley

6188   Thou art so witty, wicked, and so thin,
Thou art at once the Devil, Death, and Sin.*—Young to Voltaire*

6189   Enthusiasts, Lutherans, and monks,
Jews, Syndics, Calvinists, and punks,
    Gibbon an atheist call;
While he, unhurt, in placid mood,
To prove himself a Christian good,
    Kindly forgives them all.

6190   Of all those arts in which the wise excel,
Nature's chief masterpiece is writing well.

6191   It is surprising how many receivers of stolen goods take to writing books.

SEE ALSO
Bores 526
Time 5401

RELATED SUBJECTS
Art
Books
Letters
Literature
Pen
Poetry
Words

Y

YOUTH

6201   Young men have a passion for regarding their elders as senile.
    —Henry Adams

6202 In sorrow he learned this truth—
      One may return to the place of his birth,
      He cannot go back to his youth.   —*John Burroughs*

6203 I write of youth, of love, and have access
      By these to sing of cleanly wantonness.   —*Catullus*

6204 Life is but thought; so think I will,
      That youth and I are house-mates still.   —*Coleridge*

6205 No young man believes he shall ever die.   —*Hazlitt*

6206 Youth had been a habit of hers for so long, that she could not part
      with it.   —*Kipling*

6207 Nobody is quite so blasé and sophisticated as a boy of nineteen
      who is just recovering from a baby-grand passion.
                                                         —*Helen Rowland*

6208 Youth is a wonderful thing. What a crime to waste it on children.
                                                         —*G. B. Shaw*

6209 Children and fools are we to mourn the happy dead;
      Come, rather let us mourn youth's fading flower instead.
                                                         —*Theognis of Onegara*

6210 The youth gets together his materials to build a bridge to the
      moon, or, perchance, a palace or temple on the earth, and, at
      length, the middle-aged man concludes to build a woodshed
      with them.   —*Thoreau*

6211 The Youth of America is their oldest tradition. It has been going
      on now for three hundred years.   —*Oscar Wilde*

6212 Man is young as long as he can repeat his emotions; woman, as
      long as she can inspire them.

6213 The heyday of youth isn't in it with the pay day of manhood.

6214 To refuse to grow old is the unmistakable sign of youth.

6215 To him in vain the envious seasons roll,
      Who bears eternal summer in his soul.

SEE ALSO	RELATED SUBJECTS
Death 1377	Age
Debt 1392	Children
Fools 2267	Love
Love 3737	

ACKNOWLEDGMENTS

Thanks are due to:

E. P. Dutton & Company for permission to reprint Epigram 5012, by Arthur Guiterman, from the volume, "Lyric Laughter."

Little, Brown & Company for permission to reprint Epigram 1727, by Ogden Nash, from the volume, "The Face Is Familiar."

The Viking Press for permission to reprint Epigrams 1167 and 1168, by Dorothy Parker, from the volume, "Not So Deep as a Well."

If any required acknowledgments have been omitted or any rights overlooked, it is by accident, and forgiveness is desired.

INDEX OF
EPIGRAM SUBJECTS

INDEX OF EPIGRAM SUBJECTS

A

B

C